Comparative Entrepreneurship

Comparative Entrepreneurship

The UK, Japan, and the Shadow of Silicon Valley

by
D. Hugh Whittaker

with
P. Byosiere, S. Momose, T. Morishita,
T. Quince, and J. Higuchi

OXFORD
UNIVERSITY PRESS

OXFORD

UNIVERSITY PRESS

Great Clarendon Street, Oxford OX2 6DP

Oxford University Press is a department of the University of Oxford.
It furthers the University's objective of excellence in research, scholarship,
and education by publishing worldwide in

Oxford New York

Auckland Cape Town Dar es Salaam Hong Kong Karachi
Kuala Lumpur Madrid Melbourne Mexico City Nairobi
New Delhi Shanghai Taipei Toronto

With offices in

Argentina Austria Brazil Chile Czech Republic France Greece
Guatemala Hungary Italy Japan Poland Portugal Singapore
South Korea Switzerland Thailand Turkey Ukraine Vietnam

Oxford is a registered trade mark of Oxford University Press
in the UK and in certain other countries

Published in the United States
by Oxford University Press Inc., New York

© D. Hugh Whittaker, 2009

British Library Cataloguing in Publication Data

Data available

Library of Congress Cataloging in Publication Data

Data available

Typeset by SPI Publisher Services, Pondicherry, India
Printed in Great Britain
on acid-free paper by
by the MPG Books Group

ISBN 978–0–19–956366–1

10 9 8 7 6 5 4 3 2 1

Contents

v

Figures and Tables

Figures

Tables

Contributors

D. Hugh Whittaker is Professor at the University of Auckland Business School, and Visiting Professor of Doshisha University, Kyoto.

Philippe Byosiere is Professor at the Doshisha Business School, Doshisha University, Kyoto, and Visiting Research Professor at The University of Michigan-Ann Arbor, USA.

Shigeo Momose is Emeritus Professor of the Faculty of Politics and Economics, Meiji University, Tokyo.

Tadashi Morishita is Professor of the Faculty of Politics and Economics, and Director of the Incubation Centre, Meiji University, Tokyo.

Thelma Quince is Educational Research Associate, School of Clinical Medicine, University of Cambridge.

Junpe Higuchi is Associate Professor of the Faculty of Economics, Wakayama University, Wakayama.

Acknowledgments

First and foremost, we would like to thank all the participants of this study – both respondents to the questionnaires and those who took part in interviews – for their generosity in sharing their time, reflections, and insights with us. This generosity is hard to repay directly, but is essential for this kind of research.

At the ESRC Centre for Business Research we have benefited from the assistance, advice, and general support of many people, including Anna Bullock, Cissy Bullock, Brendan Burchall, Andy Cosh, Diana Day, David Keeble, Sue Moore, Jocelyn Probert, and especially Alan Hughes. Similarly, at or affiliated with the Institute for Technology, Enterprise and Competitiveness (ITEC) at Doshisha University, we owe much to the very competent office staff, seminar and workshop participants, Jacques Payet, and especially Keiko Matsunaga, Eiichi Yamaguchi, and Yoshi-fumi Nakata. At Meiji University Faculty of Economics we thank Masaaki Ito, and at the University of Auckland Business School, Sanjay Bhowmick, Ian Hunter, Christine Woods, and especially Wendell Dunn and Ben Fath. In addition we have benefited greatly at various points or on an ongoing basis from comments or writing by Robert Cole, Ronald Dore, Elizabeth Garnsey, Takeshi Inagami, Sanford Jacoby, Masahiro Ogawa, Mari Sako, and Saras Sarasvathy. There are undoubtedly more people we could add to this list.

We also gratefully acknowledge financial support from the ESRC, British Academy, and Daiwa Anglo-Japanese Foundation in the UK, and the Japanese Ministry of Education, Culture, Sports, Science and Technology (MEXT) 21st Century Centre of Excellence Programme, Omron Corporation, and Meiji University Institute of Social Sciences in Japan.

We are also grateful for the encouragement and support of David Musson, Matthew Derbyshire and Kate Walker of Oxford University Press, as well as Jacqueline Daniel for guiding this project into its final book form.

Introduction

Are entrepreneurs the same everywhere? Do they strive for the same things? Are the processes of entrepreneurship similar? Are they equally collaborative? Or are all of these shaped by their environments? If so, how?

We know a lot about national differences in management practices, corporate governance, employment relations, and their embeddedness in institutional contexts, but we know surprisingly little about how entrepreneurs and entrepreneurship differ across countries. Many studies attempt to show how and why *levels* of entrepreneurship so differ, or compare specific aspects of entrepreneurship, like founding motivations, but they do not address the above questions as a whole. The gap is curious, given the huge growth of research on entrepreneurship in recent years.

This book addresses that gap through a comparative study of entrepreneurs and entrepreneurship in the UK and Japan. These countries are often associated with liberal market economies (LMEs) and coordinated market economies (CMEs) respectively. Institutions in LMEs and CMEs are seen to favor different types of innovation; we will explore whether this applies to processes of entrepreneurship as well.

Although the book is not about technology entrepreneurship per se, its focus is on high-tech manufacturing, where we would expect to find a high level of novel and innovative activity. If we are going to find systematic differences in degrees and types of innovation and processes of entrepreneurship, we are likely to find them here. To answer our questions, we present the findings of two original surveys and twenty-five case interviews in both the UK and Japan. These look at entrepreneurs' careers, opportunity and business creation, founding teams, attitudes to growth and risk, R&D and innovation, competitive strategies, growth limitations, leadership and HRM, and collaborations.

We find some important similarities, particularly in the way businesses are founded and opportunities created, which are at odds with common stereotypes. We also find clear and systematic differences in many of the individual aspects which point to different approaches to entrepreneurship overall. We have called these approaches "project entrepreneurship" and "lifework entrepreneurship" respectively.

These approaches, in turn, can only be explained by the respective environments the entrepreneurs operate in, especially differences in markets. From the evidence we construct a "wasgij" picture of "utility" and "relational" markets.[1] The approaches also encompass different orientations to time, which we refer to as "programmed" and "open-ended" time. These are generalizations, of course, but the constructs can help us to understand entrepreneurship in other countries as well.

They can also help us to understand the limited success of policies in both countries inspired by (certain interpretations of) Silicon Valley, referred to in the book's subtitle. These include a focus on start-ups, often by youthful entrepreneurs, well-defined business concepts and plans, high growth backed by venture capital, and clear exit strategies. The entrepreneurs in this study live "in the shadow of Silicon Valley," but many flourish by being adapted to their respective environments.

As this suggests, our interest is in real-life entrepreneurs, and the contexts in which they pursue opportunities and grow businesses. It is not in fitting entrepreneurs into a theory of "the market," whether as a disruptor or restorer of equilibrium. Rather, it is in real entrepreneurs in real marketplaces, in real time. These are subject to change, of course, but we do not expect lifework entrepreneurship to give way to project entrepreneurship, or both to Silicon Valley-inspired entrepreneurship, at least in the mainstream of both countries, in the near future.

The structure of the book is as follows. Chapter 1 sets the scene and clarifies some important terms and concepts. First we look at the remarkable reemergence of entrepreneurship over the past quarter century, and the accompanying growth of entrepreneurship studies. With this growth have come disputes about just what entrepreneurship is, and is not. We will clarify our view and provide a working definition. We will then look at attempts to compare *levels* of entrepreneurship in different countries, and common explanations rooted in culture and institutions. Further, we will look briefly at the comparison of types of innovation in the "varieties of

---

[1] A wasgij is the reverse of a jigsaw, in which the picture to be pieced together is what the characters in the given picture are looking at.

capitalism" writing, and some fledgling attempts to create a framework for comparative entrepreneurship. This will help to clarify our own approach, which treats entrepreneurship as a process, and institutions and culture as, in principle, situational and dynamic.

In Chapter 2 we look at opportunity and business creation. Although founding a business is not a requirement of entrepreneurship in our definition, it is important either as a vehicle to pursue an opportunity already conceived, or for providing a vehicle from which opportunities can be discovered. Applying the AMO – ability, motivation, and opportunity – approach, we first look at the entrepreneurs' backgrounds, and find systematic differences in career paths between the two groups. We then look at motivations for starting a business, as well as how the entrepreneurs went about doing it. Here, reflecting differences in backgrounds, there was some evidence of a greater "technology push" emphasis in Japan, and market positioning or balance in the UK. There were strong similarities as well, however. To use a baseball metaphor, starting a business for these founders was about getting a base hit, not a home run. This was partly to do with the processes of becoming independent, "soft" starts, uncertainties, and balancing multiple objectives.

Implicitly, Chapter 2 treats entrepreneurship as something done by individuals. This is not the case, of course. Chapter 3 complements the discussion by looking first at "umbilical" ties with former employers – one-third of entrepreneurs in both countries were helped by a former employer – and then at cofounders, both internal and external, how many, their relationship with the respondent, and what they were seen to contribute. The extent of cofounding was similar, but their identity and contributions were very different. Collegial teams were more common in the UK, and a dominant founder supported by family or a "right-hand man" in Japan. These differences are intimately related to project and lifework entrepreneurship and their underlying logics.

If the entrepreneurs do not set out to hit home runs, are they risk-averse? In Chapter 4 we look at personal business objectives, as well as attitudes toward risk and growth. Again we find similarities, as well as some key differences. We then look at engagement in R&D, patenting, and innovation, which most engaged in, to varying degrees. From our data we construct a category of "high performers"; businesses which have produced a novel innovation and grown by at least 10 percent in the past two years – roughly one-third of the total in both the UK and Japan. This allows us to further compare whether the members of the select group are similar to each other, regardless of country differences, or whether they retain or indeed amplify country differences. Is "high performance" a matter of best practice, or best fit?

Complementing this analysis, in Chapter 5 we look at competitive orientations and growth limitations. First we examine the nature of the markets the entrepreneurs sell in, through measures of reliance on subcontracting and major customers, and number and location of competitors. We then look at perceived competitive advantages in these markets, and find them systematically different in the two countries, with high performers accentuating the differences. Somewhat unexpectedly – but understandably in the light of the entrepreneurs' backgrounds, founding motivations, and personal business objectives – these coalesce around (niche) market positioning on the one hand, and competence building on the other. Regarding limitations, all those listed were felt more acutely by the Japanese entrepreneurs, with the exception of finance, which is ironic since Japan was in the midst of a combined credit squeeze and recession.

Chapter 6 looks at the way the entrepreneurs sought to attract, retain, and motivate the employees they needed to achieve their objectives, as well as leadership and culture. By and large, the entrepreneurs were looking for the same kinds of people, but there were striking – and again counterintuitive – differences in their espoused HRM orientations, with an emphasis on supportive organizational environment in the UK, and personal growth and challenging work in Japan. These reflect differences in social and gender relations, as well as labor market differences, but they also highlight the different engagement of the entrepreneurs in their businesses, and hence leadership. HRM and leadership orientations were reinforced by company culture, and the differences were upheld or even accentuated by the high performers.

The final empirical chapter looks outside rather than inside the businesses, at interfirm collaborations. Here again there were clear differences, intensified by the high performers, which contradict certain "varieties of capitalism" writing but were consistent with the respective approaches to entrepreneurship. UK entrepreneurs reported more collaborations than their Japanese counterparts. UK high performers reported even more, Japanese high performers even less. The findings vindicate our approach of putting data first, and deriving observations on institutional influences second. We conclude the chapter with an analysis of university–business interactions, which were much more varied and haphazard than some of the writing on (and promotion of) clusters assumes.

The last two chapters integrate and explain our findings. Chapter 8 begins with a summary of similarities and differences between the UK and Japanese entrepreneurs and their businesses from the previous six chapters. We then seek to explain the differences. Our view is that the different approaches to entrepreneurship in the two countries cannot be explained satisfactorily by references to different social influences on the way entrepreneurs think and act, at least as conventionally conceived. Some can be explained by greater marketization in the UK, and institutions, actors, and ideology supporting this. But along with a number of economic sociologists, feel that the nature and embeddedness of market transactions themselves are crucial in influencing the respective approaches. Instead of focusing on labor markets, we illustrate this with a discussion of product markets.

Our final chapter begins by exploring a different kind of embeddedness, in "time." First we explore whether the differences are in fact the result of comparing entrepreneurship in industrial Japan with postindustrial UK, and if there is any evidence in newly emerging industries of a change in Japan toward the approach to entrepreneurship common in the UK. Thus we address the question of convergence.

Second, however, we also look at the fundamentally different orientations to time embodied in project and lifework entrepreneurship. These orientations have important implications for attempts to promote venture capital backing of fast growth businesses, which requires an orientation to time and engagement in the business that even many of the UK project entrepreneurs did not match. Policy promotion and entrepreneurship education will accelerate the development of some entrepreneurial businesses, but the majority are likely to retain these time orientations for the foreseeable future. They will continue to develop in the shadow of Silicon Valley. As both project and lifework entrepreneurship have distinctive strengths, an alternative policy agenda might be the promotion of a judicious mix of the two.

Throughout the book our emphasis is on people – especially entrepreneurs – and perceptions of entrepreneurial processes. It is not on finance, risk analysis, quantified performance, or formal models. Those wishing to know more about our research design, assumptions, methods, implementation, analysis, and interpretation should refer to Appendix 1. This clarifies what we mean by "high-tech" manufacturing, characteristics of the businesses in the surveys, and how we conducted our research and created our integrated data set. It further clarifies some of the issues behind our approach to analysis and interpretation, including our use of combined methods and process-oriented research, as well as how we have combined the "dancer" with the "dance" of entrepreneurship.

This study is limited to the UK and Japan, but we believe it can shed light on entrepreneurship in other countries as well. It can also provide an entrepreneurial perspective for those interested in comparative institutions, "varieties of capitalism," and economic sociology.

1

Comparative Entrepreneurship

Much of the twentieth century was dominated – economically and in terms of scholarly interest – by large firms and organized capitalism. Even Schumpeter, who contributed greatly to our early understanding of the entrepreneur, saw innovation being reduced to corporate routine carried out by teams of specialists (Schumpeter, 1942), and in the late 1960s, Galbraith saw no rationale for entrepreneurs or small business owners in the new industrial state (Galbraith, 1967).[1] There were some laments for the passing of the entrepreneur, small business owner, and self-made inner-directed man (Riesman, 1950; Whyte, 1956). In the UK, the commission of inquiry which wrote the Bolton Report (1971: 342–43) made a plea for their continued importance in the face of serious decline: "The contribution of small businessmen to the vitality of society is inestimable. Above all their spirit of independence is a strength to the nation, as deeply needed now as it has ever been."

This report is seen as a landmark in official and scholarly thinking about small firms and entrepreneurship, as was research by Birch (1979; 1981) on firm size and job creation in the USA at the end of the 1970s. In many industrialized countries, the turbulent 1970s marked a turning point, as large firms faced multiple challenges of inflation and competition from upstarts like Japan. There followed a wave of restructuring which saw average firm sizes drop and a shift of employment to the service sector. The significance and desirability of the small firm resurgence was hotly debated (e.g., Sengenberger, Loveman, and Piore, 1990; Leighton and Felstead, 1992). Piore and Sabel (1984) interpreted it as a "new industrial

---

[1] See Audretsch (2007) for a fuller exposition of the "death" and reemergence of the entrepreneur.

divide," with the industrial, Fordist age giving way to a new age of specialized small firms, interacting in flexible networks.

Audretsch and Thurik (2001) portray a fundamental shift in the last decades of the twentieth century, from "managed" to "entrepreneurial" economies, more enthusiastically embraced in Europe by the UK and the Netherlands, but less enthusiastically by other (coordinated market economy) countries. The shift involves significant trade-offs, they suggest, which the latter have been reluctant to make. Japan might be included in this group as well.[2] The authors see the "twin forces of globalization" – competition from lower wage economies, and telecommunications and computer revolutions – as drivers of the shift.

With this transformation came a renewed interest in the entrepreneur and small business owner. A trickle of research grew into a strong surge, with multiple streams, giving rise to calls for greater rigor and theoretical sophistication (Low and MacMillan, 1988) and the creation of a coherent field of research with delineated boundaries. By the mid-1990s, however, the streams had become torrents. Far from disappearing, the entrepreneur now featured in start-ups, large firms, nonprofits, politics, and even in institutions and norm changing. Once elusive, the entrepreneur was now ubiquitous, but potentially all things to all people.

To avoid generating further confusion, we begin this chapter by clarifying what we mean by entrepreneurs and entrepreneurship. This is important for justifying our approach and selection criteria, which include non-founders. Having provided a working definition, we introduce studies comparing *levels* of entrepreneurship in different countries, and offering reasons for different levels. This highlights the apparently anomalous nature of Japan (and others), and brings our very different approach into sharper focus. We then look at comparative institutional studies, notably from "varieties of capitalism," and their alleged influence on innovation, again to highlight points of similarity and difference. Finally, we look at fledgling attempts to construct a framework for comparative entrepreneurship research, in which we will locate this book. This will provide conceptual clarification needed before we report our empirical findings in Chapters 2–7.

---

[2] In fact in Japan, despite the dominance of large firms in policy and scholarly interest, there had not been a decline in small firms from which to spring a resurgence. Start-up activity remained high until the early 1970s, and easily exceeded closures. Such activity declined in the 1980s, however, and by the 1990s closures began to exceed start-ups in many industries (cf. Whittaker, 1997).

What is entrepreneurship?

Much of the early research on entrepreneurship focused on the entrepreneur – frequently separating the "dancer" from the "dance" (Gartner, 1988) – and the supposed distinctiveness of the entrepreneur compared with other groups such as administrators. Though now routinely dismissed, there were many interesting and insightful studies. Collins, Moore, and Unwalla (1964) distinguished entrepreneurs from "hierarchs." With an echo of Veblen, using the same data set and focusing on the entrepreneurs, Smith (1967) distinguished two types – craftsmen and opportunists – with different backgrounds, motivations, and approaches to developing their business.[3] Liles (1974) asked "Who are the entrepreneurs?" and provided interesting insights in terms of individuals' life cycles, which we will refer to again in Chapter 2. Stevenson (1983) created polar constructs of promoter and trustee, and contrasted entrepreneurial and administrative behavior or domains along a number of dimensions (of the "dance"). The list could go on.

There were also problems, however. One was that the "if-we-can-just-find-out-who-the-entrepreneur-is-then-we'll-know-what-entrepreneur-ship-is" approach (Gartner, 1988: 59) failed because study after study failed to confirm the distinctiveness of the entrepreneur, and entrepreneurs are not entrepreneurial all the time, leading Gartner to famously claim that "'Who is an entrepreneur?' is the wrong question." In the same year Low and MacMillan (1988) criticized past research for failing to create common ground necessary to synthesize all the insights generated. To create this common ground, they called on researchers to clarify their purpose, theoretical perspective, focus, level of analysis, time frame, and methodology.[4]

Both these critiques proposed reuniting the "dancer" with "the dance," and treating entrepreneurship as a behavioral phenomenon. Gartner (1988: 62) went further and asserted: "If we want to understand the phenomenon of entrepreneurship in order to encourage its growth, we need to focus on the process by which new organizations are created." Low and MacMillan (1988: 141), too, suggested that research should "seek to explain and facilitate the role of new enterprise in furthering economic progress."

---

[3] Stanworth and Gray (1991, chapter 7). Chell (1986) identifies (early life) "psycho-dynamic," "social development," and "trait" approaches to explaining entrepreneur distinctiveness.

[4] Cf. also Aldrich and Wiedenmayer (1993).

One stream of writing emerging from the late 1980s was thus focused on new business creation (Gartner, 1988; Carter, Gartner, and Reynolds, 1996; Gartner and Cater, 2003). Another stream also emerged which was critical of this approach. According to this stream it is not enough to know who an entrepreneur is or what an entrepreneur does, including creating small businesses. Rather, the crucial processes occur when individuals encounter opportunity. Here entrepreneurship is seen as "how, by whom and with what effects opportunities to create future goods and services are discovered, evaluated and exploited" (Venkataraman, 1997; Shane and Venkataraman, 2000: 218). These processes can occur in the context of new business creation, in existing businesses, or even outside of firms. The form entrepreneurship takes will depend on personal and environmental factors, such as availability of capital for start-up, intellectual property (IP) protection, incentives in large firms, and so on (cf. also Shane and Eckhardt, 2003).

"Opportunity" is by no means a simple concept. Are opportunities recognized, discovered, or created? Tensions arise from the links of these views to different theoretical schools – neoclassical, Austrian, and behavioralist – but some have also seen them as complementary, and empirically valid at different stages of market creation (Sarasvathy et al., 2003; cf. also Endres and Woods, 2006). In fact, they might be seen as a spectrum, with recognition linked with arbitrage, or exploitation of existing markets by bringing supply and demand together, discovery as supplying previously nonexistent supply or demand, and creation as producing both supply and demand.

As Sarasvathy and colleagues also note, an alert entrepreneur might discover a potential opportunity, but the potential can only really be gauged through market validation, often after much hard – and creative – work. Shane and Eckhardt (2003: 169) agree: "The only reliable confirmation that a previously unseen or unknown valuable opportunity has in fact been discovered occurs when a market has been created for the new item." Here opportunity recognition, discovery, and creation are also processes of varying duration, and entrepreneurship is determined by outcomes, not just cognitive processes.

Shane and Venkataraman (2000) and Gartner (2001) agree that the emphases on individuals and opportunities, and new firm creation, are complementary. Others have tried to bring these two approaches into a single definition of entrepreneurship. Bygrave and Hofer (1991: 14), for instance, see the entrepreneur as "someone who perceives an opportunity and creates an organization to pursue it," and the "entrepreneurial process" as all the activities associated with the perceiving of opportunities and creation of organizations to pursue them. This definition implies that opportunities come first and business creation follows. But a perceived opportunity might not be a "real" one in hindsight, and a "real" one might only be discovered after business creation. In fact, Ronstadt (1988) shows that many compelling opportunities only become apparent *after* a business has been created; it is only by entering the "corridor" of business creation that the opportunities through side doors become apparent. The entrepreneur may then decide to start a new business, as Ronstadt suggests, but in principle he or she may decide to pursue the more compelling opportunity in the existing business.

These qualifications are important. If opportunity discovery or creation and new business creation are loosely linked, and if "opportunity" is determined by final market outcome, we are forced to acknowledge the ambiguous and contingent nature of entrepreneurship. We are also forced to recognize that at any point in time it may be unclear whether a would-be entrepreneur is pursuing a "real" opportunity that will find a market.

One way through the dilemma is to recognize "degrees of entrepreneurship." Aldrich and Martinez (2001: 44; also Aldrich and Kenworthy, 1999) distinguish between "reproducers" (or "imitators" as others have called them) and "innovators." They also claim that "the continuum from reproducer to innovator is defined by outcomes, not intentions." Citing Bhave (1994), moreover, Davidsson (2004: 10) argues: "No entrant is a perfect clone of an existing actor. Trying to include an innovativeness criterion in the definition of entrepreneurship would create problems." Logically, an entrepreneur or entrepreneurial business may be located at one point of the spectrum at a certain point of time, and at another point at another point of time. Significantly, Aldrich and Kenworthy suggest, and our study will confirm, that most nascent entrepreneurs start out as small reproducers and not as "home-run" innovators.

The reversible, indeterminate, indeed creative nature of the entrepreneurial process is further highlighted in Sarasvathy's "effectuation" theory, which stresses the pursuit of "ambiguous, changing and *constructed* goals" (2001: 244; emphasis in original) through the deployment of means over which the entrepreneur has control. Here means as well as ends influence cognitive and behavioral processes, and the deployment of means influences ends ultimately pursued as much or more than ends influence means.[5] In fact, we see entrepreneurs as frequently having multiple goals,

---

[5] This is analogous to structures or competences influencing strategy in contingency theory and strategic management writing.

such as making ends meet in the short term, whilst pursuing a longer-term opportunity. Multiple goals imply trade-offs and compromises. Entrepreneurs are influenced by desirability as well as feasibility (Christensen et al., 1994). If we want to understand processes of entrepreneurship (the dance), then we cannot ignore the entrepreneur (dancer), or environmental influences on both.

As this brief and highly selective account shows, entrepreneurship defies simple, watertight definition. In this book we will treat it broadly, as *processes in which opportunities are discovered or created, and turned into market outcomes by organizational means*. While we have sympathy for those seeking to pin down entrepreneurship precisely, and delineate a distinctive field of research and teaching – against the odds formerly in many business schools – our encompassing approach is deliberate, for reasons which will become clear.[6]

An entrepreneur is someone who is central to these processes, who makes key entrepreneurial decisions (Casson, 1982). As we are interested in entrepreneurs as much as entrepreneurship, we will concentrate on small businesses, where individuals or small teams typically make these decisions. Moreover, we will focus on industries known for high levels of innovation, but we do not apply selection criteria beforehand to filter out "non-entrepreneurs." Later, in Chapter 4, we will identify a group of growing, novel innovating businesses in both the UK and Japan, which we call "high performers," and we will compare them with "non-high performers" (who are not necessarily reproducers or imitators).

Levels of entrepreneurship

Are levels of entrepreneurship the same everywhere? This question has been asked by many people, who have offered a range of views and explanations. In *The Protestant Ethic and the Spirit of Capitalism*, Weber (1904–05; 1935) argued that heroic entrepreneurs alone could not create the capitalism of northern Europe. Rather, its origins lay in the indirect influence of Protestant – especially Calvinist – beliefs. Seeking to build on Weber, in *The Achieving Society* McClelland (1961) proposed that the combination of need for achievement, power, and affiliation differed not just between individuals, but between societies, giving rise to different levels of entrepreneurship.

---

[6] For some, our working definition may be *too* restrictive, as it fails, for instance, to include social entrepreneurship, or entrepreneurship outside organizations.

With the shift in focus we noted from individuals and traits to processes, new approaches have been developed, first of all in measuring levels of entrepreneurship. Here the new business creation definition has been favored over the opportunity approach, as it is more amenable to statistical data collection and analysis. Where business creation figures are lacking, alternatives such as numbers of small business owners or self-employed have been used. For example, researchers in Europe have developed a harmonized database called Comparative Entrepreneurship Data for International Analysis (COMPENDIA) using measures of unincorporated and incorporated self-employment, based mainly on OECD labor force statistics. With this, they have compared levels in twenty-three countries between 1972 and 2002.

In these thirty years, across eighteen European countries, the self-employment rate initially fell, but began to rise again from the 1980s to reach 11.0 percent of the labor force in 2002. In the USA and the UK it rose between 1972 and the late 1980s, but dropped back somewhat from the late 1990s to 9.5 percent and 10.7 percent respectively in 2002. In Japan it rose between 1972 and 1980, but from the 1980s it began a steady decline, to 9.2 percent in 2002. Over the thirty years, the UK ranking rose from 18th to 12th, and the US ranking from 16th to 13th, while Japan dropped from 4th to 14th (Van Stel, 2004; cf. also Verheul et al., 2002). Topping the table in 2002 were Mediterranean countries, followed by several anglophone countries.

Self-employment is not the same as entrepreneurship, however. It measures neither business creation nor opportunity discovery or creation. An alternative initiative surveys intentions and engagement in new business creation. The Global Entrepreneurship Monitor (GEM) consortium was started in 1997 by researchers at Babson College in the USA and the London Business School, and by 2004 had grown to encompass thirty-four countries. GEM calculates a "total entrepreneurial activity" (TEA) index consisting of the proportion of 18- to 64-year-old "nascent entrepreneurs" – people who have taken some action to start a new business in the past year – and owner-managers of new businesses, which have paid wages for more than three months but less than 42.[7]

In this measure the USA and some anglophone countries appear in the upper middle or top band (after countries like Uganda, Venezuela, and Argentina) and the UK in the lower middle, while Japan languishes at the tail (with Italy, France, and Croatia). If this is a real measure of

[7] See www.gemconsortium.org

entrepreneurship, it is conspicuous by its absence in Japan and only moderately better in the UK.[8] However, it appears to measure intentions as much as actual behavior. Using GEM 2004 data, Burchell and Hughes (2007: 8) calculate 20.7 million individuals engaged in TEA in the USA, compared with a total level of self-employment of just 14.2 million in 2000![9]

Another group has used Eurobarometer survey data to calculate seven entrepreneurship engagement levels, ranging from "never thought about starting a business" and "thought about it but gave up" through "thinking about it," "taking steps for starting up," and "having a young business" to "having an older business" and "no longer an entrepreneur." Here the USA scores higher on intentions and preliminary steps than most (Western) European countries, but the differences disappear when it comes to businesses actually set up, and when it comes to older businesses (three or more years), the US score is actually lower than that in most of the European countries (Grilo and Thurik, 2006).

Depending on whether one focuses on intentions, nascent entrepreneurship, or subsequent outcomes, then, a very different picture of entrepreneurship levels appears. Countries with high start-up rates tend to have high closure rates as well, while those with low start-up rates have low closure rates. The former might be an important vehicle for Darwinian upgrading, but if we accept Shane and Venkataraman's opportunity view of entrepreneurship, the latter might be just as entrepreneurial, only in different ways. Table 1.1 looks at "high-tech" manufacturing industries in Japan, the USA, and the UK, industries in which we would normally expect to find high levels of entrepreneurship. The table shows that even with the tightest criterion, there is a greater share of small-firm employees in at least half of the industries in Japan. How, if Japan's start-up rate is so low?[10]

The answer is simple. Closure rates are also low, and many existing small businesses have diversified into these industries. (As we noted, start-up rates in Japan were high until the 1970s, giving the country a massive small-firm base, which may have shrunk, but is still very substantial.

---

[8] The 2003 GEM survey introduced a second measure of entrepreneurial activity – "firm entrepreneurship" – of firms of the owner-managers providing goods or services new to the marketplace, as a proportion of all firms, and as a proportion of all jobs. This was subsequently dropped (cf. Reynolds et al., 2004: 6–13).

[9] In New Zealand, too, the figures suggest 340,000 people engaged in nascent entrepreneurial activity in 2004, which is more than the total number of businesses.

[10] Japanese start-up rate figures are not very reliable, and tend to underestimate actual start-ups because of the survey method and infrequency of surveys. Matsuda (2006) argues that they could in fact be rising sharply.

Table 1.1 Small business employment share in high-tech manufacturing industries: Japan, the USA, and the UK (%)

	Japan (2003)	USA (2004)	UK (2003)
Chemicals	11.4	15.2	10.1
Pharmaceuticals	7.3*	15.9	4.0
Special-purpose machinery	41.4	32.5	37.3
Ordnance	6.8	15.6	10.7
Office machinery and computers	19.5	16.8	17.1
Electricity distributing, generating, and control equipment	33.5	21.9	24.6
Electronic components and other equipment	14.4	15.8	21.2
Radio, TV communication, and related equipment	15.0	18.6	15.3
Medical instruments	34.2	27.6	33.3
Instruments for checking, testing, navigating, industrial control, and other purposes	30.3	17.5	25.0
Optical instruments	31.4	19.0	31.3
Aerospace	7.4	12.0	2.7

Notes: UK figures are for businesses with 1–49 employees, Japanese figures for 4–49, and US figures for 0–99.
* 2005 figure
Definition of ''high-tech'' based on Butchart (1987) and Hecker (1999).

Sources: Japan: Ministry of International Trade and Industry, *Kogyo tokei*; USA: http://www.census.gov/; UK: Department of Trade and Industry, SME Statistics for the UK.

A large base, moreover, mathematically suppresses start-up rates.) There is no a priori reason, according to Shane and Venkatarman's view, why diversification should not be as entrepreneurial as a new start-up, or a second-generation business owner as entrepreneurial as the first. In fact, in Japan innovative "venture" businesses tend to be older than the average business (Whittaker, 1997). It is for this reason that our definition of entrepreneurship specifies opportunities turned into market outcomes by "organizational means" rather than "new business creation," and why we have not limited our attention to founders, except in Chapters 2 and 3, which look at founding and opportunity creation processes.[11]

Measuring levels of entrepreneurship is one thing; accounting for them is another. GEM researchers have identified a number of factors which appear to be related to TEA levels, including demographics, education levels, and household wealth. And the interaction of these factors appears to be different in "developing" and "advanced" countries. Taking this observation further, they have identified a U-shaped curve where the horizontal axis is per capita GDP, and the vertical axis is the ratio of TEA among 18- to 64-year-olds. Entrepreneurial activity is high in countries with low per capita GDP because of "necessity entrepreneurship." It declines as per capita GDP increases, but then increases again as "opportunity entrepreneurship." Thus, entrepreneurship is high in pre- or early-industrial countries, declines when large manufacturing firms – and presumably secure jobs – become established with industrialization, and rises again with the relative decline of manufacturing and expansion of services. This third stage corresponds to the "resurgence" of small firms and entrepreneurship amongst a number of developed countries from the 1980s (Acs et al., 2005: 38–41).

Interestingly, those countries plotted above GEM's parabolic curve – those with higher than average levels of TEA at a particular per capita GDP level – are the USA, Australia, Canada, New Zealand, Israel, and (only just) the UK; essentially Anglo-Saxon or liberal market economies. Those plotted below the curve, on the other hand – those with lower than

---

[11] Support for this position comes from a study of turbulence, in which the sum of entry and exit rates is scaled by industry size. As Van Stel and Diephuis (2004) point out, we need to know not just the amount of turbulence, but also its composition, since the effects of entry are different from those of exit. They use a measure called volatility – turbulence minus the absolute value of net entry – to measure turbulence not reflected in changes in the number of firms. Using data from fifteen "innovative" (or high-tech) industries in six countries, they find the greatest volatility in the USA, and the lowest in Japan (the UK was not included). Although they find that net entry and volatility contribute positively to employment growth, they fail to find an "optimal" level of volatility for industry-level growth by country.

average levels of TEA at a particular per capita GDP level, but wealthy nonetheless – are the Scandinavian countries and Japan, and to a lesser extent some other Continental European countries. This lack of fit in both directions might be interpreted in several ways, but one is different styles of entrepreneurship, or at least innovation, rather than a prevalence in one group and a lack in the other.

Similarly to GEM, Hofstede and colleagues (2004) looked at a range of economic, cultural, and "dissatisfaction" variables from COMPENDIA data, and found a strong link between self-employment and dissatisfaction. Poor European countries have high levels of dissatisfaction and high levels of self-employment. As income levels rise, dissatisfaction falls, and so does self-employment, until as countries make a postindustrial transition either unemployment (and presumably dissatisfaction) rises or new opportunities associated with a service-based economy spark a rise in self-employment.

The U-curve thesis has become more sophisticated as control new variables are added (Wennekers et al., 2005). Whether the thesis, and indeed the whole resurgence thesis, will require reexamination in the light of the recent tapering off and decline in start-up rates in some postindustrial countries, the UK included, is an interesting question.

A second and more popular approach to explaining levels of entrepreneurship is "culture." This approach has a long history, dating back to Max Weber, and earlier. Culture might influence levels of entrepreneurship directly, through the cognitive or affective dispositions of would-be entrepreneurs, or indirectly by fostering a supportive or obstructive environment (Davidsson and Wiklund, 1997).[12]

"Culture" is a slippery concept, but Hofstede's constructs have been extensively used. Hofstede sees culture as "the collective programming of the mind which distinguishes the members of one group or category of people from those of another" (1991: 5). In this view the mind is not hardwired – deviation is possible – but mental programming results in reactions to situations which are "likely and understandable." Based originally on surveys of IBM managers between 1967 and 1973, Hofstede developed a number of dimensions for measuring culture, including

---

[12] Regarding the second, environmental influence, Etzioni (1987) argued that "legitimation" plays a key role in determining levels of entrepreneurship. The higher the level of legitimation, the more resources will be dedicated to educating and training entrepreneurs, the more the polity will reward entrepreneurs, and the higher the respect and the psychic rewards for entrepreneurs. More recently, there has been interest in influences such as popular and legal attitudes toward failure and second chances (Armour and Cumming, 2005; Burchell and Hughes, 2007).

"power distance," individualism, masculinity, and uncertainty avoidance (Hoftstede, 1980), which researchers have used as independent variables for explaining levels of entrepreneurship.

Shane (1992; 1993), for instance, found that national rates of per capita innovation (measured by patents granted to nationals of thirty-three countries in various years) is positively correlated with individualism and power-distance, and negatively associated with uncertainty avoidance. He found, however, that the association was becoming weaker over time, and cited "anecdotal evidence that many collectivist and hierarchical Asian nations are becoming more innovative" (Shane, 1993: 59)!

While conducive to quantitative research, Hofstede's framework has been criticized on a number of grounds. Hunt and Levie (2003) attempted to correlate Hofstede's four indices (and "authority" and "well-being" from Inglehart's [1997] World Values Survey) with GEM's TEA, but could find no relationship, except a modest link between *corporate* start-ups and uncertainty avoidance. They conclude – as do Hayton and colleagues (2002) – that "culture in terms of these constructs is not a key driver of entrepreneurship" (Hunt and Levie, 2003: 6).[13]

Tan (2002) points out that "culture" and "nation" cannot be used interchangeably, and that in fact the latter appears to be more decisive in explaining entrepreneurs' strategic orientations. A third approach has therefore been to link levels of entrepreneurship with national institutional variables such as tax levels and social security provision (e.g., Parker and Robson, 2004). These efforts have become increasingly sophisticated. Kostova (1997) and Busenitz and colleagues (2000) have attempted to create "country institutional profiles" for entrepreneurship consisting of regulatory, cognitive, and normative dimensions.

Sweden, noted above as an outlier on the GEM parabola, has received particular attention. Introducing a special journal issue on institutions and entrepreneurship in Sweden, Karlsson and Acs (2002: 66) noted:

It appears as if there is a negative correlation between entrepreneurship and the total taxes as a share of GDP, the public spending as a share of GDP, the average corporate tax level, the marginal personal income tax rate, the degree of equality in the income distribution, labor costs, the degree of rigidity in the labor market, the degree of non-participation in higher education, and so on.

---

[13] More recently, Hofstede himself has found stronger links between self-employment and dissatisfaction than culture, as noted above. There are alternative conceptions of (direct) cultural influence based on needs theory, such as need for achievement (McClelland, 1961) and need for autonomy (Brockhaus, 1982).

They do warn, however, that the correlations "should be treated as circumstantial evidence only" (ibid.). Regarding a similar set of claims by OECD chief economist Cotis to the 2007 GEM Forum, Dore (2007) comments wryly: "Ironically, according to the paper of the OECD chief economist just cited, Sweden comes top of 20 OECD countries on a combined index of 'innovative activity'."[14]

Summing up, there are a number of problems with comparative levels of entrepreneurship writing. On the plus side, its importance in raising interesting questions and testing formal hypotheses should not be underestimated. On the other hand, first, the increasingly complicated algebra needed to improve reliability makes it accessible to fewer and fewer people. Second, the approach largely fails to account for entrepreneurship in countries like Japan and Sweden. Third, and crucially for us here, it does not actually tell us much about entrepreneurship itself. It gives us variables, when there is an acknowledged need for studying entrepreneurship as a process. We do not get a dancer *or* a dance, or an understanding of interactions with cultural or institutional environments.

Varieties of capitalism and types of innovation

Outside of the field of entrepreneurship there is already a flourishing school of research and writing about country institutional profiles, less quantitatively driven, with roots in neo-institutionalism. Neo-institutionalism has typically paid scant regard to entrepreneurship (Aldrich, 1999) or indeed actors and agency, but this has been changing, with a growing interest in the microfoundations of institutions (DiMaggio and Powell, 1983; 1991)[15] and new currents such as "actor-centred institutionalism" (Scharpf, 1997; Mantazavinos, 2001), which have found their way into comparative institutional studies and "varieties of capitalism" (VOC) writing (Crouch, 2005).

---

[14] The Economist Intelligence Unit rated another notable GEM outlier and laggard, Japan, the world's most innovative country in 2007, followed by Switzerland, the USA, and Sweden (press release, May 18, 2007).

[15] DiMaggio and Powell's (1983) concept and typology of institutional and competitive "isomorphism" has been influential. Aldrich and Martinez (2003), too, have developed a typology of cognitive, moral, and regulatory legitimacy which creates isomorphic pressures. These pressures are counterbalanced by resistance, experimentation, and boundary pushing as "naturally occurring behaviours" (pp. 363–4).

One influential formulation of VOC is Hall and Soskice's (2001) typology of liberal market economies (LMEs) and coordinated market economies (CMEs). LMEs are characterized by high reliance on market mechanisms for coordination, while CMEs prefer "strategic interaction supported by non-market institutions." The anglophone countries dominate the former, and a number of Continental European countries and Japan, the latter. The authors claim that "the fluid market settings of liberal market economies encourage investment in switchable assets, while the dense institutional networks of coordinated market economies enhance the attractiveness of investment in specific or co-specific assets" (Hall and Soskice, 2001: 49). These differences in investment patterns, they further claim, result in different patterns and sectoral concentrations of innovation: radical innovation in LMEs, and incremental innovation in CMEs.

Every aspect of this series of propositions has been challenged – the placing together of countries in two market economy types, the purity and stability of the types, whether radical and incremental innovation can be separated like this, the nature of the patent data used to justify the innovation typology, and so on[16] – but the essence of the argument is intuitively appealing. It is not that institutions directly facilitate or impede levels of entrepreneurship, but they influence investments and commitments, and hence innovation patterns. Countries have "comparative institutional advantages" for different types of innovation.[17]

Following this logic, Casper and colleagues (1999: 15) found "in both software and biotechnology German firms have selected the market segments that best 'fit' their inherited institutional environment: software services in software and platform technology in biotechnology." Similarly, Casper and Whitley (2004: 89) claim:

While the UK and, to a limited extent, Sweden, have developed similar institutions to those found in the US that help govern "radically innovative" firm competences, Germany has invested in institutional frameworks associated with "competency enhancing" human resource practices that give its firms an advantage in more generic technologies in which organizational complexity is higher.

---

[16] Especially Crouch (2005). In contrast to Hall and Soskice, the Economist Intelligence Unit rated both LME USA and CME Japan as providing the "strongest environments" for IT industry competitiveness in 2007 (press release, July 11, 2007). On similarities and differences between Japan and Germany, see also Yamamura and Streeck (2003), Thelen (2004), and Dore (2000).

[17] Baumol (1993) also argued that it is not so much levels of entrepreneurship which differ between countries, but its expression, productive or unproductive, which is influenced by institutions.

Thus listed biotechnology firms in Germany (and Sweden) specialize in platform technologies while their UK counterparts specialize in therapeutics, whereas in software, the German firms specialize in enterprise software and the UK firms in standard software, with a balance in Sweden which also includes middleware.

Rather than promoting a different market sector focus, or radical versus incremental innovation, Dore (2007) sees institutions as encouraging different *paths* to innovation. In the market path, individual or group inventors work out a way of making money from their invention, create a business, and seek funding and try to capture the profits. In the organization path, innovation in corporate R&D labs is carried out by employee researchers, funded by corporations and subsequently commercialized by corporations. The prevalence of the former in the USA and the latter in Japan is linked to differences in labor markets, capital markets, and other institutional and sociocultural influences.[18]

The VOC approach to innovation and (occasionally) entrepreneurship is very different from that of levels of entrepreneurship. Rather than starting with levels and seeking to explain it through culture or institutions, it frequently begins with institutions, and traces what kinds of innovation or entrepreneurship flourish or are stunted as a result of their influence. There are at least two problems with this from the point of view of our study here.

First, if we start with institutions, there is a temptation to select the kinds of innovation or entrepreneurship which result in the closest fit, and to ignore tensions and contradictions that could lead to new insights. Poorly done, it can lead to "just so" stories with a circular logic. More specifically, if we begin with institutions and their influences, we will probably end up with a poor sense of agency, derived from institutions rather than in dynamic tension with them. Rather than starting off with an "a priori paradigm case methodology," then, deriving our institutional patterns empirically should produce a more satisfactory understanding of the relationships between entrepreneurs and their institutional environments (cf. Crouch, 2005: 31).

Second, if we were to follow this approach for our comparative study of entrepreneurship in the UK and Japan, using Shane and Eckhardt's (2003) typology, we would probably concentrate on independent startups and acquisitions in the UK, and (large business) corporate venturing

---

[18] Kneller (2007) gives a detailed account of these "two worlds of innovation" which is much more critical of Japan.

and spin-offs in Japan. This might make sense in that the bulk of R&D expenditure in Japan is indeed in large businesses (although as Roper (1999) notes, "objective" measures typically understate the amount of R&D and innovation actually carried out in small firms), but we would be comparing apples and lemons, and we would not be able to answer the questions we started out with.

By focusing on entrepreneurs with small businesses in both countries, we do run the risk of comparing apples with apples where they do not grow naturally, but as we saw in Table 1.1, the prevalence of small firms in Japan in many high-tech manufacturing industries where rates of innovation are high suggests that this is actually open to question, and comparing apples with apples may generate insights missed by the predominant varieties of capitalism approach. While we do require our entrepreneurs to be people who can make key entrepreneurial decisions about pursuit of opportunity and allocation of resources (Casson, 1982), we do not require them all to be founders; some in the UK acquired their position through management buy-outs or buy-ins or succession, while some in Japan are second-generation successors, with a small number of buy-outs. We are comparing apples with apples, then, but not all of the same type.[19]

Finally regarding VOC, there are ambiguities and sometimes conflicting interpretations in views of the relationship between agents – firms, innovators, or entrepreneurs – and markets, which are core institutions. Hall and Soskice (2001: 8) see coordination of firm activities in LMEs as primarily occurring through hierarchies and markets, with an emphasis on markets, while in CMEs "firms depend more heavily on non-market relationships to coordinate their endeavours with other actors and to construct their core competences." However, market transactions do take place in CMEs, and as Block (2003) and others have argued, markets themselves are socially embedded, meaning there may well be differences in the way market transactions are carried out. A growing body of research in economic sociology points in this direction, and this is indeed what we shall find in Chapter 8.

Our approach to institutions, in brief, is that of a "wasgij" – the reverse of a jigsaw, in which the picture to be pieced together is what the characters in the given picture are looking at. In this case, we must first construct the empirical picture – a jigsaw of comparative entrepreneurship – and then figure out what the entrepreneurs are looking at. Thus our starting

---

[19] Industry-wise, too, there are different weightings within our "high-tech manufacturing" of which we must be mindful.

point is similar to our starting point with culture. Having rejected a non-socialized view of entrepreneurs and entrepreneurship on the one hand, we have no wish to embrace an over-socialized view on the other. To understand how contexts influence entrepreneurship, *and potentially vice versa*, we must do it through a nuanced approach which sees culture and institutions as situation-dependent, sometimes ambiguous and in conflict, negotiated and adapted rather than imprinting mechanisms (cf. McGrath et al., 1992). We may end up with systematic national differences and strong influences on entrepreneurship, but we do not start with them.

Comparative entrepreneurship

There are a number of studies which compare specific aspects of entrepreneurship in different countries, like founding motivations (e.g., Scheinberg and MacMillan, 1988), but surprisingly little effort has been made to study processes of entrepreneurship comparatively. Noticing this gap, Baker and colleagues (2005) have proposed a "framework for comparing entrepreneurship across nations."[20] Based on, and critical of, Shane and Venkataraman's opportunity discovery, evaluation, and exploitation (DEE) framework, they propose a comparative discovery, evaluation, and exploitation (CDEE) alternative, which takes into account contextual – especially institutional – influences in each of the D, E, and E stages. Social divisions of labor strongly influence the discovery stage, appropriability regimes and opportunity costs the evaluation stage, and resource availability the exploitation stage. These differ according to the environment. From population ecology the authors present a spectrum, ranging from rich agglomeration environments which facilitate *de novo* start-ups, through "broadly developed niches" which require specialized assets to be developed internally, and "entrepreneurial patience," to less-developed niches, where would-be entrepreneurs are "burdened by a lack of environmental munificence" and their enterprises are frequently local in scale and scope (Baker et al., 2005: 499).

The authors are no doubt right that "the study of comparative entrepreneurship requires that researchers bring social context into the foreground" and that "the 'nexus' of enterprising individuals and entrepreneurial

---

[20] Thomas and Mueller (2000) also make a "case for comparative entrepreneurship," but it is not compelling in our view. It makes a heroic leap from traits to entrepreneurship, and an even more heroic leap from university students who were surveyed to entrepreneurs who were not.

opportunities is strongly shaped, and sometimes dominated, by social structures and processes" (p. 501). The framework is neat, and the typology of environments is potentially useful. While reasonable as a theoretical statement, however, CDEE asserts rather than demonstrates how entrepreneurship emerges and unfolds in different contexts. As we have suggested, and as we shall see, the processes of entrepreneurship are not necessarily linear, and probably more complex than this framework suggests.

In our view, the Panel Study on Entrepreneurial Dynamics (which GEM grew out of) could provide a robust framework for comparative entrepreneurship research. It combines the new business creation and opportunity perspectives, views entrepreneurship as a process, and seeks to discover empirically how nascent entrepreneurs go about starting firms, what kinds of efforts are successful, and why some of the start-ups grow while others die, taking into account social, political, and economic contexts. Theoretically and empirically informed, it involves a large group of leading researchers, and while originally focused on the USA, has inspired similar studies in other countries which could be used for comparison.

Large-scale projects and longitudinal projects are very difficult to coordinate and manage, however, and here both difficulties are combined. When overall projects are divided into discrete units, moreover, it is not easy to integrate the results. Thus practical issues must be considered alongside theoretical and empirical ones. Our study is broadly resonant, but is more modest in terms of questionnaire sample size and involves only two countries. This has its weaknesses, but also advantages in terms of manageability.

We also employ a multiple-method strategy with surveys, and case (rather than follow-up) interviews. Our initial survey of owner-managers of "entrepreneurial businesses" was carried out in Japan, without a comparative study in mind. A slightly modified survey was then carried out in the UK, targeting entrepreneurs in "high-tech" industries, and focusing on entrepreneurs' professional and educational backgrounds, reasons for leaving employment, reasons for starting their new business, cofounders, and resources. The comparison between these surveys raised a host of new questions, and we decided to carry out a further survey, designed for comparison, with questions on attitudes to growth and risk, perceptions of competitive advantage and growth limitations, HRM orientations, innovation, and collaboration. We subsequently interviewed twenty-five of the respondents in both countries to help interpret and contextualize the data. (Further details are given in Appendix 1.)

There are several ways we could have approached our analysis. We could have emphasized technology, or industries, or regions, but it soon became clear that national differences or contexts were very important, and upon further analysis, this was for some of the reasons that VOC scholars have written about. It was not just that "environments" (or "cultures" or even "institutions") were very different, but more specifically the markets the entrepreneurs engaged in, as well as social relations. While rooted in entrepreneurship studies then, instead of trying to stake out boundaries, our treatment of comparative entrepreneurship ultimately looks outward, to comparative institutional studies, economic sociology, and (potentially) national innovation systems.

Concluding comments

This chapter has briefly sketched the reemergence of the entrepreneur and some of the ensuing debates about entrepreneurship. We provided a working definition of entrepreneurship – *processes in which opportunities are discovered or created, and turned into market outcomes by organizational means* – to guide us in our study. In doing so, we avoided the cultural biases inherent in start-up-based definitions, which typically cast the world's second largest economy as virtually devoid of entrepreneurship. (Indeed, resolving this apparent puzzle through our approach will be a contribution in itself.) Our entrepreneurs do not have to be founders, but they do have to be key decision-makers.

We critiqued some levels of entrepreneurship research, additionally, for its treatment of explanatory concepts like culture. Whatever else its merits, this research ultimately tells us little about entrepreneurship processes, entrepreneurs, or their interactions with their environments. We also reviewed some of the VOC writings, particularly that of Hall and Soskice (2001), who distinguish between LMEs (which includes the UK) and CMEs (which includes Japan), and suggest that their different institutional arrangements encourage different types of innovation. While the underlying thesis is appealing, we do not start out with it, and even if we end with something broadly similar, our entrepreneurs are real decision-makers, and not puppets pulled by institutional strings. We do describe two types of entrepreneurship, moreover, but concede there could be more.

Finally, we considered some nascent approaches to comparative entrepreneurship. Baker and colleagues' CDEE framework is neat, but it asserts rather than demonstrates empirically how entrepreneurship emerges and unfolds in different contexts. In the next six chapters we will present our empirical findings. Throughout, we focus on the entrepreneurs and their perceptions, beginning with their careers, motivations, and business and opportunity creation.[21]

---

[21] We do consider finance to be important, but our view, supported by the findings of Chapter 5, is that human resources – of the founder, founding team, and employees – are *the* key resource.

2

Opportunity and Business Creation

We begin our exploration of entrepreneurship in the UK and Japan with opportunity and business creation.[1] We want to find out whether these processes in the two countries are basically similar, or whether there are systematic differences. Either outcome is potentially interesting. To guide us, we adopt the "AMO" framework, which sees performance – or the opportunity and business creation processes here – as a combination of ability, motivation, and opportunity.[2] Ability provides the skills, but without motivation they will not be mobilized. Conversely, motivation without ability is likely to result in failure. More generally, how an entrepreneur engages in opportunity and business creation will depend not just on the nature of the possible opportunity, but on the entrepreneurs' abilities and motivation as well.

Perhaps in their desire to stake out a distinctive field of entrepreneurship studies, many researchers have paid only passing attention to entrepreneurs' backgrounds.[3] Yet as we shall see, these are critical not just for the accumulation of abilities or skills, but in influencing motivations, uncovering the beginnings of opportunities, and providing a trigger which leads to new opportunity and business creation. We might predict extensive differences in the backgrounds and *abilities* of entrepreneurs in both countries, given previous comparative research on labor markets and employment relations (e.g., Dore, 1973; Whittaker, 1990). But how much and in

---

[1] We will use opportunity "creation" in preference to "discovery" since in high-tech manufacturing, opportunities typically have to be constructed, even if *potential* opportunities are recognized or discovered. We use the expression "opportunity and business creation" (OBC) because opportunity creation and business creation are intertwined at the start-up stage. We will also call entrepreneurs "he" in Chapters 2–7 because the overwhelming majority of those surveyed were male.

[2] Cf. Davidsson (1991), Christensen et al. (1994), Lundström and Stevenson (2005); also Boxall and Purcell (2003).

[3] There are, of course, exceptions. For a review and note on the PSED approach see Brush and Manolova (2004).

what ways do these matter when it comes to creating opportunities and businesses?

Given labor market and employment relations differences, we might predict differences in *motivation* as well. Blocked promotion or disagreements with bosses might be needed to prompt quitting employment and embarking on the path of entrepreneurship in Japan, while motivations and triggers might be more diverse in the UK. Economic turbulence in the 1980s might figure in the backgrounds of the UK entrepreneurs, but not in the Japanese, where corporate restructuring in manufacturing at least was less common until the late 1990s.

Differences in the economic environment would influence not only motivations, but also the nature of *opportunities*. When it comes to opportunity creation, the "varieties of capitalism" perspective might lead us to expect a greater prevalence of imitation or incremental innovation in Japan and novel innovation in the UK, and potentially different approaches to innovation itself. These are very general expectations, however, and we need a much more concrete understanding of the entrepreneurs' backgrounds, motivations, and pursuit and creation of opportunities to begin our study.

In the first section we compare the backgrounds of entrepreneurs, and in the second section we compare motivations, or at least reasons for starting a business. The analysis is based on responses to the first ("Founders and Founding") survey, and considers founders only. We then look at opportunity and business creation (OBC). As these are typically complex processes, in which a business can be created to pursue an opportunity or an opportunity can follow the founding of a business with considerable trial and error, they are difficult to capture in survey responses. Instead we turn to our case interviews. In addition to founders of high-tech manufacturing businesses, these include some non-founders and a small number of high-tech services (software and technology consulting). Again, details of our methods and surveys are given in Appendix 1.

We find considerable and unexpected (by us) similarities, and at the same time some fundamental – and unexpected – country differences.

Backgrounds

In answering his question "Who are the entrepreneurs?" Liles (1974) claimed that two conditions are critical: how ready potential entrepreneurs see themselves, and how many distractions or obligations hold them back. Readiness typically increases with time, as people enter employment, master specialized routine tasks, assume increasing responsibility, and finally master complex problems. As they approach their peak, however, the restraints kick in. The (American) entrepreneur "now has two cars instead of one, a larger house, and takes more expensive vacations. These costs, closely following if not overtaking income, as a practical matter are only adjustable upward. And until the children have finished school, it is unusual to find sufficient funds for anything approaching financial flexibility" (Liles, 1974: 40). Liles calls the zone in which readiness is high and restraints are low – late 20s to late 30s – the "free choice period." A trigger is also needed, however, which can be identification of an opportunity, or deteriorating job satisfaction, combined with support, especially from a spouse.

Popular images of youthful IT business founders may make this view seem dated. Lack of mastery of "complex problems" can be overcome by support teams mobilized by venture capitalists, or the increasing incidence of two-income families, which potentially lessen some of the financial constraints. Entrepreneurship has been unleashed and the "free choice period" extended. Or has it? Perhaps not, if the entrepreneurs in this study are anything to go by.

The importance of looking at entrepreneurs' backgrounds was brought home to us by the answers of UK entrepreneurs to an open question in the first survey, in which they were invited to "recall any critical events or experiences which influenced (a) your approach to business, and (b) the development of your business." As many as three-quarters responded to this question, and one-third referred to previous employment. Some referred to skills developed, and, importantly, confidence in them:

In the previous employment I had the opportunity to operate within an environment which I solely controlled. . . . I gained confidence in my own abilities.

Along with skills went opportunity recognition:

I was producing designs for the control of air conditioning and refrigeration equipment, and I realized I could produce these controls better than any other potential suppliers at the time.

I saw a need for improved medical appliances used in body waste collection. The current products caused patient discomfort. My pharmacy gave me the financial security and government grants to develop and manufacture our products.

Previous employment was also linked to motivation:

1. Working with incompetent, lazy, disorganized bosses. 2. Working in academic life – too slow and repetitive. 3. Working for more effective, interesting clients. 4. Clients

who gave us the opportunity to get started. 5. Opportunity for FREEDOM from gerbils, small minded book-keeping dolts, dishonest bosses, arrogant creative people.

Finally, a pressing or impending situation quite often provided a trigger:

(a) The opportunity afforded by the closure of the R&D operation was critical for the start up of the business; (b) Familiarity with the market was essential to the conviction that a chance be taken and success would follow.

Indeed, for both the UK and Japanese entrepreneurs the average age of founding of their (current) business was 37, which is toward the high end of Liles' "free choice period." This means that most had considerable work experience before founding, and may be indicative of the skills and resources typically required for high-tech manufacturing businesses.[4] Let us look more closely at that work experience which may prove critical for OBC. We preface our analysis by noting that the UK entrepreneurs were asked specifically about the company they had spent the most time in prior to starting their own company, while the Japanese entrepreneurs were asked to report on prior work experience in general. If anything, then, the figures understate the range of UK entrepreneurs' experience, since a high proportion had changed job several times.

Previous functional work experience is summarized in Table 2.1 under the categories of R&D, production (including drafting/design and production engineering), staff (accounting, planning, personnel), and sales and marketing. According to the table, the one category more Japanese entrepreneurs reported experience in compared to the UK entrepreneurs was production. More UK entrepreneurs had experience in the other three categories, especially staff and sales and marketing. In addition, three-quarters of the Japanese group reported experience in just one area, compared to half the UK group. Some 60 percent of the Japanese group *only* had experience in a technical area (R&D, production), compared with one-third of the UK group. On the other hand, a significant minority – roughly a third in both countries – only had experience in nonproduction areas.

Some had all-round experience. A third of the UK entrepreneurs but only a very small proportion of the Japanese entrepreneurs had experience in both technical and nontechnical areas. In fact, a quarter of the UK

---

[4] Many started thinking about starting their own business "after working for several years" (60 percent of UK entrepreneurs, 37 percent of Japanese entrepreneurs). Interestingly a quarter of Japanese entrepreneurs started thinking about their own business before they started work, and a quarter soon after starting work – far more than UK entrepreneurs. This dream, however, was prolonged, as starting ages were the same. Some of the UK entrepreneurs had previously started other businesses, moreover, which meant that the average age of founding their *first* business was lower.

Table 2.1 Previous work experience

	UK % ($n = 148$)	Japan % ($n = 90$)
Previous functional experience		
R&D	41.9	34.2
Production	38.5	45.2
Staff	23.9	12.3
Sales and marketing	51.3	28.8
Previous management experience		
Senior manager	47.0	24.3
Middle/junior manager	33.3	42.9
Other	19.7	32.9
Size of previous business (employees)		
1–19	17.1	7.0
20–99	24.8	63.6
100–299	17.1	14.1
300 +	41.0	42.2

entrepreneurs said they had experience in all four areas, compared with only 6 percent of the Japanese entrepreneurs. Caution is needed in interpreting these figures – backgrounds are often more complex than the responses suggest, as we found from our interviews – but they do appear to point to greater diversity and broader functional backgrounds of UK entrepreneurs, and narrower backgrounds, often in a technological area, of the Japanese entrepreneurs. (Quite a few of the Japanese entrepreneurs' experiences in sales and marketing, moreover, had a strong technology focus.)

Next, let us look at previous management experience, dividing the responses into "senior manager" (Chairman, CEO, MD, other director/senior manager), "middle/junior manager" and "other." Table 2.1 suggests more extensive senior management experience on the part of the UK entrepreneurs; almost half had experience at this level compared with a quarter of the Japanese entrepreneurs, whose management experience was mainly at the middle/junior management level.[5] Some of the difference might be related to the size of the businesses they had worked for; a similar proportion worked in large businesses, with more than 300 employees, but a higher proportion of UK entrepreneurs had worked in micro businesses, with fewer than 20 employees, whereas more Japanese entrepreneurs had worked in small businesses, with 20–99 employees. Although not shown in the table, most had worked in similar industries to the one they had established their business in, but there was slightly more variation among the UK entrepreneurs.

---

[5] The Japanese figures are comparable with those of Peoples' Finance Corporation (PFC) surveys, although these typically only distinguish between directors and managers (Kokumin kin'yu koko, 2002, 2004).

Table 2.2 Previous job-changing experience

Number of job changes	0	1	2	3	4 +
UK	20.9	16.7	32.4	28.4	22.6
Japan	14.4	43.1	31.9	18.1	7.0

In terms of job-changing experience, Table 2.2 shows that, contrary to popular stereotypes, slightly more Japanese entrepreneurs had changed jobs at least once prior to starting their own business, but the UK entrepreneurs had changed jobs more on average.[6] In addition, we note that one in five of the UK entrepreneurs had started more than one business. We do not have comparable Japanese data. Our case interviews show this happened occasionally in Japan, but not as frequently.

Overall, the survey data suggest broader functional job experience, more management experience, and sometimes entrepreneurial experience on the part of the UK entrepreneurs. These might give them more cognitive resources to perceive, and confidence and skills to create, opportunities, while Japanese entrepreneurs, with their more focused, technical backgrounds, might be expected to follow a narrower technological or production path, with a technology-push rather than a market-pull emphasis.

Finally, let us consider education levels. Table 2.3 shows that a similar proportion – just under half – had university degrees. Not surprisingly, the proportions were higher for younger entrepreneurs, and those of more recently founded businesses. A much higher proportion of the UK entrepreneurs had a postgraduate as well as an undergraduate degree. Postgraduate degrees in Japan have traditionally been undertaken by students aspiring to an academic career, whereas companies have preferred to hire graduates from a four-year undergraduate degree program. Only in recent years has the bar shifted to the masters level in engineering, and may be shifting now in humanities and social sciences.

As for degree type, from the functional work experience background we might expect more Japanese entrepreneurs to have a technological education, but this is not the case. In fact, a higher proportion of UK entrepreneurs had a science or engineering degree than their Japanese counterparts. Some additionally had a humanities or social science degree,

---

[6] These figures should be treated with some caution – it is possible that some Japanese respondents might have indicated the number of companies worked at previously, rather than job changes. On the other hand, in the same PFC survey just noted, Japanese founders had changed jobs on average 2.8 times before starting their own business (Kokumin kin'yu koko, 2002). Amongst our Japanese interviewees, too, there was often an intermediate business between a company they had been employed in the long term, and the business they started up.

Table 2.3 University education and degree type

	Education level			Degree type		
	No degree	1st degree	Postgraduate degree	Science/ engineering	Humanities/ social science	Both
UK	53.8	13.1	33.1	75.6	17.8	6.7
Japan	54.4	43.3	2.2	70.7	26.8	2.4

usually an MBA, which was less common for the Japanese graduates, reflecting the scarcity or recency of MBA education in Japan.

In combination with the previous work experience data, this suggests that many of the UK entrepreneurs started out in science or engineering jobs, but then moved into other functional areas and/or management before starting their own business. Japanese entrepreneurs, however, started with engineering or science jobs, in manufacturing companies, and from these data at least, many did not stray from those jobs.[7] From the case interviews, the following quotes are illustrative.

Having done my apprenticeship, I went as a drawing office technician. Then I got a job at T as an electronics engineer, and then went into software engineering. I went into marketing as a product specialist, and then as a service manager. Then I had a complete change of career. The guy I worked for at the time was a bit of an industrial bully, and the company knew it. I was one of the only people who would talk back to him, so they put me in charge of personnel and quality. That was a great eye opener to skills other than technical. . . . Then I had an opportunity to become operations director . . . and eventually we splintered off. So I have broad knowledge, rounded. The only experience I didn't get was accounting. (UK18)

I started with a technical background . . . and became engineering manager. Partly due to an interest in the business side I became involved in management and became part of the management team. (UK9)

I began to think of quitting to become independent when I was 38, but I consider the trigger was (my company's) decision to quit LED, which I had been doing research on, and thought there was a future in it. When I quit, I did not have any orders or customers, just a desire to make my own company. (J1)

In sum, there were both similarities and differences in backgrounds. The average age at founding was the same. Few entrepreneurs started their business (in the UK, their *first* business) before their late twenties, and most started them in their thirties or forties. This was the time when many

[7] Moreover, while most social science or humanities graduates were assigned to staff or sales and marketing jobs, sometimes even nonengineering graduates were assigned to production in Japan. Nongraduates might be assigned to either.

had family responsibilities – young children and a mortgage – and could be expected to shun risk, but it was also the time when they had accumulated skills, resources, and experience crucial for starting their own business. Most had changed jobs, and as we shall see, this sometimes involved being part of an entrepreneurial team, as a stepping stone to creating a new business. Finally, education levels were broadly similar; around half had a university degree, although more UK entrepreneurs had a higher degree as well.

There were also differences that were partly predictable. Not only did the UK entrepreneurs have broader functional experience, but they had more senior management experience as well. The Japanese entrepreneurs had narrower functional experience, focused in technical areas of R&D and production (although a similar proportion to the UK had experience in nontechnical areas only). They also had less senior management experience, and had changed jobs less often.

The question that concerns us is whether these similarities and differences are also related to OBC processes, and if so, how? Before we look at this, though, we need to consider the reasons or motivations they considered were important in founding their business, again drawing on the first, Founders and Founding, survey.

Reasons for starting the business

Career backgrounds and skills are likely to influence the way nascent entrepreneurs create opportunities and businesses, but there will be other influences as well. Feasibility needs to be backed by desirability. There is by now an accumulation of research on reasons or motivations for starting businesses, some of it drawing on needs or expectancy theory.[8] Our aim in this section is not to test specific motivation theories; rather we want to explore reasons given for starting the business, which can shed light on this second cognitive dimension.

Scheinberg and MacMillan (1988) propose six broad factors in business start-ups which vary across countries – need for approval, communitarianism, wealth, personal development, independence, and escape. Shane et al. (1991) identify four factors – recognition, independence, learning,

---

[8] See Gatewood (2004) for a brief summary of expectancy and related theories applied to entrepreneurship.

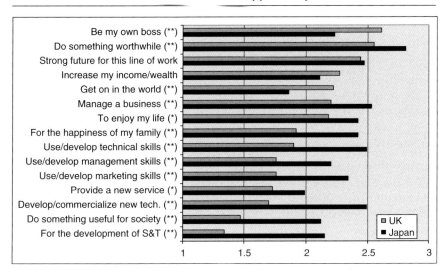

Figure 2.1 Reasons for starting a business

Note: 1 = insignificant; 2 = significant; 3 = crucial
** differences significant at .01; * differences significant at .05

roles – while Birley and Westhead (1994) propose seven.[9] These factors will naturally depend on the items listed in surveys. Our items derive from the original Japanese survey (which was not designed for comparison). It used fifteen items, and a three-point scale.

The results are summarized in Figure 2.1. In terms of both means and ranking, there are striking differences between entrepreneurs in the two countries, although one of these should be treated with caution. The item most strongly emphasized by the UK founders was "I wanted to be my own boss." Unfortunately, we cannot necessarily infer that this was less important for the Japanese entrepreneurs because the Japanese item read "I wanted to be a company president."[10]

Wanting to do something worthwhile and a strong future in this work ranked highly in both countries, but increasing income and getting on in the world differed sharply. So sharply, in fact, that it seemed as if many of the Japanese entrepreneurs were saying: "If I wanted to increase my income and get on in the world I would not have become an entrepreneur.

[9] See Carter et al. (2004) for a brief review and preliminary treatment of the PSED (Panel Survey on Entrepreneurial Dynamics) research. One Japanese study which explores start-up motivations, and links to subsequent growth, points to the influence of immediate social networks, and social contribution and self-actualization motivations (Yasuda, 2004).

[10] The English was changed to make it more understandable to UK respondents, but this compromised the comparison. Translations for other items are comparable. An extra UK item – "I wanted to commercialize an existing technology" – has been dropped from the comparison because it did not rank highly on the UK list and was not in the Japanese list.

(I would have kept working at my prestigious company.)" Conversely, and perhaps predictably from the previous discussion on backgrounds, they ranked commercializing a new technology and using technical skills much more highly than their UK counterparts.

We wanted to know whether these answers were simply different emphases, or whether they reflected different underlying constructs as well, so we did a factor analysis. The results are summarized in Table 2.4. In the UK, five factors explained roughly two-thirds (63.1 percent) of the variance. The first consists of six items, five of which were ranked most highly. The desire to be their own boss, to manage a business, to get on in the world, to increase their income, and to do something worthwhile suggest a strong orientation toward personal advancement, or "getting on."

The second factor encompasses the three skill use items, and we label it "skill deployment" from previous employment. The third factor also consists of three items, the first two of which may be considered contributions to society. It is interesting that commercializing a new technology most strongly loaded onto this factor, and that the three items were ranked lowest by the UK entrepreneurs. We call it, somewhat awkwardly, "technology and society." If "getting on" represents the group of items most strongly identified with, this factor represents the items most weakly supported, or even rejected. The last two factors may be called "happiness" and, again somewhat awkwardly, "business opportunity." It is interesting to note that commercializing a new technology only very weakly loaded onto this factor.

Overall the picture suggested by the UK factor analysis is a strong desire for getting on or personal advancement in an area which had some future, and using skills accumulated from previous employment, in a way in which the founders could be happy. Social contribution per se was downplayed as a start-up reason, and technology itself did not appear to be very important – the items relating to it were dispersed over several factors.

Turning to Japan, we find not five but four factors, explaining 60.1 percent of the variance. The first encompasses six items, although the loading of the sixth is weak. Here the three UK "technology and society" factor items appear, linked to the highly ranked items of using technical skills, strong future in this line of work, and doing something worthwhile. Together they present a complex of reasons for founding, but with a strong focus on technology, looking toward the future. There is less emphasis on personal advancement, and more on doing something meaningful for self

Table 2.4 Reasons for starting the business: UK and Japanese factors

UK	Japan
1. Getting on Own boss, manage a business, get on in the world, increasing income, doing something worthwhile 2. Skill deployment Use management, marketing, technical skills 3. Technology and society Development of science and technology, something useful for society, commercialize a new technology 4. Happiness Enjoy my life, happiness of family 5. Business opportunity Provide a new service, strong future for this line of work	1. Technology (ad)venture Commercialize a new technology, development of science and technology, something useful for society, use technical skills, strong future for this line of work, do something worthwhile 2. Personal satisfaction Manage a business, increase my income, enjoy my life, happiness of my family 3. Other skills Use marketing, management skills, provide a new service 4. Advancement Own boss, get on in the world

Note: Based on principal component analysis, varimax rotation with Kaiser normalization. See Appendix 2, Tables A2.1 and A2.2 for details.

and society with technology. We call it "technology (ad)venture," not in a frivolous sense, but in the sense of stepping toward the future with a focus on technology.

The second factor brings together managing a business, increasing income, enjoying life, and family happiness. It suggests a desire to combine work/personal advancement, and family/happiness, by escaping from the limitations and frustrations of the "salaryman" life of previous employment. We call this factor "personal satisfaction." The third factor encompasses two of the skill use items – technical skills was part of the first factor – and providing a new service. We call this "other skills" and see it as a relatively minor current, contrasting with the first factor. The final factor – desire to be their own boss (company president) and getting on in the world – suggests "advancement" in a socially recognized sense. Overall, the picture of a strong technological orientation in starting the business, with a desire for a more satisfactory, independent working life and work–life balance is quite different from the picture suggested by the UK factor analysis.

Where do these differences come from? Clearly there is some link between the technical backgrounds of the Japanese founders and "technology (ad) venture" on the one hand, and the more varied UK backgrounds and "getting on" on the other. Does this mean that differences derive mainly from skills or work backgrounds? Do UK entrepreneurs with a similar technical background give similar responses to Japanese technologists, or are they closer to UK founders with nontechnical backgrounds? To answer this we divided the sample into two different groups, those with a technology-only background, and those with at least some experience in other functions. One-third of UK entrepreneurs and 60 percent of Japanese entrepreneurs fell into the former group. T-tests and Spearman ranking correlations show unambiguously that the differences are national. UK technologists are not at all like Japanese technologists, but they are like other UK founders. The same applies to the Japanese technologists. We must therefore look for other reasons for the differences.

Opportunity creation: "base hits" versus "home runs"

I left them basically because I saw this gap in the market. While I was working for them I saw this American company also go for this gap and they raised millions of dollars to get it off the ground, and they were very successful, and they were lucky as well. I thought well, we ought to do it as well. I had the skills and the contacts. So we did it all by ourselves, absolutely no money from outside. (UK2)

I left the company because I believed in my invention. . . . I began to search for a factory to make my invention, and also plunged into sales, soon after quitting the company. (J6)

The third part of "AMO" is opportunity, which we will explore in the next two sections. It is difficult to access OBC processes through questionnaires; given their complexity and varied nature, we think they are better approached through qualitative methods, such as in-depth interviews. Thus we switch to our case interviews of twenty-five UK and twenty-five Japanese entrepreneurs, noting again the somewhat differently weighted composition of the respondents (inclusion of non-*de novo* start-ups, some high-tech services, and innovative businesses) compared with the first survey. We lose our ability to do statistical comparisons, but we do gain new insights.

The different routes of OBC are depicted in Figure 2.2. After leaving school or university, the interviewees either went into long-term employment, or – somewhat less often – through a succession of jobs with different companies. Prior to becoming an entrepreneur in the sense we are using here, quite a few were involved in "quasi" entrepreneurial activities, as heads of units in large companies, junior members of buy-out teams, or even as cofounders of other enterprises. While this was more often the case in the UK, it was not uncommon for the Japanese entrepreneurs, either.

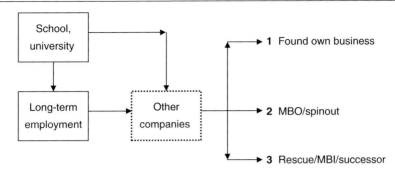

Figure 2.2 Routes to opportunity and business creation

Subsequently there were three routes to entrepreneurship: founding their own new business, management buyout (MBO) or spinouts, and successors or quasi successors, in the sense of being brought in to rescue the company of a friend or relative. Not surprisingly, the first of these routes on the one hand, and the second and third on the other, were associated with somewhat different OBC processes.[11] In this section we summarize our findings under three headings which highlight the emergent and multidimensional nature of OBC. The first of these is imitators and innovators, already introduced in our discussion of "degrees of entrepreneurship"; the second is means and ends; and the third is the concept of "soft" and "hard" starts, which we will explain.

Imitators and innovators

Most of the opportunities the entrepreneurs *started out* to pursue were modest. Very few were aiming for a "home run" in the sense of a world-first product incorporating a fundamentally new technology for a yet-to-be-created market. In some cases, in fact, they were more intent on maintaining the status quo than in pursuing an opportunity, such as when their company was going to relocate physically, or refocus strategically. These threats were recast as opportunities.

Most entrepreneurs were closer to the imitator or reproducer end of the degrees of entrepreneurship scale, with a few notable exceptions – some serial entrepreneurs in the UK, and some from routes 2 and 3, including

[11] Route 1, or new start-up entrepreneurs, made up roughly two-thirds of our interviewees. They also made up two-thirds of the high-tech manufacturing respondents in the CBR 2004 survey, while spin-off, buyout, and nonbusiness spin-offs made up one-third (Cosh and Hughes, 2007*b*).

successors in Japan. The former had been involved in previous start-ups. Some had been called on to adjudicate in subsequent business plan competitions, or to advise others with ideas for new ventures, which gave them exposure to potential new opportunities. They were unambiguously aiming at innovation.

This is the tenth business I've started. . . . This one we started in '94. P. our technical director and myself had been in the previous business and were looking round for another opportunity to invest in, but really to take full control of. At that stage I was invited by the DTI to [help set up a group, one of the members of which] asked if I could come along and talk to some of the students about commercializing technology. . . . What took my eye was a student's project about neural network technology. We set about how we would look at it and did some market research here and in the US, with some people I knew, and decided there was a bigger market for the technology elsewhere. (UK15)

As for the Japanese successors and some of the others in routes 2 and 3, our interpretation is that (*a*) they were free from the immediate pressures of feeding themselves and their employees; (*b*) they were free from the immediate pressures of gathering and organizing resources (although they were sometimes under pressure to dispose of them); and (*c*) they were able to, or had to, stand back and take a more objective view of the business and its future, or lack of it in its present form, while (*d*) their ties with key stakeholders were sufficiently loose that they could contemplate radical change (as in Granovetter's [1983] "strength of weak ties").

The real battle was internal. This was about the time I was meant to take over as president. I argued in front of the board that if I was going to become president, I wanted to quit steel construction. My father in law did not like that at all, and there was an argument. I was prepared to quit and go independent, but he finally came round. (J24, who went on to make semiconductor production machines, then satellite equipment)

I had the opportunity to take over the factory of a relative, which I happily did because I was tired of doing book work with no experiments or real-world engineering work. We were subcontracting for O. When O reduced our work, I put more effort into motors, and we succeeded in becoming a maker. (J7)

In the UK, too, the more innovative entrepreneurs tended to be either the serial entrepreneurs or the MBO entrepreneurs. The former were no longer interested in pursuing new business creation for independence reasons, having "been there, done that," but were still sufficiently interested in a bigger challenge, with potentially bigger rewards. The MBO entrepreneurs, like the Japanese successors, also had an existing business and income stream to start with, but had to take a critical look at where they were going from the outset.

From this we can see that OBC is multidimensional in nature. Some dimensions will be stronger or weaker depending on whether it is a novice entrepreneur starting a new business, an expert or serial entrepreneur, a successor, or an MBO team. Novice entrepreneurs – the majority of our interviewees – have to cope with most if not all of the multiple dimensions simultaneously, including: (*a*) creating an income source, (*b*) gathering resources and organizing them, and (*c*) pursuing an opportunity. Handling these multiple tasks simultaneously is likely to push them toward the imitator end of the spectrum. Entrepreneurs coming through routes 2 and 3, however, did not need to concern themselves with some of these dimensions, and could concentrate their energies on more ambitious innovation.

Overall, however, the founders typically started with modest innovation ambitions, aiming for a base hit rather than a home run. In fact, to stay with the baseball metaphor, it may have been sufficient simply to get into the game. They did not necessarily remain imitators, but their starting point did influence how they subsequently developed their business.

Means and ends: strategic intent

Few entrepreneurs start out with a fully worked-out business plan, which they then proceed to implement (Bhide, 2000). The route 1 entrepreneurs in this study were no exception. There was little evidence of business planning, not only in a formal sense, but sometimes in an informal sense as well:

We basically fell out with the managing director who did not understand computer systems and we decided to set up a software house. Or a consultancy as it became. We had nothing to do, we had no plans. We hadn't thought about it at all. We told our wives that this was what we were going to do, and that was the most planning that there was. (UK13)

I made up my mind to quit S when I was 36, before I became a general manager. I was working in development at the time, and the job was very interesting. . . . When I quit, I had no plan, I only had a network of engineers at the major electronics companies. Before quitting, though, I did visit some venture companies for discussions. They welcomed me because they thought I might join them. (J19)

Sarasvathy (2001, 2008), too, shows that entrepreneurs typically create opportunities not by setting clear goals and aligning means to achieve them, but with a set of means which they deploy creatively and allow goals to emerge over time. She calls this "effectual" thinking, in contrast to goal-oriented "causal" thinking, and likens it to explorers setting out on voyages into uncharted waters. The best entrepreneurs, Sarasvathy argues, use a combination of effectual and causal thinking depending on the circumstances, but they prefer effectual thinking in the early stages of a new venture, and may not transition well into later stages which require more causal thinking.

Broadly speaking, the entrepreneurs in this study support this perspective. Route 1 entrepreneurs, especially, proceeded through trial and error, using the principle of "affordable loss." If their thinking was "effectual," however, the balance appeared to tilt toward causal thinking among routes 2 and 3 entrepreneurs, especially when their plans required substantial external finance.[12] Reactions to writing a formal business plan, moreover, ranged from derision at the implausibility of the exercise, given the range of uncertainties, to appreciation at being forced to set goals and milestones toward which to work. In terms of informality and propensity to use effectual thinking, as far as we can tell in retrospect, there appeared to be little difference between the UK and Japanese entrepreneurs.

Soft and hard start-ups

Researching UK and US high-tech start-ups, Connell has written of "soft" start-up strategies and companies, which in order to get started "carry out bespoke developments for individual customers, perhaps built around some core proprietary technology. It is often possible to get customers to pay for a significant portion of development costs up front" (2004: 4). They do this to cope with uncertainties and minimize risks, as shown in Figure 2.3. By contrast, "hard" start-ups attempt to leap straight into a product launch. They are "all about an excellent product idea, a strong management team and fast execution ahead of competitors" (ibid.). They need significant investment, but the product is highly scalable, which offers the potential for large exit profits for investors.

Almost all of the businesses in this case study – UK and Japanese – fell unambiguously into the "soft" category. Many started out by essentially

---

[12] Only 10 percent (6.8 percent) of UK (Japanese) entrepreneurs in the second survey sought venture capital, and 7.5 percent (4.1 percent) got it. In the majority of cases, this was well after start-up. Start-up finance was overwhelmingly from savings or bank loans, with an emphasis on the former in the UK, and the latter in Japan, where there is a wider range of banks, including some specifically for SMEs.

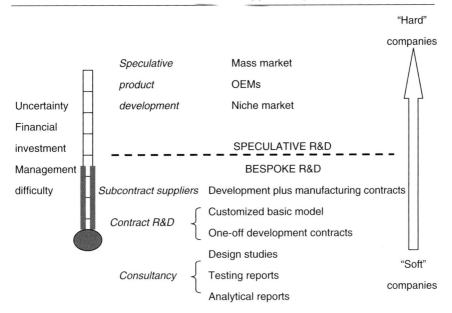

Figure 2.3 "Hard" and "soft" start-ups
Source: Connell (2004: 4)

selling their skills, as consultancies, supplying contract R&D, or subcontracting, sometimes for their former employer (see Chapter 3). In most cases they were dealing with one, or sometimes two or three, customers. This not only provided them with a means to make ends meet, and an effectual step forward, but also gave them confidence that there was demand for the opportunity they were trying to figure out, helped them to refine the opportunity through interaction with the customer, allowed them to strengthen weaker functions, and gave them credibility with other customers.

Connell lists a number of well-known Cambridge start-ups that have followed this route, and indeed argues that most successful UK technology businesses also fall into this category.[13] In the USA, too, companies like Sun Microsystems Inc. made a soft start with Defence Advanced Research

[13] The "soft" start concept originally comes from Bullock (1983). In their review of the "Cambridge phenomenon," Garnsey and Cannon-Brookes (1993) find insufficient evidence to support the "soft" to "hard" transition claim. Their definition of "soft" appears to be somewhat narrower than ours, however, and their view is compatible with our finding (below) that many businesses fail to make the transition.

Projects Agency (DARPA) funding and purchases in its early stages. A soft start is particularly helpful for entrepreneurs with technical backgrounds and limited management skills (Connell, 2004, 2006: 1). And so it was in both the UK and Japan:

[G] decided they were not going to continue with automated vehicles and robotics, so I was looking for other things to do, basically. I had the opportunity to set up with a group of people, so three of us left G. We set up this little consultancy in automated vehicles and in that sense we were subcontractors writing software. We didn't aim for patents or have any new technology. We thought we had particular skills that not many other people possessed and we thought we could sell those skills. We did that for five or six years. Then we decided we had done that, and that the company was not going to grow any further doing that. One of the problems we faced was that every company wanted us to work for them and not for anybody else. There were lots of secrecy clauses and "thou shalt not do this" clauses, and really we only worked for one company. (UK12)

Having been given the leg up by the single customer (in fact their former employer), after five or six years the group went on to develop their own products:

Our first unit was a laser scanner for automated vehicles which we designed ourselves. When that went into the field we felt it was the start of our becoming a real company and not just a group of software engineers trotting around the world having a good time. (UK12)

There were many similar cases. Innovative start-ups are said to confront the "Valley of Death" and "Darwin's Sea," but our cases suggest a different metaphor. "Soft" start-ups confronted "Independence Fen," a swamp that must be crossed before reaching terra firma. It is the swamp of consultancy, bespoke R&D and subcontracting, and many businesses get stuck there. To give an example from Japan, J18's founder began his career as an aeronautical engineer. When his company relocated, he decided to become independent, on a consulting basis for his former employer. He called his company M Technical Consulting Office. He started doing work for shipbuilders through his former employer, and when shipbuilding went into decline, he made a successful switch to automated production lines. However:

I liked interesting work. That's what I placed most emphasis on. I did think of products, but the ideas always came when I was really busy, working seven days a week, and not able to do anything about them. I could also have sold the company, but I was doing what I wanted to do, and then I wouldn't have been able to do it.

Newspaper people came around calling us another Sony, but I knew I didn't have the management skills for a large company. (J18)

Indeed, consultancy and bespoke R&D can be very interesting for engineers, and quite a few tend to get "lost" in the swamp without reaching terra firma. The metaphor assumes their destination is terra firma beyond the swamp, but some like the founder of J18 prefer to stay there. Our cases suggest that this kind of start is normal, and that "hard" starts are exceptional.

In sum, most of our case entrepreneurs started out as imitators or reproducers, without clearly defined goals, and with soft activities. These were not differentiators between the UK and Japanese entrepreneurs, especially those of route 1. The broader experience base of the UK entrepreneurs did not mean that they started out pursuing a home run. Those that were further toward the innovation, hard, and perhaps causal ends of the scales were those who already had an organizational and business base to work from, but they were in a minority. That does not mean that differences in backgrounds and motivations were irrelevant for OBC. We still have to consider one more dimension, as well as an underlying, major difference which emerged from the case interviews. We turn to these now.

Market-pull, technology-push, and underlying approaches to entrepreneurship

From backgrounds and founding reasons, we might predict a tendency toward market-pull, or at least a greater awareness of markets on the part of UK entrepreneurs, and a tendency toward technology-push in OBC on the part of Japanese entrepreneurs. In fact, it was remarkable how seldom Japanese entrepreneurs even used the word "market," whereas the UK entrepreneurs were much more likely to talk about a "market opportunity."[14] There were more frequent references to competitors in the UK as well. If nothing else, the UK entrepreneurs had to be more mindful of markets because of the very real risk that their key customer might get taken over or change course abruptly, threatening them with the instant loss of a large share of their turnover. There was less of this kind of volatility in Japan.

---

[14] The differences could be more apparent than real; a "strong future in this line of work" for the Japanese entrepreneurs might not be so fundamentally different from a "market opportunity" for the UK entrepreneurs.

More specifically, there may be two kinds of market-pull. We found a small number of entrepreneurs for whom their specific technology was secondary and most likely temporary, and who always appeared to have an eye out for market openings that they might pursue, opportunistically (as in opportunity "discovery"). They usually did not have a strong background in technology, and most were not university graduates, but had worked their way up through a succession of companies in the past. The second kind of market-pull was of entrepreneurs with a background in technology, but who appeared to be sensitive to market opportunities for these. Both types were probably more numerous in the UK.

At the other, technology-push extreme, there were a number of Japanese interviewees who clearly were more interested in technology than in managing and growing a business – mostly former researchers of corporate R&D labs. A small number of UK interviewees who had spun out of universities or government research institutes fitted this category as well.

In the middle were technologists with sales and often management experience, who were trying to create a technology-based business. They were also more numerous in the UK, but quite a few Japanese entrepre-

Table 2.5 Entrepreneurs' backgrounds, motivations, and OBC

Entrepreneur orientation	UK (project)	Japan (lifework)
Market-pull		
Education	Especially high school	High school, university (special circumstances)
Career	Progression of businesses	Progression of businesses
Motivation	Make money, prove worth	Gain respectability
Route	Routes 1, 2	Routes 1, 2
Balanced		
Education	Engineering/science/social science, sometimes MBA	Engineering/science/social science
Career	Technical → management →	Technical → sales →
Motivation	Challenge, solve problems, create business	Develop strong business through technology
Route	Routes 1, 2, 3	Routes 1, 2, 3
Technology push		
Education	Often Ph.D	Engineering/science/social science
Career	University, government lab.	Large firm technologist
Motivation	Sometimes restructuring, other circumstances	Pursue technology development
Route	Mainly 1	Mainly 1

Source: From case interviews

neurs also started in this space, or moved into it over time, either from the market-pull direction (by studying technology) or the technology-push direction (having become more interested in growing a business). Within this space, there appeared to be different emphases between the UK and Japanese entrepreneurs. The former were trying to create a technology *business*, focusing on strategic and operational issues that created current value for the business. The latter were trying to create a *technology* business, attempting to balance short-term market pressures while building up technology resources over the long term. The differences are summarized in Table 2.5.

Project and lifework entrepreneurship

This distinction is important. When we take a step backward from the detail of our case interviews, moreover, it is clear that there was something quite different about the UK and Japanese entrepreneurs' approaches to OBC and indeed entrepreneurship itself. The differences concern a dimension which has received very little attention to date, or has been lumped together with a lifestyle-versus-business orientation. They were addressed most directly when the entrepreneurs were talking about the future, but they appear to have been present in OBC as well.

The dimensions can be seen as a scale. At one pole, OBC is a "project," in which the entrepreneur makes a partial or conditional investment, or a more complete investment for a limited period of time, but with a willingness to consider other options should the project fail to meet his original goals, or should his goals change.[15] With a partial or conditional commitment, the entrepreneur might sell the business or stake in it and try something else. At the other extreme, opportunity creation and building a business is a "lifework," in which entrepreneurs invest themselves totally, such that their identity becomes intertwined with the business. With total commitment, they will try harder to make the adjustments *within* the OBC processes, rather than considering options outside the business should it fail to satisfy them.

On this scale, most of the Japanese entrepreneurs were clustered toward the "lifework" pole, and the UK entrepreneurs were spread out more toward the "project" pole. Some of the UK founders had started their business on a part-time basis, experimentally, to test the waters before committing significant time or financial resources, with a means of exit

---

[15] Casson and Wadeson (2006) consider entrepreneurial opportunities as projects, but not in the sense discussed here.

in case the project did not take off. Some had started or acquired more than one business, and many served as directors of, or investors in, other businesses, as projects also. The following quotes are illustrative.

I'm a business angel. I bought a software business some time ago, but I recently sold that. I quite fancy pharmaceuticals and I have an interest now in this organic vitamin company. I help other small businesses if they require my expertise.... That's what I want to move on to. I foresee a company of about 30–50 million will buy us. It's a personal thing. It gets more challenging every day, but its an operational challenge as opposed to an intellectual challenge. The operational side of me is getting exhausted, and I'm not learning any more. (UK10)

I actually think we'll be bought. We are bringing in some nice product. We have a very good reputation. We are a British Quality Award winner.... I think we'll be bought up by a multinational. (UK3)

On the other hand:

Our motto is "A boy's courage is for 100 years." We are blind to profit and loss in our boyhood. So it is with business.... I want to devote my life to this technology, and I hope to create jobs in poor countries with it. (J25)

Actually I had invested in a couple of joint ventures. One went under, the other was selling lots of machines but getting no money. It was a double blow.... You shouldn't stray off your main business. (J18; such "straying" was unusual)

Project and lifework orientations can be linked to founding reasons; the project approach flourished where there was emphasis on personal advancement, while the technology (ad)venture represented a sharp break with past employment, and a commitment to working with technology in the long term. Perhaps this was necessary to gain social approval, from the Japanese entrepreneurs' own families, friends, and business associates, whereas social expectations in the UK were consistent with personal advancement and entrepreneurship-as-project. A change in course in the latter would not be deemed a failure, whereas it would in the former. In Table 2.5, it would appear that the lifework orientation pulled even those in the top "market-pull" segment downward, to emphasize the accumulation of technology resources and competences, as we shall see in Chapter 5.

Concluding comments

Let us bring the observations in this chapter together, highlighting both similarities and differences in OBC. Most entrepreneurs were employed before they started a business, and this was important for the formation of skills, for developing attitudes and motivations toward OBC, for alerting future entrepreneurs to opportunities they might pursue, and frequently for providing the trigger as well. The UK entrepreneurs had broader functional experience, experience at a higher level of management, had changed jobs more often, and had sometimes started other businesses. A similar proportion had degrees, but more UK entrepreneurs had postgraduate degrees, often MBAs. The Japanese entrepreneurs had careers focused more on technology, and with less senior management experience. There was often an intermediate job or jobs between quitting their first (supposedly lifetime) employment and setting up their own business.

There were links between these backgrounds and reasons the entrepreneurs gave for starting their business. In the UK it was about personal advancement, or getting on, using the skills they had built up from their past career. In Japan it was about embarking on a technology (ad)venture, in areas close to those they had worked in in the past, but with a future as well. It was also about creating a more satisfactory, independent working life and work–life balance. The differences were national rather than a technologist–nontechnologist distinction.

When it came to OBC, there were clear similarities. OBC is multidimensional, and includes (*a*) earning enough money with which to live and support (solely or partially) a family, (*b*) gathering and organizing resources to create a business, and (*c*) pursuing an opportunity. This complexity, and a desire to reduce associated risk, or at least uncertainty, pushed both UK and Japanese entrepreneurs toward the imitator end of the imitator–innovator scale. The exception was certain entrepreneurs in both countries with an existing platform (routes 2 and 3), with fewer dimensions to worry about. Few if any began with well-worked-out business plans, and most appeared to emphasize means, or shorter-term goals in the pursuit of vaguely perceived long-term goals (like explorers setting out on voyages into uncharted waters). Again, the partial exception was those with an existing business platform. Finally, start-up entrepreneurs in both countries pursued "soft" starts, and quite a few became caught up doing "soft" work.

At the same time, there was some evidence of a more technological approach on the part of the Japanese entrepreneurs, and greater emphasis on market opportunities (either opportunistic, or in a commercialization sense), or at least a balance, in the UK. The differences were by no means clear-cut, however, at least among the interviewees. Moreover, we found

49

systematic differences of another, unanticipated kind, namely a "project" approach to OBC and entrepreneurship, which was common in the UK, and a "lifework" approach, which was common in Japan. These are not the same as business and lifestyle approaches, and they relate to different logics underlying entrepreneurship. We will return to this fundamental distinction at various points in the following chapters.

3

Ties and Teams in Start-up

In Chapter 2 we treated opportunity and business creation as an individual undertaking. In reality, of course, entrepreneurship involves the participation of a range of people, in various capacities. This chapter will look at some of these.

It has become fashionable to write about the social relations of entrepreneurship in terms of networks. Networks are necessary to secure resources, to access customers or markets, and to engineer legitimacy. Not surprisingly, there are, once again, a range of viewpoints concerning the rationality of network creation and leverage, and the effectiveness of different types of networks. But the social nature of entrepreneurship is even more basic than much of this writing acknowledges. Social relations influence the very cognitive processes of opportunity discovery or creation. Koller (1988) found that half of the entrepreneurs in his survey discovered their opportunity through their social network, and Singh (2000) has shown that such networks have both a quantitative and qualitative impact on opportunity recognition. This was clear from our study as well:

Shortly after we moved house we got to know our neighbours. N. had just been appointed an ENT consultant, and one day he was complaining about how expensive grommets were. I said can I see one, and when he showed me, I said I think I can find somewhere to do this cheaper, and better. That's where it started. (B7, paraphrased)

In this chapter we will focus on two sets of social relations during start-up: relations with former businesses or "umbilical ties," and founding teams. Concerning the former, there is a small, specialized stream of research which looks at spinouts and employee start-ups, but our research suggests that relations with former businesses are common and important, and should be considered in mainstream research on opportunity and business creation as well. They add a further dimension to the significance of former employment. We will explore the similarities and differences between the UK and Japanese entrepreneurs regarding umbilical ties with their former employer, mainly using data from our first Founders and Founding survey.

Subsequently, we turn to quantitative and qualitative aspects of founding teams. We ask whether Japanese entrepreneurs complement their more technologically focused background with inputs from others at the founding stage, or on the contrary, whether these backgrounds make it difficult for them to collaborate with others. We also ask how the UK entrepreneurs seek to complement their broader skill and experience base. Or does that base make it easier for them to work with others? Do they seek junior partners to help them leverage these bases, or do they do it alone? Do both groups, in fact, seek to work with those with complementary assets, or do they look for affinity, emphasizing trust? We address these questions with data from the second, Comparative Entrepreneurship, survey, which will be used subsequently unless otherwise noted.

Umbilical ties and spinouts

Interest in employee start-ups and spinouts has grown in recent years. Klepper (2001) reviews four perspectives – capitalizing on discoveries made during employment, developing innovations that employers are slow to pursue, exploitation of knowledge learned in employment, and parent–child analogies – as well as a number of studies in high-tech industries. Echoing our findings of Chapter 2, he writes:

(S)pinoffs did not generally introduce significant innovations in their products, nor did they pursue very ambitious strategies. They produced products closely related to the ones their parents produced, or in the case of disk drive ones their parents apparently developed but chose not to produce. They relied less on distinctive technologies of their parents and more on the experiences of their founders to craft their initial strategies. Last, although they did not appear to be terribly innovative or challenging to the competitive positions of their parents, founders of spinoffs commonly reported frustration with their parents as a major reason for leaving to start their own firms. (Klepper, 2001: 655–6)

Here we can sense several aspects to relations between the employing firm and the departing employee. In our first survey, one-third of the UK and Japanese founders (34 percent and 31 percent respectively) reported being helped by their former company when they started their present business.

The most common kind of help was customer or client connections (54 percent and 36 percent respectively). The same proportion of the UK entrepreneurs received technological assistance, but only a quarter of the Japanese. A significant minority also received financial assistance (27 percent and 16 percent respectively). And while a third of the UK respondents received management and planning assistance, only 4 percent of the Japanese respondents received this kind of help. On the other hand, three-quarters of the Japanese group reported receiving "other" forms of assistance. We cannot be sure what these were, but subcontracting orders were likely to feature prominently. These subcontracting relations also showed up in our case interviews, and at least one of the case companies was given old equipment to start out with.[1]

From this we can see that in many cases the former company, rather than being neutral or hostile to efforts of employees – or managers or even directors – to start their own business, actually supports them. The quid pro quo for this is that the start-up will not become a direct competitor. Case interviews suggest that this happens in various ways. The parent company might wish to exit a business, but has ongoing obligations to customers. Or it might wish to discontinue an R&D effort, but not abandon it completely ("just in case"; cf. Chesbrough, 2006). Here it might actually be helped by an employee spinning out to do these tasks. Or it might recognize that it cannot stop the employee, and offer favors which it might call in at some point. Here is one example:

When T (previous company) fell into difficulties in the 1970s, new management was brought in from the bank, who did everything from the management logic. Don't sell one off machines, and this and that. But you can't keep customers if you just do profitable things, and so I made a company which my brother in law was nominally head of taking in repair work we were no longer allowed to do at T. . . . T made silicon-based equipment, and we didn't want to become a competitor. We went for opto-electronics. Other people weren't into it yet, and I knew it would grow. (J16)

Sometimes there was even benevolence, when the former employer recalled someone who helped them when they were in a similar position. The result, however, was that these umbilical ties exerted a subtle influence on the way new opportunities were pursued, and the way the business was

---

[1] The UK entrepreneurs also received help in the form of sales and marketing advice (29 percent), legal advice (10 percent), emotional or moral support (19 percent), and other (10 percent). The first three were inserted into the UK survey to try to tease out some of the "other" category dimensions which had shown up in the Japanese survey.

developed initially. This applies in both countries, but is perhaps particularly the case in Japan. On the other hand, the lower level of technological support extended to Japanese founders suggests that the technological aspects of their business pursuit were really their own affair. Or at least that is how they chose to portray it.

Founding teams

Next, we turn to founding teams, which are "at the heart of any new venture" (Cooper and Daily, 1997: 128). Such teams can enrich the skill set and resources available for start-up, provide stability and balance, enhance networks, and increase legitimacy (Vesper, 1990; Hirata, 1999; Aldrich, Carter, and Ruef, 2004). One study estimates the proportion of businesses with *full-time* partners at start-up in the USA at 30 percent, while other studies have shown this proportion to be higher in high-tech and high-growth ventures – typically around two-thirds or more – and lower in low-tech or limited-niche businesses.[2] Whether teams create faster-growing businesses, or high-potential businesses make it easier to recruit teams, is not necessarily clear.

The composition of entrepreneurial teams matters. A study by Beckman (2006) holds that founding teams whose members worked in the same company in the past are more likely to engage in "exploitation," as they have shared understandings and can act quickly, while members from a range of different companies, with different backgrounds, are more likely to engage in "exploration." The ideal combination for growth, by implication, is a team which combines people with common and diverse prior affiliations.[3] Other studies, however, have pointed to the importance of friendship in entrepreneurial teams for improving early performance, and subsequently solving thorny problems (Francis and Sandberg, 2000). Gartner and Carter (2003: 240) also found that "[t]eams appear to be composed, primarily, of strong ties that are based more on trust and familiarity, rather than on skills and competence."[4] Commonly – in about a third to half of cases – one of the partners is a spouse.

[2] Cooper and Daily (1997) provide a review. See also Timmons (1990; high potential businesses require a team), Roberts (1991; teams and high-tech ventures), and Davidsson and Honig (2003; faster gestation and development in team-based start-ups, and start-ups with strong social networks).

[3] Cf. also Eisenhardt and Schoonhoven (1990).

[4] Cf. Ruef et al. (2003); also Kamm and Nurick (1993) and Birley (1985).

Trust in start-ups can help to reduce transaction costs, reduce complexity, and facilitate speed, but trust might also encourage overconfidence and lock-in (Welter and Smallbone, 2006). Goel and Karri (2006: 479–80) argue that over-trusting entrepreneurs regularly place bets in the opposite direction to the Williamsonian entrepreneur. They do so because of the need for "swift trust" in a nascent venture, and not because they are irrational, but because they use effectual logic, and cannot or choose not to predict the future. Sarasvathy and Dew, too, claim that in a world of Knightian uncertainty, goal ambiguity, and fuzzy future preferences "it is at least as likely that opportunities for entrepreneurial action will be shaped by a variety of relationships arising from every aspect, aspiration and accident of human life, as it is that visions of particular projects and their predicted gains will induce participants to enter contractual relationships in order to harvest the expected returns" (Sarasvathy and Dew, 2005: 402).

However, stresses involved in creating businesses can place severe strain on friendships, which can then impede business development, to the extent of crippling it. In Quince's (1998; 2001) study, 60 percent of the businesses surveyed had been founded collaboratively, and of these, 43 percent had experienced a fragmentation of the founding team, the majority acrimoniously. Her participants recounted a number of benefits of team collaboration, particularly economic benefits, but the affective aspects of close interpersonal relationships provided the "glue." They stressed the importance of shared visions, values, and objectives, but if the glue came unstuck it had debilitating consequences, including delayed decision-making, damaged morale, loss of customer confidence, bitterness and resentment, and sometimes even the dissolution of the business.

Turning now to our study, we define a team as two or more people who are present during the nascent phase of start-up and who jointly establish a business, with an equity stake.[5] Using the second, Comparative Entrepreneurship, survey we have excluded entrepreneurs who were not part of the original founding team according to this definition, leaving 83 entrepreneurs from the UK and 115 from Japan.

First, we asked how many owners there were when the business was created, and whether they were internal or external to the business. The answers are summarized in Table 3.1. Only a quarter of the businesses in both the UK and Japan had external owners at the time of founding, suggesting overwhelming internal control. Of those that did have external

[5] This follows Kamm et al. (1990); also Aldrich et al. (2004).

owners, they were somewhat more numerous in Japan. The majority of businesses in both countries had at least one other internal owner, but they were more common in the UK (roughly 70 percent versus 60 percent). Again, however, where there were internal owners, there tended to be more of them in Japan.

Next, we look at the share of equity held by other owners (Table 3.2). A number of Japanese respondents indicated no equity holding by co-owners. Whether this was a misunderstanding, or whether they considered ownership in non-equity terms was not clear. Where there were other co-owners, they were likely to hold a minority stake. In the UK, however, internal co-owners often held a *majority* stake between them. In other words, while the number of internal co-owners tended to be small in the UK, they held significant stakes, suggesting a more equal form of participation, as in a partnership. Ownership in Japan was more widely dispersed, but did not challenge the dominance of the founding entrepreneur.

This becomes more apparent when we consider the resources contributed by the other owners or, conversely, the resources the respondents said only they contributed. Of all the resources or capabilities in Figure 3.1, a higher proportion of Japanese respondents than the UK respondents said they were the sole contributors. The differences were especially marked when it came to customer or client connections and entrepreneurial talent. On these, the Japanese entrepreneurs saw themselves overwhelmingly as the sole contributors. Similarly, there was a marked difference in

Table 3.1 Number of co-owners (%)

		0	1	2	3+
Number of other internal owners	UK	28.2	46.2	17.9	7.7
	Japan	39.3	22.3	19.6	18.8
Number of other external owners	UK	72.8	17.3	4.9	4.9
	Japan	71.7	9.7	4.4	14.2

Table 3.2 Equity held by co-owners (%)

		0	<50%	50%+
% equity held by other internal owners	UK	0	36.7	63.3
	Japan	(18.6)	47.1	34.3
% equity held by other external owners	UK	0	63.6	36.3
	Japan	(12.1)	57.6	30.3

Note: Includes only businesses indicating internal and external co-owners, respectively

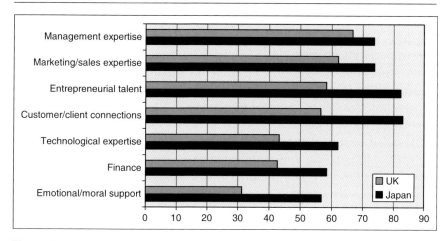

Figure 3.1 Resources contributed by the entrepreneur only (%)

contribution of technological expertise. And not only were the Japanese entrepreneurs more likely to see themselves as the sole contributors of key resources or competences, they were more likely to feel that they were the psychological or emotional center of the business as well, as suggested by the figures on emotional or moral support. (Only two-thirds of the UK entrepreneurs answered this item, moreover, whereas most of the Japanese entrepreneurs did, suggesting that it was more meaningful for them.)

Finally, we consider how the respondents knew the other cofounders. Almost one in five of the UK entrepreneurs noted that one of the cofounders was a spouse or partner. Where the spouse or partner choice was selected, other categories were not, meaning husband–wife partnerships constituted one distinct subcategory. The proportion of spouse (only) partnerships was similar in Japan, but unlike the UK, the spouse was often present in other ownership combinations as well, bringing the total to over one-third. To this we might add "immediate family," which was selected by one in ten UK and Japanese respondents, but in combination (especially with the spouse) by a further 7 percent in Japan. Overall, there was much greater representation of family in the founding team in Japan.

The most common category in the UK, on the other hand, was "colleague," which was chosen exclusively by 43 percent, and as part of a combination by another 10 percent. This compares with Japanese figures of 19 percent and 16 percent respectively. These colleagues were people the founders had worked with in their previous employment or business. They contributed both complementary skills or resources, and trust and personal compatibility. There was another significant category in Japan (a quarter in total, exclusively or in combination), however, which hardly figured in the UK (less than 10 percent), namely "other business acquaintance." This might be a former customer or supplier the founder had had dealings with over the years, or someone who introduced an idea or opportunity. Finally, friends featured in about 10 percent of the responses in both the UK and Japan.

Overall, it appears that the balance in the UK was tilted toward cofounding with colleagues on a roughly equal basis, while in Japan it was tilted more toward family, but sometimes with colleagues on a less equal basis. Our case interviews confirm this picture, with some very interesting nuances. Certainly, as some of the quotes in Chapter 2 suggest, there were collegial founding teams in the UK:

The business I was working in was automated vehicles and robots. And they decided that that was not going to continue so I was looking for other things to do basically. I had the opportunity to set up with a little group of people, so three of us left G. (UK12)

In fact, there were often fine differences in share ownership – 35/25/25 and 3×5 percent, for example – but there was an emphasis on the team dimension. In our Japanese interviews, we found some cases in which an intermediate business had been founded similarly, but the business had subsequently fragmented, and the interviewee either left, or was left with most of the capital.[6]

After working for N. Company for ten years I left with three others to form T. Company. I was the youngest. Within one year we grew to forty employees, but in the second year we were down to fifteen because the US Federal Communications Commission changed its regulations. Two of the others left shortly afterwards. I gradually became uncomfortable and left. I traded my 46% of shares for technology to start my next company. (J11, paraphrased)

Company "politics" was a cause of fragmentation, but so were disputes over which technology to back. The end result appeared to be businesses with clear control by a single entrepreneur. In the UK, fragmentation – and recombination – was also common. This happened when priorities changed (as we might expect from project entrepreneurship) and a partner moved on, a founder reduced his stake and involvement, and so on.

---

[6] In fact, a number of UK respondents to the first survey also noted problems with founding teams: "First business was with an over-ambitious partner, who preferred to compete rather than work together." "[H]eld back by non-committed/forward-thinking partners, now bought out."

The breakup was amicable. He got a lot of his money and his Porsche back. He didn't really ever want to work setting up a business. He lives in some style. He does a bit of consultancy, flits around the industry. (UK3)

Thus it appears that certain pressures pushed the Japanese entrepreneurs in the direction of (single) entrepreneur dominance after some experimentation or idealism. One or two mentioned the *un*desirability of team management. That does not mean that they were "one-man" businesses, as we shall see. In the UK, on the other hand, if the collegial team did not work out, or if priorities changed, adjustments were made to the ownership structure, but this did not necessarily push the businesses in the direction of single entrepreneur dominance. In fact, adjustments were frequently being made to the capital structure by tie-ups with competitors, partial acquisition by or of customers, infusions of venture capital, and so on. Founding team adjustments were one category of rearrangement.

High performers

In Chapter 4 we will introduce a category of businesses, representing a third of the Comparative Entrepreneur survey respondents in both countries, which had introduced a novel innovation and grown by at least 10 percent in the past two years. We call these "high performers." Anticipating this category, let us consider briefly whether the founding teams in these businesses were different from those of the remaining "non-high performers," and whether there were similarities regardless of country. In brief, the differences between the UK and Japan were maintained, but with some important qualifications. In the UK the number of internal cofounders did not differ much between high and non-high performers, but the share of equity ownership was somewhat more dispersed in high performers. There were also few differences in the number of external owners, but the share of equity ownership was *less* dispersed. In the UK context, then, a strong founding team with limited external ownership (and control) might confer innovative and competitive advantages.

In Japan there was little difference between high performers and non-high performers, either in the number of internal or external owners. However, the share of equity held by other internal owners was slightly *less* for high performers; further enhancing control by the entrepreneur, while the share held by other external owners was slightly *greater*. It is possible that external owners play a different, more supportive, role in Japan, or that they are more silent than in the UK.

59

Differences in resources contributed by other owners, or conversely by the entrepreneur only, again were mostly modest. In the UK, high performers considered they solely contributed somewhat more resources than the non-high performers, except (marginally) for technological expertise, and entrepreneurial talent! In Japan they considered they themselves contributed somewhat less in most areas except for financial and management expertise. This is potentially significant when we consider who the other owners were. In the case of both the UK and Japan, there were fewer spouses among the high performers – significantly fewer in the case of Japan (27 percent for high performers versus 43 percent for non-high performers) – while there were significantly more colleagues (61 percent versus 44 percent in the UK, 35 percent versus 20 percent in Japan).

It seems that the combination of trust and complementary assets or resources provided by colleagues in the founding team is beneficial. In the case of Japan they provide more resources to high performers, but the relationship with the entrepreneur is possibly more hierarchical (as in a senior manager spinning out with subordinates, or those remaining after a more fluid intermediate arrangement), as the entrepreneur provides more financial and management expertise. In the UK, similarly, differences between high and non-high performers were greatest in respect to financial and management expertise, suggesting greater de facto control within the team by the entrepreneur in the case of high performers. In other words, the combination of complementary resources and expertise, combined with entrepreneur control, appears beneficial in both countries. Fewer spouses and family members also appear beneficial, but the balance is different, with greater collegiality in the UK, and more hierarchical control in Japan.

This interpretation of Japan is admittedly impressionistic, and open to empirical challenge, but it fits with a small but growing literature on founding teams, and in particular a stream on the role of the "right-hand man." The "right-hand man" is usually promoted internally, although in some cases he (used advisedly) may have come from a large company while in his forties as a "second career" (Tomita, 2002), and hence may have his own external networks which can be used for recruiting or securing resources (Inamura and Nakauchi, 2006). His presence is positively related to profits (Wakisaka, 2003), especially if he is a nonfamily member (Tomita, 2002). Significantly, the "right-hand man" assumes a supporting role to the owner-founder, but is not a full or equal partner.

Implications

When we put these findings together with those of Chapter 2, an interesting picture emerges. In Chapter 2 we saw (from the survey; the picture from the interviews was a little different) that the Japanese entrepreneurs had narrower functional experience, and less experience at senior management level. Their experience was deep, and focused in technical functions. We might expect them to have attempted to balance their technical expertise with other kinds of expertise and resources when they started their business. What we find, however, is that their cofounders were considered to have contributed fewer key resources than in the UK. Many of the cofounders were family members, including spouses, suggesting a weighting toward trust and familiarity over complementary assets.

A number of explanations might be offered. Perhaps the Japanese entrepreneurs were unable to articulate a vision or plan for their business sufficiently to attract other types of cofounders. Or perhaps starting a new business was so arduous and risky that even if they were able to articulate a vision or plan, the likelihood of someone such as a colleague abandoning secure employment to join them was low. As we saw in Chapter 2, one main factor among the reasons for starting a business in Japan was "personal satisfaction," which is highly dependent on the individual.

Or perhaps it is related to the question of control. For having cofounders who contribute important resources implies sharing, and having to negotiate, control over key decisions. The popular image in Japan of starting a new business – paradoxically for those who believe or assume that cultural orientations like "groupism" are not context-dependent – is that of an individual struggling against the odds to establish both legitimacy and business viability. The reality, as suggested by our findings so far, might not be too far from this image. In fact, conforming to this image might be part of the very process of establishing legitimacy.

The importance of "control," in turn, is related to the "lifework" orientation identified in Chapter 2. The founder invests himself fully in his work, and expects to continue to do so. The personal stakes for gaining legitimacy and succeeding are high, while the chances for success are uncertain. It is in many ways a highly personal journey along a tortuous path that others are not expected to share in fully. Nonetheless, family ownership was less prevalent, and collegial ownership was more prevalent, in high-performing businesses, where co-owners also contributed more. In other words, control and complementary contributions were probably more effectively combined, and this probably happened from the outset.

These businesses, one can imagine, were also more likely to be in the middle "balance" sector of Table 2.5.

The UK entrepreneurs opted for a balance, probably leaning toward complementary assets, through cofounding with colleagues. It may be that they were more conscious of the need for complementary assets in the first place, given their management experience. It was more than this, though. In our UK case studies, there were quite a few business started by two people, frequently colleagues. They tended to share the founding tasks, and this sharing was seen as one of the positive and pleasurable aspects of the process, not to mention a mechanism of reducing risk. Control through ownership was often de-emphasized in order to emphasize expertise, contributions and collegiality, with a willingness to adapt the ownership structure if necessary.

Again, the UK entrepreneur appeared to start his business as a project. If he could do it with colleagues, so much the better – it would be more enjoyable, and would grow more quickly in the shorter term. The attitude was (liberally interpreted): it is difficult to predict what will happen in the longer term, but if it does not work out, adjustments can be made, and, if necessary, the project can be stopped, and a new one started. Such is life. High performers were even more collegial, and the entrepreneur appeared to play a somewhat different role – that of an integrator and possibly stabilizer of potentially centrifugal forces.

Roughly half the businesses in both countries had seen at least one of the internal founders leave the business. Although we do not have survey data on why this is so, our cases suggest a greater propensity in the UK for cofounders, too, to treat the business as a project. They might leave because they got bored, their priorities had changed, or they wanted to do something else. Personality clashes, differences in vision, and issues of control were mentioned, but less frequently. If we include changes to the capital composition, or change without fragmentation, the figure would be even higher.

Of course, this was how the remaining founders chose to present their history. By contrast, the Japanese founders were much less likely to talk (spontaneously) about changes in the composition of the founding team, and we seldom came across cases in which cofounders were deemed to have left because they wanted to try something else. When pressed, however, examples emerged. Frequently fragmentation had occurred during or just after crises, precipitated by the economic environment (asset bubble burst, Asian Financial Crisis, etc.), and sometimes, as noted, by disagreements in the early years over technology paths.

Concluding comments

Entrepreneurship is conceived and carried out through social relations. In this chapter we looked at two sets of relations which are important in opportunity and business creation – relations with former businesses or "umbilical ties," and founding teams.

One-third of entrepreneurs said they were helped by their former employer when starting their business. This was most commonly in the form of customer or client connections, technical advice, and financial and management assistance in the UK. The basis of this assistance appeared to involve a fair amount of goodwill. Japanese founders were also introduced to customers or clients, and some of the other forms of assistance, and they also received "other" types of support such as subcontracting orders, with expectations of reciprocity (such as prioritizing the former company's rush orders in return). These relations undoubtedly influenced the "soft" start of many of the businesses, in subtle ways.

Our definition of founding teams had an ownership component, which we divided into internal and external owners. A minority of businesses had external co-owners, but most had internal co-owners (70 percent in the UK, 60 percent in Japan). After exploring the distribution of ownership, contributions of co-owners, and who the co-owners were, we concluded that the nature of founding teams was different in the two countries. In the UK they were more collegial, often with shared responsibilities between two or three cofounders. In Japan they were more familial, and hierarchical, supporting the founder. We linked these differences speculatively to past careers, but more strongly to the nature of business founding; the stresses and social expectations in Japan which encourage the lifework approach, and the greater emphasis on personal choice in "getting on," which encourages the project approach in the UK.

There were some interesting similarities and differences in the high performers. Here cofounders provided more resources than in non-high performers in Japan. There were fewer spouses and significantly more colleagues amongst the founding teams. There appeared to be a balance between authority of the entrepreneur and resources contributed by cofounders. This balance was important in the two countries, but it appeared to be different. UK high performers were characterized by strong internal control on the part of the founding team, with the entrepreneur as an integrator, while Japanese high performers were characterized by stronger hierarchical control by the founder. There was also somewhat more external ownership, which may play a different role than in the UK. The country differences were therefore sustained, in a modified form.

We will build on these findings when we explore other types of social relations, especially employment relations and leadership in Chapter 6.

4

Entrepreneurial Orientations and Business Objectives

The next two chapters look at business orientations and activities. One stream of entrepreneurship research argues that founders, executives, or businesses can be distinguished along a number of dimensions which are indicative of entrepreneurial-ness, and that these have a tangible effect on business development and bottom-line performance (Miller, 1983; Miller and Friesen, 1983). The most common dimensions are pro-activeness, risk taking, and innovation, but some studies add other dimensions such as autonomy and competitive aggressiveness (Lumpkin and Dess, 1996). This stream is called "entrepreneurial orientations" (EOs).

In this chapter we will cover some of the same ground. We do not wish to prove that EOs are a predictor of performance, but we do want to know what our entrepreneurs think about, and how they rate on, some of these issues. We have seen that entrepreneurs in both the UK and Japan start out more as imitators than innovators, but do they stay like this? Some readers may have a nagging suspicion that "real" innovative entrepreneurs have slipped through the net we have cast over high-tech manufacturing. Have they?

By the end of the chapter we will have identified a group of "high performers" in both countries. We can then – as we did in Chapter 3 – compare these groups in different aspects of entrepreneurship to see whether UK and Japanese high performers are essentially similar to each other, or whether they are more similar to their non-high-performing compatriots; in other words, whether they diminish, maintain, or even intensify national differences.

We begin by reviewing some of the writing on EO, and why we do not pursue it as a causative model. We then look at some of the things the entrepreneurs rated as important in developing their opportunities and businesses, or "personal business objectives." Next we consider growth objectives and attitudes toward risk, and then engagement in R&D, intellectual property, and innovation. Finally, we combine a measure of innovation and sales growth to identify our "high performers." Logically speaking, we should separate our discussion of entrepreneurs' attitudes from R&D, IP, and innovation, which are organizational outcomes, since a lot goes on between these. We combine them in this chapter, however, for presentation purposes, and because we need the high-performer construct for the following chapters.

Entrepreneurial orientations

The premise of much EO writing is that attitudes shape behavior, which creates an entrepreneurial outcome; without certain attitudinal dispositions, we are unlikely to get entrepreneurship. The most common dispositions or dimensions cited are pro-activeness, risk taking, and innovation, but autonomy and competitive aggressiveness are included as well. The premise might be simple, but demonstrating it is not, and caution is needed when working with these concepts. The same questions have been asked by a number of researchers (cf. Covin and Slevin, 1989: 86), but the answers have been dubbed, respectively, entrepreneurial behavior, strategic posture, entrepreneurial posture, as well as entrepreneurial orientation (Wiklund, 1998). Applying the content–process distinction from strategy research, Lumpkin and Dess (1996) link entrepreneurship to the former and EO to the latter (without really clarifying in what ways EO is a process). On top of this, some researchers believe we should pay more attention to entrepreneurial *intensity* (EI), which is concerned with the *degree* of entrepreneurship, rather than directionality of EO (Liao and Welsch, 2004).

It is commonly asserted, and occasionally demonstrated, that EO dimensions of pro-activeness, risk taking, and innovation co-vary; people who score high on one dimension will score high on others. Lumpkin and Dess, however, argue that there may be different combinations along their five dimensions, linked to different types of entrepreneurship (as in Schollhamer's [1982] acquisitive, administrative, opportunistic, incubative, and imitative types). Different combinations (and intensities) might be appropriate for different environments, moreover.

Some assumptions of EO are, first, that questionnaire responses actually elicit some fixed, measurable, stable, and relevant quality, and second, that these translate seamlessly into behavior. In fact, EO research often mixes if not conflates cognitive dispositions or intentions and behavior (Brown et al., 2001). There are further problems of linking an individual entrepreneur's behavior with business performance (Hart, 1992), which depends on a number of factors such as the environment (Naman and Slevin, 1993; Zahra and Covin, 1995) and resource availability (Wiklund, 1999). When intervening environmental or organization variables are introduced, moreover, they may be conceived as moderating effects, mediating effects, independent effects, and interacting effects (Lumpkin and Dess, 1996).

Finally, performance, or effectiveness, is difficult to measure. Turnover growth and profitability are commonly used, but to entrepreneurs these may be means to other ends, or relatively unimportant. "Derived" and "prescribed" notions of performance differ, as do "official" and "operative" or espoused and actual goals within the latter (Kirchoff, 1977). All this suggests that caution must be exercised when talking about EOs, and particularly in trying to link them with performance.[1]

Despite all of this, we are still interested in entrepreneurs' attitudes. We want to know what the entrepreneurs consider important in creating and developing their businesses, their attitudes to growth, and to risk. Do they think the same way about these, or are there differences? Let us look at general attitudes or "personal business objectives" first.

Personal business objectives

We asked the participants of the second, Comparative Entrepreneurship, survey to rate the importance of a number of objectives for them in their business, on a 1 (not at all) to 5 (crucial) scale. The results are summarized in Figure 4.1.

The top UK mean scores were for "building a business with a reputation for product/service excellence," "providing a stable and positive environment for employees," and "conducting business on the basis of fairness and moral integrity." These may almost be described as a "stakeholder" orientation and suggest a greater emphasis on means than ends. The

---

[1] "(T)here often seems to be a strong normative bias toward the inherent value in entrepreneurial behavior, and an assumption or explicit depiction of a positive relationship between behavior and desired organizational outcomes such as sales growth and profitability.... Further, the press applauds entrepreneurial behavior" (Dess, Lumpkin, and Covin, 1997: 678).

lowest ranked were "preparing the business for future stock exchange/AIM listing," "making a contribution to science and technology," and "building a business which contributes to the well-being of society." Public listing did not appear to figure much in UK entrepreneurs' consciousness, whether as a means of raising capital, or as a means of exit. Altruism, too, was rejected. The other financial gain items were assigned medium-to-low importance (in both countries), which is worth noting given the frequent assumption that entrepreneurs are primarily motivated by the prospect of profit, or the possibility of obtaining high rewards, and will incur substantial risks to do so.

The top three objectives of the Japanese entrepreneurs were "building a business which will continue to exist without me," "building a business with a reputation for product/service excellence," and "maximizing my enjoyment and satisfaction from work." Rather than a "stakeholder" orientation, there appears to be greater emphasis on the relation of the entrepreneur to the business, possibly a legacy concern. "Building a business which will continue to exist without me" might be interpreted in several ways, and might even appear to contradict our argument (from Chapter 3) of the self-perceived centrality of the entrepreneur to the business in Japan. Indeed, "maintaining my involvement in the business" was ranked second lowest by the Japanese entrepreneurs, significantly lower than the UK entrepreneurs.

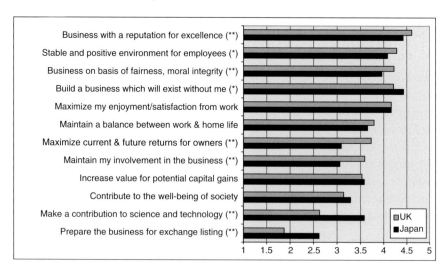

Figure 4.1 Personal business objectives

Note: ** differences significant at .01; * differences significant at .05

The contradiction is more apparent than real. Building a business which would continue to exist without the entrepreneur means a business which can be passed on, either to family or to a new generation. An entrepreneur does not want a "lifework" to dissolve when he retires. He wants to build something which will last, beyond his involvement. *Because* it is a lifework, he wants to create one which will continue to exist without him. As for maintaining involvement in the business, while ideally he wants to build a business which does not need him, paradoxically he has to devote all his energies to the business in order to bring this about.

The other bottom-ranked objectives for the Japanese respondents were "preparing the business for future stock exchange/(OTC) listing" and "maximizing current and future returns for the investors/owners." Here there was a more emphatic rejection of financial gain objectives, but while public listing was ranked bottom in both the UK and Japan, the Japanese average was significantly higher. Indeed, in a number of the Japanese cases, the entrepreneur was actively preparing for public listing. They saw this not as part of an exit strategy, however, or even primarily as a way of raising capital, but as a way of increasing public trust, which would make it easier to recruit good people, motivate employees to work hard toward a new goal, and increase succession options – a suitable outsider could more easily be recruited to take over the business if the company were public – thus increasing the chances of a solid legacy.

I wanted to live quietly as a small firm owner. But there are young employees who went out of their way to join the company, while their friends were working for large, famous companies. So we must be listed for their pride. That was a kind of obligation for me. (J2)

There were some differences in personal business objectives by age in both countries. Social contribution became more important for those over 50.[2] Financial gain did not change significantly, but public listing was somewhat more important for younger UK entrepreneurs. Finally, the objectives of high performers were not markedly different from those of non-high performers, especially in terms of financial gain objectives.

---

[2] Older UK entrepreneurs ranked building a business which would continue to exist without them, building a business which contributed to the welfare of society, and conducting business on the basis of fairness and moral integrity more highly than their younger counterparts, while older Japanese entrepreneurs ranked providing a stable and positive environment for employees, making a contribution to science and technology, and conducting business on the basis of fairness and moral integrity more highly.

Factors

Overall, Figure 4.1 shows a very different weighting given to many of the objectives by UK and Japanese entrepreneurs; eight are statistically significant, mostly at the .01 level. Stepwise discriminant analysis correctly predicts 79 percent of the responses as either UK or Japan (77 percent for the UK, 80 percent for Japan). The strongest discriminators are making a contribution to science and technology, which the Japanese entrepreneurs rated much higher, and maximizing current and future returns for the investors/owners, which the UK entrepreneurs rated much higher.

To tease out the underlying constructs, again we carried out factor analysis, first with the combined group, and then separately with the UK and Japanese groups. The results are summarized in Table 4.1. Principal component analysis yielded four factors, the first of which consisted of many of the top-ranked items. We call it "principles." In the UK, it consists of four items, with a fifth – fairness and moral integrity – also loading weakly. This item loads more strongly onto the second factor in the UK, however, along with maximizing enjoyment and satisfaction, and maintaining involvement in the business. Together, they seem to capture the nature of the UK entrepreneurs' "involvement" in their project. The third factor – "social contribution" – combines contribution to science and technology and well-being of society, and somewhat surprisingly (for us), exchange listing. As noted, this item was ranked bottom by a long way in the UK, and did not appear to impinge on the entrepreneurs' consciousness very often, but it is interesting that it loaded onto this factor, as it did in Japan as well. The fourth factor combines maximizing current and future returns with increasing the value of the business for potential capital gains. We call it "(UK) financial gain."

The first Japanese factor is the same as that of the UK, with the addition of conducting business on the basis of fairness and moral integrity. The second Japanese factor is the same as the UK social contribution factor, but with the interesting (weak) addition of maximizing enjoyment/satisfaction. The third factor, also interestingly, combines maintaining involvement in the business with maximizing returns for owners. We call it, awkwardly, "investment." The fourth factor consists of the single item increasing the value of the business for potential capital gains. Overall, the factor constructs appear to be reasonably similar, particularly with regard to "principles," which we need to elaborate on.

Table 4.1 Personal business objectives: factor comparison

UK	Japan
1. UK principles Business which will exist without me, balance between work & home life, stable/positive environment for employees, build reputation for excellence 2. Involvement Maximize enjoyment/satisfaction, fairness and moral integrity, maintain involvement in business 3. UK social contribution Make a contribution to S&T, prepare for exchange listing, contribution to well-being of society 4. UK financial gain Maximize returns for owners, increase value for potential capital gains	1. Japan principles Stable/positive environment for employees, build reputation for excellence, business which will exist without me, balance between work & home life, fairness and moral integrity 2. Social contribution and satisfaction Make a contribution to S&T, prepare for exchange listing, contribution to well-being of society, maximize enjoyment/satisfaction 3. Investment Maintain involvement in business, maximize returns for owners 4. Japan financial gain Increase value for potential capital gains

Note: Based on principal component analysis, varimax rotation with Kaiser normalization. See Tables A2.3 and A2.4 for details.

What do we mean by "principles"?

"Principles" suggests that the pursuit of other business goals such as financial gain passes through a filter of principles, which are important for the entrepreneurs' personal and business identities. They can also be seen as an extension of effectuation logic, in which means are emphasized over ends or ultimate goals, not just at the time of start-up, but on an ongoing basis as well.

The question about business objectives itself was prompted by UK entrepreneurs' responses to an open question in the first survey, in which they were asked to recall any critical events or experiences which influenced their approach to business, or the development of their business. Comments about personal business objectives or orientations had three basic themes: excellence, quality, and service; customer orientation; and employee involvement/respect. Comments like the following were common:

To provide products and services of outstanding quality. Realizing that to survive and be successful in business we must have a culture which is based on quality goods and services.

Driven by the satisfaction associated with quality and integrity (though this is not always perceived or appreciated by customers).

When I was an employee, I saw continual customer dissatisfaction caused by co-workers who lacked technical expertise and pressure to achieve unrealistic objectives. My core principle has been – Product Quality – to ensure long-term customer relationships and satisfaction.

Your staff are your business.

In a climate of redundancies and "devaluation" of engineering skills in the late '80s, we wanted to form a company that provided job interest, stability, salaries, involvement (participation) and responsibility for employees.

To look after employees, customers and shareholders with due regard to other interests.

As was the case in creating their business, the entrepreneurs' personal business objectives or orientations were shaped by their past experiences. A strong link was also made between motivating employees and satisfying customers. We interpreted this as a kind of "stakeholder" orientation. Thus it was no accident that the top three UK choices were building a business with a reputation for product/service excellence, providing a stable and positive environment for employees, and conducting business on the basis of fairness and moral integrity.

The Japanese entrepreneurs we interviewed espoused similar views. They wanted to provide an environment in which their employees were challenged, too, and their contributions recognized, as we shall see in Chapter 6. But the overriding concern for them was to create or maintain a viable, ongoing business, by establishing a reputation for product or service excellence (as well as maximizing their personal satisfaction, which had been cramped in their former employment).

I want the company to be independent. I hope it will contribute to society through solar cells, and that the employees will be happy and excited in their work, and that the shareholders will willingly support it. (J1)

I want my employees to enjoy working and to know how happy accomplishing tasks is. I send my young people overseas as much as possible to get them experienced. I want them to know what the main point is, especially when they are meeting with customers. (J14)

I needed to create an environment in which they [employees] could respond speedily to customer needs and build trust. (J24)

I'd be happy to give up the presidency at any time, if there were a good successor. But they would have to be superior to me, or at least to have a strong potential and sense of responsibility for the future of the company. (J2)

As there were multiple objectives in start-up, there were multiple objectives in maintaining and developing the business as well, and also an emphasis on means, which may well have shaped the ends pursued. This applied to both the UK and Japan, with somewhat different nuances.

Growth aspirations, risk, and uncertainty

The entrepreneur has always been associated with risk, from Cantillon, who is said to have coined the term "entrepreneur" at the beginning of the eighteenth century, through Mill, who popularized the term in the mid nineteenth century, to the present day. Knight's (1921) distinction between calculable risk and uncertainty did nothing to weaken the association. Entrepreneurs themselves deny that they like to take risks. Liles (1971: 46) puts it bluntly: "I believe the entrepreneurs I know would describe [people who like to take risks] as fools," or in the words of Sahlman et al. (1999: 2): "As a highly successful entrepreneur once put it, 'My idea of risk and reward is for me to get the reward and others to take the risk.' " In an influential paper, Brockhaus (1982) found that entrepreneurs are moderate risk takers, as are most people. He concluded that risk taking is *not* a distinguishing feature of entrepreneurs. And yet the association refuses to go away.

As most people to not use Knight's distinction, and given that there is considerable uncertainty involved in opportunity and business creation, and moreover that entrepreneurs might embrace this uncertainty, then the persistence becomes more understandable. Sarasvathy (2001: 7) recalls: "(S)everal of the expert entrepreneurs I studied explicitly stated that being in a market that could be predicted was not such a good idea, since there would always be someone smarter and with deeper pockets who could predict it better than they could."

In this section we will approach "risk" in two ways. First, we look at the entrepreneurs' growth aspirations for the next three years. As Storey (1994: 119–20) notes, many business owners do not aspire to growth, and many who do, do not achieve it. How about the entrepreneurs in this study? Second, we consider responses to an open question about their attitude toward risk in the development of their business.

Table 4.2 tabulates growth aspirations. We see that by no means all entrepreneurs, or even the majority of them, were aiming for substantial growth. The UK entrepreneurs as a group sought higher levels of growth than the Japanese entrepreneurs. The high performers sought more growth than the non-high performers, but the difference was much smaller in Japan than in the UK, and even the UK non-high performers sought more growth than the Japanese high performers.

Table 4.2 Growth objectives for the next three years

	UK				Japan	
	All UK	HP	Non-HP	All Japan	HP	Non-HP
Become smaller	0.9	0	1.6	5.0	5.2	4.9
Stay the same size	9.7	2.5	12.5	28.4	20.8	33.3
Grow moderately	47.8	40.0	57.8	53.2	59.7	48.5
Grow substantially	41.6	57.5	28.1	13.5	14.3	13.0

Note: HP = high performer

Does this mean that the UK entrepreneurs are more pro-active or aggressive, have higher aspirations, a greater tolerance of risk even? Perhaps. These results surprised us, given the overwhelmingly cautious remarks about growth from the first UK survey[3]:

Biggest experience has been that too much growth too quickly can kill a company quicker than no growth.

Don't expand too quickly.

Keep the brakes on!

These remarks were sometimes preceded by comments – and cautionary tales – about recession in the early 1990s. By 2000, buoyant economic conditions appear to have raised aspirations. Indeed, growth aspirations were significantly related to growth experiences over the past two years. This might also explain the extreme caution on the part of the Japanese entrepreneurs. Not only were they in the midst of a decade-long deflationary downturn, with a shift of production overseas and restructuring by major customers, but the fallout of the IT bubble bust of 2001 was beginning to engulf them as well. For many survey respondents, including high performers (though not so much, it should be said, our interviewees), survival was their focus, and in some cases this meant retrenchment:

My orders have dropped by 50% [with the IT slump]. My self-capital is at 35%, so I can manage financially, but I'm going to be forced into restructuring. I am going to keep a small number of trusted employees, however.

When the Bubble burst, in 1992, we made a big loss, but survived. This time it's worse. We are using up internal reserves, and relying on relations we have built up with banks.

It's the worst it's ever been. The directors have taken a cut in pay, we've laid off some employees, and encouraged our subsidiaries to take measures [substituting full time employees with part timers].

[3] They are also considerably higher than even the fast growth and innovator businesses reported in the Cambridge 1999 CBR Survey (Cosh and Hughes, 2000: 40).

When we take out these environmental influences, it is possible that the UK entrepreneurs were more growth-oriented, but we cannot say for sure, and we still have to recognize that over half the UK entrepreneurs wanted to grow moderately at most.

Perceptions of risk

Let us now look at how the entrepreneurs themselves thought about risk. Given the above comments about risk, we proceed with considerable caution. Rather than using a standard test (such as the Jackson Personality Inventory or Kogan-Wallach Choice Dilemma Questionnaire), we asked an open question about their approach to risk in the development of their business.

The UK entrepreneurs expressed a range of views, from conservative, complete avoidance ("Retirement has more appeal than risk") right through to declarations of the need for high levels of risk taking ("Prepared to take a high level of risk to achieve ambitious targets"). The extremes were roughly balanced in terms of numbers, but the most common statements were of caution, acceptance of moderate risk or calculated risk, after analyzing a situation thoroughly first.

All business has to involve some risk, but we have run our own business on the strategy of evaluating risks prior to taking them, monitoring the risk and pulling the plug at any stage.

Risk is necessary, but should be calculated and minimized.

A number indicated that they were willing to take risk – it was part of business – but not to the extent that it could jeopardize the business. In other words, "affordable loss" (Sarasvathy, 2001).

There are times when we have taken risks which to others appeared excessive, but to us seemed well managed risks. We have never been willing to risk the whole business, although with hindsight there have been occasions where we had, fortunately with a positive outcome.

A small number reported a growing appetite for risk once their business was on a solid foundation, while some commented on a diminishing appetite for risk, either because there was a lot of risk in the early days which they were glad to see the end of, or because they did not want to jeopardize their achievements, especially as they were getting older. Commonly mentioned risk-reducing strategies were diversifying the customer base and the product line up, limiting the amount of risk taken on at any one time, or limiting it in certain parts of the business. Other self-declared strategies included consulting with partners and encouraging others to "co-own" risk.

Several entrepreneurs distinguished between product or R&D-related risk and financial risk, indicating that they were prepared to accept the former, but minimized the latter. Perhaps they felt they had a greater chance of influencing the outcome of the former, or at least would fail only through their own shortcomings, while financial risk put them at the mercy of others.

We have attempted to grow the business organically, using our own resources and funding and concentrating on our chosen market segment of the industry. Our product development risk is high, but we adopt a conservative approach to funding and exposure.

Like the responses to growth, these comments seemed more upbeat – receptive to the notion of taking some risk, albeit cautious or calculated – than those in the first UK survey, in which comments like the following were common:

Being told by the bank that they were not concerned with my business, only the safety of their money.

Getting development finance and real capital – without being indentured like a serf – is impossible. . . . Given this situation, we have been risk averse.

Having been through two major recessions (73/74 and 89/92) – taken more realistic approach to business expansion and risk.

Development held back by slow payment of invoices (four to five months is typical). We limit the amount of work in hand to reduce the risk of cash flow problems resulting from very late payment.

To some extent these attitudes persisted – "The UK engineering industry is risky enough without sticking one's neck out on risky projects" – but the earlier problems of late payment by major customers or banks pulling in loans as well as recent memories of recession had diminished, and the entrepreneurs were more positive about business expansion.

Needless to say, this was not the case in Japan. Here also "caution" and "calculated risk" were keywords, but a different keyword was "stability."[4] This was seen as a virtuous state, not easily attained. Threats to stability

---

[4] The wording of the Japanese question was slightly different from the English question. It asked about approaches to "management crisis and risk" rather than simply "risk." This was intended to make the concept of risk more meaningful, but the result may have been to frame the issue in participants' minds slightly differently. We have triangulated the answers with other open questions and interviews, however, so the comparison is meaningful.

had to be anticipated, and early efforts made to reduce or eliminate their impact. If the UK entrepreneurs expressed a willingness to take on risk in the development of new products or R&D, the single most common response of the Japanese entrepreneurs also concerned product development and R&D, only it was to reduce risk, and establish or reestablish a basis for future stability.

I focus on the product cycle, and try to develop next-generation products, implementing strategic strengthening aimed at stability and profit leveling.

In order to avoid financial risk, I have made positive efforts to approach financial institutions, always engaged in cutting edge R&D, and tried to gain customer trust by improving quality, and obtaining ISO9002.

Strengthening technology development (including production technology), gathering information on technology trends and customer needs, managing inventory (reducing, appropriate levels) and building flexibility into production to cope with fluctuating volumes.

I have gained the conviction that I can get business by doggedly pursuing R&D.

Past crises were frequently mentioned, which had necessitated a concerted or even frantic response in order to survive. In addition to new product development and R&D, this included seeking out new customer needs and gaining employee cooperation to fulfill them. There was less mention of partitioning risk, but risk-reduction strategies included sharp information scanning and analysis, financial prudence, and communication with banks, and sometimes the insertion of considerable personal funds and effort, so much so that some respondents mentioned personal health as a crucial element.

My deceased husband was an engineer, and "one man" manager. He became too engrossed in work and became sick. We had to devolve work to individual employees and educate them to take responsibility (from five or six years ago). They gritted their teeth a bit, but they did it.

Overall:

On the production side, I am passionate about quality, and through R&D, cost control, introducing new production methods and computers in the office, strengthening production management and trying to anticipate the needs of the age. I have tried to introduce annual planning, monthly statements, grasp the movement of people, money and things in real time, and maintain clear communication with employees, banks and customers.

UK entrepreneurs sometimes recounted the perilous nature of their existence in the years immediately following start-up, or difficulties when their major customer was taken over and their orders were cut, or the ups and downs or stop–start nature of the UK economy in the past as influencing their approach to business. Quite a few conceded that risk is a part of daily business life. Once they had survived the start-up years and the business was on an even keel, however, risk was often seen as something within their discretion to maximize or minimize, depending on their general objectives and growth objectives. To use a metaphor, the UK entrepreneurs dipped their toes into the cold water of risk, and moved in cautiously up to their ankles, then to their knees. Some decided to wade in further. The water itself was like a lake, reasonably calm close to the edges, although storms could make it choppy.

For many of the Japanese entrepreneurs, however, risk was something quite different. It was not something they voluntarily took on and lived with the consequences, rather it was a state of the world into which they had thrust themselves. Using a different metaphor, they were small vessels in an ocean of risk, where the waves were dangerous near the shoreline. They wanted to get beyond the breakers and get their vessel on an even keel. This necessitated intense efforts at R&D or developing new products, and cultivating relations with stakeholders. Calmer waters were just out of reach, and a bigger boat was needed to get there. Whether this counts as "risk avoidance" is debatable, since the quest to reach calmer waters entailed what would normally be considered risk taking.

Where do these different perceptions come from? They might be considered cultural, in the sense that the entrepreneurs had absorbed notions of risk from the business and popular media, and through their daily interactions. Their realities were a social construction. From an ecological perspective, however, they might reflect the crowded and harsher nature of the Japanese environment relative to the UK environment, at least for entrepreneurs. Between these two views, the perceptions may be seen as grounded in different approaches: a "project" approach which was associated with voluntaristic notions of risk taking, and a "lifework" approach which was associated with the need to build resources and competences to prepare for all contingencies.

Finally, regarding high performers and non-high performers, if the statements are categorized into "positive," "neutral," and "negative" attitudes toward risk, in the UK more high performers professed a positive attitude than neutral, and more had a neutral attitude than negative. Amongst non-high performers, numbers in the three categories were roughly equal. For the Japanese entrepreneurs, it is difficult to make such a distinction, although as noted, our interviewees tended to be more upbeat, both about growth and about their success in reducing risk through innovation.

Innovation

Innovation is considered a defining characteristic of the entrepreneur in the Schumpeterian tradition. It is not so much an attitude, however, as something which is done, and typically not by an individual, but by people working together. We see it, therefore, as an organizational *outcome* which locates a business on a continuum between imitation (there are usually some distinguishing features, even in imitation) through innovations which are new to a business but not to the industry, to a geographical market but not to an industry, to more radical innovations which are entirely new, and create new markets or industries. Degrees of entrepreneurship are easy to talk about, but are more difficult to measure. Our metrics follow the Oslo Innovation Manual (2) 1997 edition, which distinguishes five types of innovation – product, process, logistics, service, and service delivery,[5] as well as between "novel innovation," which is new to both business and industry, and "non-novel innovation," which is new to the business but not to the industry.

Before looking at innovation outcomes, however, let us consider innovation inputs. Table 4.3 summarizes the statistical findings on R&D. The majority of entrepreneurs were involved in R&D activity on a continuous basis in the previous two years, and less than a quarter did not undertake R&D.[6] UK–Japan differences here were minor. UK entrepreneurs reported spending more on R&D as a proportion of turnover, however. Only 18 percent of the Japanese entrepreneurs spent 5 percent or more on R&D (the same proportion that spent nothing), which was half the UK figure. We are not sure whether the difference is due to different perceptions of what constitutes R&D expenditure (which is hard to pin down in small businesses), to more sophisticated accounting methods in the UK, to the impact of the business environment in Japan, or whether there are real

---

[5] Marketing and organizational innovation, which were added to the 2005 edition, were not surveyed. The same question was used in the Cambridge CBR surveys, and was intended to ensure comparability with them. There is some overlap here with Schumpeter's (1934, 1961) five types of "new combination": new good, new method of production, opening of a new market, new source of supply, and new organization of industry.

[6] These figures, like growth aspirations, were somewhat higher than those reported in the Cambridge 1999 CBR survey, but the latter only asked about R&D in the last year (Cosh and Hughes, 2000: 57).

and sustained differences in how much entrepreneurs in both countries spend on R&D. As we noted above, many of our Japanese case interview companies devoted substantial resources to R&D, and did not appear to withdraw these during downturns.

Let us also consider briefly intellectual property rights (IPRs) which seek to protect the results of R&D for commercial benefit. Half the Japanese entrepreneurs had applied for patents compared with just under a third in the UK, and more than twice the proportion had been granted them. Almost one in ten of the Japanese entrepreneurs had applied for ten or more patents, and just over 3 percent had been granted ten or more. None in the UK were so prolific. The more pro-active stance on patents on the part of the Japanese businesses might be attributed to their attempts to protect themselves from competitors and large companies, to the use of patent applications as a means of setting goals for engineers, or to the technological orientation of the founders, many of whom were involved in patenting activities (with numerical targets) for many years before they started or inherited their own business.

When it came to copyrights and trademarks, however, the situation was reversed. A quarter of UK entrepreneurs had applied for trademarks, compared with only 14 percent of their Japanese counterparts, but the gap in terms of trademarks granted was less (16 percent versus 12 percent). This might be related to the market or commercial orientation of the UK entrepreneurs. With regard to in-licensing, Japanese firms were somewhat more active – 11 percent versus 8 percent – but the levels were much lower than their own IPR activities.

In sum, numerical statistics on innovation inputs present us with a mixed picture. Most of the businesses were engaged in R&D, and many had also applied for patents. The UK entrepreneurs appeared to spend more on R&D, and were more likely to apply for trademarks, but the Japanese entrepreneurs were more aggressive on patent applications, and were somewhat more likely to in-license. High performers in the UK, we should note, were much more likely to engage in R&D than non-high performers, they spent a greater proportion of turnover on it, and were more active in patenting.[7] In Japan, however, non-high performers were just as likely to engage in R&D, and a higher percentage spent 10 percent or more of turnover on R&D than high performers (13 percent versus 7 percent)! Whatever else separates high performers and non-high

---

[7] Thirty-one percent of UK high performers spent 10 percent or more of turnover on R&D compared with 12 percent of non-high performers. Forty-six percent had applied for patents, compared with 19 percent.

performers in Japan, it is not innovation inputs. Rather, it is likely to be how those inputs are combined and turned into outputs which customers valued.

Turning to innovation outcomes, Table 4.4 presents a summary. Over half of the entrepreneurs in both countries reported introducing a novel product innovation and another quarter a non-novel product innovation, in the previous two years, reflecting the innovative character of their high-tech industries. Levels of product innovation were higher in Japan, but not markedly so. When it came to other types of innovation, however, the differences were substantial. The Japanese entrepreneurs reported more novel process, logistics, service and service delivery innovation.

These differences are probably real rather than varying propensities to recognize innovation. From our interviews, there seemed to be a tendency

Table 4.3 R&D and IPR activity

	UK	Japan
Engaged in R&D?		
No	22.3	15.5
Yes, occasionally	22.3	27.3
Yes, continuously/primary activity	55.4	57.3
Percentage of turnover spent on R&D		
0/ n/a	24.8	17.6
<1%	16.8	32.4
>>1%, <5%	22.8	32.4
>>5%, <10%	15.8	7.8
>>10%, <15%	12.9	2.0
>>15%	6.9	7.8
Applied for patents	30.8	50.7
Granted patents	15.9	34.5
Taken out licenses	7.6	11.3

Table 4.4 Innovation

	UK		Japan	
Innovations during the past two years	Novel	Other	Novel	Other
Technologically new or significantly improved manufactured product	51.8	26.4	58.8	24.0
Technologically new or significantly improved methods of making manufactured product	23.9	28.4	40.9	23.3
Technological improvements in supply, storage or distribution systems for manufactured product	10.2	13.0	27.7	30.1
New or significantly improved service product	13.8	21.1	35.2	26.3
New method to produce or deliver service or product	9.2	13.8	28.5	46.2

Note: Novel = innovation new to firm *and* to industry
Other = innovation new to firm but *not* to industry

among the UK entrepreneurs to link innovation with product, and to focus on this as a key competitive driver. Process and other types of innovation were often seen as less consequential. Rapid and thorough response to customer needs was important, and might necessitate the adoption of IT packages or solutions, but these were purchased rather than developed in-house. The exception was UK high performers, whose levels of novel product *and process* innovation were almost as high as the Japanese high performers (83 percent and 42 percent compared with 88 percent and 44 percent, respectively). Logistics and service innovation levels, however, were much lower, and little over half the level of Japanese high performers.

In Japan, on the other hand, process innovation was given almost as much emphasis as product innovation. The emphasis started early, often before products were even launched. It was driven partly by customers, and partly by trying to anticipate or recover from shocks or crises, as noted in our discussion of risk. Packaged software was purchased for the office, or for design, but when it came to production, there was an emphasis on in-house innovation – at least in the form of customization, but often as a defining competitive advantage.[8] This is consistent with the backgrounds of the entrepreneurs and their technological orientations, and possibly a harsher competitive environment in Japan, where innovative products alone are no guarantee for survival. Even when production was out-sourced, which was not uncommon in technology businesses around Kyoto, for instance, key processes in design, assembly, and interfacing with customers were retained in-house.

Then came the semiconductor slump. I thought about things and decided that our base is in making things that are difficult for others. I set up a home page and got new work from that. I spend ¥100–200 million a year on new equipment. When I started doing aircraft work I spent ¥10 million on CAD hardware and ¥10 million on software and the same again for training. Now we have the expertise to advise our customers. Out of the blue, someone from a factory in Kyushu turned up one day, said he had seen a list of our equipment, and could we make a robot arm for large LCD panels. Before we had even reached agreement on the price a truck turned up with the materials. (J24, formerly a custom manufacturer of semiconductor assembly machines)

If there were few differences between Japanese high performers and non-high performers in terms of innovation inputs, there were clear differences in terms of outputs. In most categories only half as many non-high performers reported novel innovations, although with the exception

---

[8] See also the discussion of competitive advantages in Chapter 5.

of product and process innovation, these were comparable to the UK high-performer figures.

Our data and interviews produce no evidence of a systemic bias toward radical innovation in the UK, and incremental innovation in Japan, at least from small business sources. If anything, our patent and novel innovation data suggest a greater likelihood of radical innovation in Japan, but we did not probe patent quality. It did appear that technology and technological innovation was seen as the basis of continued viability and competitiveness in Japan (see also Chapter 5), and that our interviewees sought to develop competences in technologies with long-term potential. This often meant focusing on two or three technology niches, sometimes in process technology, with growth potential.

Over the past two decades we have developed three core technologies, and we aim to develop new products by combining them. Lasers are becoming the strongest area. We got involved in YAG lasers eighteen years ago. I visited many companies to figure out what the possible markets were, and opted for fine lasers rather than high power ones. It was the right decision, and customers helped a lot. The market is too small for companies like Toshiba and NEC, but it's a good size for us. (J13)

In the UK, technology was important, and some interviewees also sought to develop competences in two or three niches to reduce risk or prepare for the future, but these were often product-based. With the exception of high performers, there appeared to be less concern with developing core technologies, perhaps because the entrepreneurs had more business and personal options, in terms of sales, acquisition, portfolio adjustment, and adjustment of personal involvement.

High performers

Finally in this chapter, we wish to set out how we identified a group of highly innovative businesses which could add a further dimension to our comparison. Our choice of high-tech industries was intended to ensure we had many innovative entrepreneurs and businesses in our sample. A further filter would help us to identify the most innovative. We wanted to know whether they negated, maintained, or even amplified national differences.

Our "novel innovators" were prime candidates for such a group. Some businesses may be wildly innovative, however, without finding customers.

We therefore decided to introduce an additional requirement for our selected group: a certain level of growth in turnover. This additional requirement meant that they were likely to be effective in both exploration and exploitation, or in reaping the benefits of past innovation whilst sewing the seeds for future growth. We opted for turnover growth of at least 10 percent in the past two years.

The proportion of businesses meeting both requirements dropped from 61 percent in the UK and 69 percent in Japan – the proportion of novel innovators – to just over one-third (35 percent) in both countries. We call these innovative, growing businesses "high performers." We cannot assume the remainder are imitators or reproducers – they may have introduced very novel innovations more than two years ago, or have been about to introduce them, or they may have introduced a novel innovation without capturing its benefits (yet), or they might have been growing strongly without introducing a novel innovation. For want of a better expression we simply call these businesses "non-high performers."

We decided against additional requirements such as a certain level of profitability. The Comparative Entrepreneurship survey was conducted during the IT slump and prolonged recession in Japan, and before the slump and at a time of relative buoyancy in the UK. There are additional problems with using profitability as a performance indicator here, and some studies have shown a negative relationship between profits and innovation (Cosh and Hughes, 2000). We therefore decided against using this measure. In passing, however, we note – surprisingly – that levels of profitability as a ratio of turnover were quite similar between the UK and Japan, and it might be added, similar between our high performers and non-high performers in both countries.

As we have seen in this chapter, the high performers had significantly higher growth aspirations than non-high performers in the UK, and espoused a more positive attitude toward risk. It is possible, however, that these are the result of past growth experiences, and that they are as much the result as the cause of growth and innovation. High performers also had higher growth aspirations in Japan, although the differences were not nearly as marked, and it was difficult to make a distinction in terms of attitudes toward risk. There were some differences in terms of innovation inputs, as we noted, as well as outputs. We shall see whether there are differences in other areas as well, including perceived competitive advantages, HRM orientations, and interfirm collaboration.

Concluding comments

In Chapter 2 we saw that most of our entrepreneurs started out closer to the imitator end of the imitator–innovator spectrum. In this chapter we have seen that most did not stay there, but moved toward the innovator end of the spectrum. The majority was engaged in R&D continuously, and patenting activity was quite high. Roughly two-thirds of the entrepreneurs in both countries reported introducing a novel innovation – new to both company and industry – in the past two years, and more had introduced innovations new to their company. These innovations were carried out as the businesses moved from "soft" to "hard" phases of development by introducing their own product, as they attempted to introduce new product lines or move into new lines of business, and as they tried to cope with threats and opportunities in the short and long term.

Thus our broad similarities of founding are carried forward into growth stages, in the form of progress toward becoming innovators. As they did so, moreover, entrepreneurs in both countries emphasized the importance of "principles" in their business, which may also be interpreted as "means." They wanted to build a business with a reputation for product or service excellence, to provide a positive and stable environment for employees, and to conduct business on the basis of fairness and moral integrity. These principles complemented the "hard" edge of commitment to R&D and innovation.

Within these broad similarities, there were differences. First, there were significant differences in the scores given to many of the personal business objectives. The strongest discriminators were making a contribution to science and technology, which the Japanese entrepreneurs rated much higher, and maximizing current and future returns for the owners/investors, which the UK entrepreneurs rated much higher (but still in the middle of their ratings). These differences are consistent with the founding reasons explored in Chapter 2, as well as the respective lifework and project orientations to entrepreneurship. The Japanese entrepreneurs also rated building a business which would continue to exist without them, and preparing for public listing, significantly higher. Neither of these suggested preparation for exit or partial commitment, however, and were consistent with the lifework approach.

The UK entrepreneurs wanted to grow moderately or substantially, while the Japanese entrepreneurs wanted to grow moderately, if at all. This may or may not indicate basic and enduring differences in attitudes toward growth; it was strongly related to recent growth experience, and the Japanese economic environment made this difficult. The UK economic environment was more favorable, and optimism appeared to have grown between the first and the second survey.

Most entrepreneurs expressed cautious attitudes toward risk, or the importance of prudent, calculated risk consistent with affordable loss. In the UK, however, increasing or decreasing risk was seen as something within the power of the entrepreneur, while in Japan being in business meant existing in a state of risk, requiring innovation, hard work, and cautious maneuvering to manage. Whether this, too, was a product of the economic environment, or rather was embedded in the respective entrepreneurial and industrial cultures, is hard to say, but we suspect the latter.

Finally, the UK entrepreneurs, especially the high performers, said they spent more on R&D than their Japanese counterparts, while the Japanese entrepreneurs registered higher levels of patenting. They also reported a broader range of innovation outcomes, while the UK entrepreneurs focused on product innovation. This might indicate more extensive incremental innovation in Japan, but it does not suggest a stronger orientation to radical innovation in the UK.

This chapter has told us something about the "entrepreneurial orientations" of UK and Japanese entrepreneurs, as well as innovation outputs, but it has not told us much about their competitive strategies, markets, or how they address those markets, as well as the kinds of things that prevent them from achieving their business objectives. We turn to these in Chapter 5.

5

Competitive Orientations and Growth Limitations

Having looked at "entrepreneurial orientations" and innovation engagement and outcomes, we now turn to how entrepreneurs try to maintain and grow their businesses in the market place. We will examine the kinds of markets the entrepreneurs compete in, and how they compete. We will also examine the kinds of limitations which prevent them from achieving their business objectives.

We hesitate to use the word "strategy." As Berry and Taggart (1998) have shown, small high-tech businesses start out with a high degree of informality and flexibility, both in terms of technology strategy and business strategy, and only as they grow do these become more formalized.[1] In fact, entrepreneurs often rely on "hustle" (or being less incompetent than competitors) rather than novel ideas or deliberate market positioning: "Successful entrepreneurs depend on person selling skills, contacts, their reputations for expertise, and their ability to convince clients of the value of services rendered" (Bhide, 1994: 155).

Not surprisingly, early attempts to apply strategic management theory to start-ups and small businesses were not particularly successful, and often mixed description and prescription. Summarizing such research, McDougall and Robinson (1990) noted that "prevailing wisdom" counseled new ventures to pursue "niche" strategies and avoid direct competition with large or established firms, but other research claimed that such strategies were self-defeating, and successful ventures were those which entered with aggressive market share and growth objectives (Biggadike, 1976; cf. also MacMillan and Day, 1987). Even if such an approach does

---

[1] Additionally, they argue, technology-push gives way to a market orientation. We have suggested that this depends on prior experience and other environmental factors.

characterize some successful ventures, however, it is another thing to offer this as a prescription.[2]

Differentiation approaches were hardly more successful. Arguing that these are overly restrictive, and do not represent the range of strategies followed by small businesses (cf. Chaganti, Chaganti, and Mahajan, 1989), some researchers have tried to create new, empirically derived classifications. Like McDougall and Robinson (1990), for example, Carter et al. (1994) use factor and cluster analysis to induce distinctive strategy configurations.[3]

This chapter follows a similar approach, without cluster analysis, and with perceived "competitive advantages" in the place of strategy.[4] Before we look at these, however, we look at subcontracting, reliance on major customers, and direct competitors. This will give us a better idea of the market context for the competitive advantages. Finally in this chapter, we consider market and other limitations which prevented the entrepreneurs from achieving their business objectives.

Niche markets

It is well known that small businesses operate in niche markets, where they are relatively sheltered from direct competition from companies with more resources and influence (Kitson and Wilkinson, 2000). Some might see this as self-defeating, but it is a reality, and a survival strategy. There are different kinds of niche market engagement, ranging from embodiment of technology in an entrepreneur, or "technical expert," to embodiment of technology in a boutique product or service, with bespoke contractors in between (Quince and Whittaker, 2002). Technical experts sometimes do international consulting, but by and large their work is localized. They work for a small range of clients, relying on their reputation and quality of their work, while the boutique producers are sometimes quite international in orientation, competing on the basis of design, novelty, and specialized nature of their product, and seeking to grow through innovation.[5]

---

[2] To succeed, such strategies require enabling competences, networks, and even aspirations. The environment matters, too; at the very least it may be "hostile" or "benign" (Covin and Slevin, 1989).

[3] McDougall and Robinson emerge with eight "archetypes" from nine factors, and Carter et al., with six cluster types from six factors.

[4] As with innovation, we have adapted the questionnaire items used in the Cambridge CBR surveys (cf. Cosh and Hughes, 2000). The same applies to our items on limitations.

[5] This typology is based on the full second survey UK data, which included high-tech services. Unfortunately, we cannot explore this distinction here as we do not have high-tech services in our comparative data set.

We consider niche markets here from the viewpoint of subcontracting, reliance on major customers, and number of competitors. First, two-thirds of both the UK and Japanese businesses did some subcontracting, while one-third (32 percent) did none. There were no differences in terms of subcontracting engagement. Of those who did subcontracting, however, there was greater reliance in Japan. The same proportion that did no subcontracting also reported relying on subcontracting for 75 percent or more of their turnover in the previous year, twice the UK proportion of 16 percent. Conversely, almost 30 percent of UK entrepreneurs relied on subcontracting for less than 10 percent of their turnover, which was more than twice the figure for Japan. Thus of those who did do subcontracting, there was heavier reliance in Japan than in the UK.

The picture is similar for reliance on major customers (Table 5.1). Just over a quarter of the Japanese entrepreneurs relied on their major customer for 50 percent or more of their turnover, which was four times the UK figure. Conversely, just over one-third of the UK entrepreneurs relied on their major customer for less than 10 percent of their turnover, compared with a quarter in Japan. One-third relied on their top *three* customers for 50 percent or more of their turnover in Japan, compared with a quarter in the UK, while one in ten in both countries relied on their top three customers for less than 10 percent of their turnover. Thus the Japanese businesses had greater levels of dependence on subcontracting, and a small number of customers, although there was a similar proportion that did no subcontracting and were not reliant on a few customers. Overall, we see an orientation toward a relatively small number of customers, rather than production for mass markets, in both countries.

Turning now to competitors, a small minority in both countries (6 percent in the UK, 9 percent in Japan) reported no serious competitors or only one (6 percent and 8 percent). Many had between two and five serious competitors, but almost 40 percent in the UK and less than a quarter in Japan reported six or more, suggesting that a substantial minority,

Table 5.1 Reliance on top customers

Turnover	Reliance on top customer (%)		Reliance on top 3 customers (%)	
	UK	Japan	UK	Japan
<10%	36.5	26.1	10.8	9.8
10–24%	44.4	31.9	27.7	30.1
25–49%	12.7	15.2	33.8	22.8
50–74%	3.2	15.2	21.5	15.4
75% +	3.2	11.6	6.2	22.0

especially in the UK, operated in more open product markets. These figures on competitors complement those of subcontracting and reliance on large customers, suggesting extensive "relational contracting" (Dore, 1983) in Japan, and less reliance with more customers and competitors in the UK, although the latter can hardly be considered atomistic market competition, either.

The location of competitors was interesting. Over a quarter (27 percent) of UK entrepreneurs who reported serious competitors said they were all outside the UK, which was twice the Japanese figure, while over half the Japanese entrepreneurs with serious competitors said *none* were outside Japan, which was twice the UK figure. The more international orientation on the part of the UK businesses may have been due to the "hollowing out" of UK manufacturing in the 1980s and 1990s as well as the proximity of, and integration into, European markets. The domestic orientation of the Japanese businesses may have been (partly) related to the larger Japanese manufacturing base, which was still relatively intact.

High performers in the UK had even lower levels of reliance on subcontracting, and on a major customer for more than 10 percent of their turnover, but other than that, there was very little difference with non-high performers. High performers in Japan showed similar levels of subcontracting reliance to non-high performers, but less reliance on their top three customers. A certain stigma is attached to "subcontracting" in the UK, and reducing reliance on it might have been seen as a means of reducing vulnerability, while innovative Japanese companies might value a degree of subcontracting, both for new, innovative ideas from these relations, and enhanced legitimacy which accrues from supplying a famous company.

As for the number of competitors, high performers in both countries were somewhat more likely to report either none, or several, and – particularly in the UK – they were more likely to have serious competitors overseas. (We do not know if the competition itself was in their domestic market, or overseas, but high performers exported more than non-high performers, and UK businesses exported more than Japanese ones.[6])

---

[6] Almost half the UK high performers exported half or more of their turnover, compared with just 20 percent of non-high performers. The corresponding figures for Japan were just 14 percent and 9 percent. Just 23 percent of UK high performers either did not export or exported less than 10 percent of their turnover, compared with 54 percent of non-high performers. The Japanese figures were 71 percent and 70 percent, respectively, although fewer high performers did not export (31 percent versus 48 percent).

Competitive advantages

We have seen that many of the businesses operated in niche markets, with a small number of direct competitors, but we need to explore *how* they did business, or competed. Was it essentially based on "hustle," general competence, and reputation, or were there other strategies, implicit or explicit? To answer this question we turn to perceived competitive advantages.

Participants of the second Comparative Entrepreneurship survey were asked to rate eleven items on a scale of 1 (not at all) to 5 (crucial). The results are summarized in Figure 5.1. A cursory glance shows that the UK averages were higher than the Japanese ones on all items except two. UK averages ranged from 3.13 to 4.45, with seven of the averages scoring over 4, while the Japanese averages ranged from 2.95 to 4.09, with most grouped in the 3–4 range. Optimism, it appears, applies not just to growth; the UK entrepreneurs were more confident about their competitive advantages as well.

There were some similarities between the two groups. Four of the top five-ranked items in the UK were also in the top five of the Japanese list.[7] These are typical "niche" items – personal attention/responsiveness to customer needs, speed of service, and specialized product/service, along with quality of product/service. Bhide's assessment appears to be at least

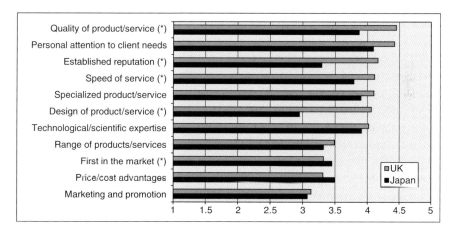

Figure 5.1 Competitive advantages

Note: * differences significant at .05

---

[7] These items also top the CBR survey list for manufacturers, and especially innovators (Cosh and Hughes, 2007: 22–3).

partially apt. Conversely, items related to open competitive markets such as marketing and promotion, range of products/services, being first in the market with new products/services and (arguably) price/cost advantages were given low ratings.

Beyond these similarities, there were important differences. Quality and design were ranked higher in the UK. This might be counterintuitive, given the fabled Japanese emphasis on quality, but this emphasis might make it a given or "table stake" in Japan, a requirement for doing business rather than a competitive advantage. Possible reasons for the much lower score on design in Japan include customer specifications (given higher reliance on subcontracting), or involvement in component rather than product manufacture. Established reputation was also rated and ranked much lower in Japan. Perhaps the Japanese entrepreneurs were saying that reputation itself is not a decisive factor in getting business (a necessary but not sufficient condition), or that their smallness or newness meant it was difficult to establish a reputation.

On the other hand, although the difference in average scores is not statistically significant, technological/scientific expertise was ranked much higher by the Japanese participants (second versus seventh). This fits well with the picture of the Japanese entrepreneurs built up so far. The higher rankings for price/cost advantages and being first in the market in Japan might stem from sectoral weightings, especially the large number of electronics businesses, versus medical products and equipment in the UK. That there were clear differences between the two groups is confirmed by discriminant function analysis, which produced a highly significant (.000) result, and classified 79.5 percent of the responses correctly (85.7 percent in the UK and 75.7 percent in Japan). The biggest discriminators were design and established reputation.

Once again we turn to factor analysis to explore underlying similarities and differences. The combined group produced three factors, which we call respectively "innovation," "market," and "client" orientations.[8] These factors are intuitively meaningful, but did the UK and Japanese groups conceive and structure the factors differently? Yes they did.

The UK entrepreneurs' responses produced four factors (Table 5.2). The first factor – "innovation" – included three of the combined group innov-

---

[8] These explain 51.9 percent of the variance. "Innovation orientation" includes being first in the market with new products/services, technological/scientific expertise, specialized product/service, and design of product/service. "Market orientation" includes marketing and promotion, range of products/services, established reputation, and price/cost advantages. And "client orientation" includes personalized attention/responsiveness to client needs, speed of service, and quality of product/service.

ation items, as well as price/cost advantages, which had a *negative* loading, meaning it was viewed as an oppositional concept. (Price/cost advantages loads weakly onto the final factor – marketing – as well.) The second factor of the combined group was split in the UK. One factor – "product lineup" – consisted of a range of products/services, specialized product/service, and quality of product/service. The other factor – "marketing" – consisted of a solitary item, marketing and promotion (with a weak loading of price/cost advantages). The remaining factor was similar to the combined group client orientation, except that quality of product/service was replaced by established reputation.

The Japanese group produced a very different picture. Here there were three factors, as in the combined sample. The first factor – "superior product" – consisted of five items – first in market, design, quality, specialized product/service, and very weakly, responsiveness to client needs.[9] The second factor – "market presence" – consisted of marketing, speed of service, reputation, and range of products. The third and final factor consisted of a negative loading of price/cost, as well as science and technology (S&T) expertise (with a weaker loading of specialized product/service). This appears to take us back to technological backgrounds, technology-push OBC, and technology-based innovation. The structure of the first factor reinforces this impression. In competitive advantage factors, then, we find some differences; let us see if these come into sharper focus through the high performers.

Table 5.2 Competitive advantages: factor comparison

UK	Japan
1. Innovation Technological/scientific expertise, first in market, design, price/cost (−ve)	1. Superior product First in market, design, quality, specialized product/service, (responsiveness to client needs)
2. Product lineup Range of products/services, specialized product/service, quality	2. Market presence Marketing and promotion, speed of service, established reputation, range of products/services,
3. Client focus Responsiveness to client needs, speed, established reputation	3. Technology base Price/cost (−ve), technological/ scientific expertise
4. Marketing Marketing and promotion	

Note: Based on principal component analysis, varimax rotation with Kaiser normalization; see Appendix 2 Tables A2.5, A2.6 for details.

[9] S&T expertise and product range also loaded onto this factor, more strongly than responsiveness, but not as strongly as onto other factors.

High performers

Are the high performers different from the non-high performers? In the UK, the average score of the high performers was higher than the non-high performers on every item except price/cost advantages. Additionally, specialized product/service and technological/scientific expertise ranked third equal versus sixth and seventh. On the other hand, established reputation was ranked higher by the non-high performers (Table 5.3). Finally, technological/scientific expertise, quality, and being first in the market were highly significantly different (at the .01 level). The greater emphasis on these, as well as specialized product/service, is not surprising given that novel innovation was one of the selection criteria for high performers.

The Japanese high performers also scored more highly than the non-high performers on all but one item – established reputation in this case, which was ranked well down the list. They scored technological/scientific expertise and specialized product/service significantly higher, and ranked them top equal versus fourth and third respectively. While the UK high performers placed even more emphasis on quality and responsiveness, however, the Japanese high performers placed slightly less emphasis on these.

Factor structures differed between high performers and non-high performers in both countries, yet again highlighting the in-built emphasis on technology and innovation of the high performers, but featuring other differences as well (Table 5.4). Compared with the Japanese entrepreneurs, both UK groups appeared to be outward-looking. The high performers, however, had a strong customer orientation, while the non-high performers expressed a textbook-like price/cost and marketing approach, mixed with speed to produce an unwieldy factor. Their "customer orientation" factor was less specific or focused as well. The strong discriminators for the UK high performers appear as reshaped low discriminating factors for the non-high performers, and vice versa. The high performers appeared to be strongly customer-focused and sensitive to the market. Although they placed more emphasis on innovation than the non-high performers, this did not act as a major discriminator.

The Japanese groups both produced three factors, with some interesting reconfigurations. With the addition of S&T expertise, the first factor of the high performers now begins to look like a competence-based approach to competitive advantage. The second, market-orientation factor was unchanged, while the third linked price/cost and speed. The non-high performers, by contrast, retained the factor structure of the overall Japanese

Table 5.3 High performers and competitive advantage rankings

	UK		Japan	
Competitive advantage	HP	Non-HP	HP	Non HP
Technological/scientific expertise	3	7	1	4
Price/cost advantages	11	9	7	6
Marketing and promotion	10	11	10	10
Speed of service	6	4	5	5
Established reputation	6	3	9	8
Design of product/service	5	5	11	11
Quality of product/service	1	2	4	2
Specialized product/service	3	6	1	3
Range of products/services	9	8	8	9
Personal attention and responsiveness to client needs	2	1	3	1
Being first in the market with new products/services	8	10	6	7

Note: HP = high performer

Table 5.4 Competitive advantages: high performer and non-high performer factors

	High performers	Non-high performers
UK	*Customer-focus* 1. Customer orientation 　speed, client attention, reputation, 　quality 2. Market position 1 　range, specialized product, first to 　market 3. Market position 2 　marketing, price/cost 4. Innovation 　design, S&T expertise	*"Market" orientation* 1. Market basics 　price/cost, marketing, speed 2. Innovation 　first in market, S&T expertise, design 3. Product 　range, specialized product, quality 4. Customer orientation 　client attention, reputation
Japan	*Competence-based* 1. Competences 　S&T expertise, specialized product, 　quality, first in market, design, 　client attention 2. Market orientation/image 　reputation, range, marketing 3. Responsiveness price/cost, speed	*Product for market* 1. Superior product 　first in market, design, quality, 　specialized product, client attention 2. Market orientation 　marketing, speed, reputation, range 3. "Value proposition" 　price/cost, S&T expertise

group, with a product focus. Responsiveness loaded onto none of the factors. The overall result is to create a mirror image of the UK divide, directed inward in a general way. The non-high performers focused on today's business, rather than building competences to combine today's business with tomorrow's innovation. The high performers, however, appeared to place dynamic "competences" at the core of their competitive advantage.

Comparing the high performers in both countries, there were marked differences, suggesting the influence of backgrounds or skill sets, and motivation, as well as adaptation to the respective business environments. High performers in the UK had a strong customer-focused orientation, while in Japan they had a strong competence-building orientation.

I saw there was this definite niche in the market. At that time there were about ... 49 customers making lenses but having to struggle to get the raw material. They were having to multisource because no-one could supply all their needs. The American company only made the raw material for its own finished products, its own lenses. So there was this straightforward, typical niche market, which we filled. (UK3)

We used to be a tier two company, but now our competitors are likely to be first tier. Most of them only do some of the work in house, but because of all the training I was telling you about we can do most of it in house. It keeps costs down, and is good for sensitive work. With our line up of skills and equipment now, we can compete very successfully. (J24)

An executive at S kindly told me they would give us work if we got into trouble, but I never accepted it. I didn't want to be an S subcontractor. We did lots of prototypes for large companies. It's not easy to be a volume producer because manufacturers seldom outsource that work, but the trigger to volume production [OEM] came from our motor for physical chemistry devices, which we had done for twenty years. A company asked us if we could do one for them with a tight deadline. We worked night and day for three days and managed it. Then they became our customer, and (their) competitors also came to us. One of our competitive edges is to do both this volume work and our own products. (J19)

Limitations

Finally in this chapter, we look at limitations to meeting business objectives. Given the greater pessimism on the part of the Japanese entrepreneurs about competitive advantages and growth prospects, we would expect them to rate limitations as more severe than the UK entrepreneurs. This is what we find (Figure 5.2). The Japanese entrepreneurs considered nine of the ten items to be more of a limitation than the UK entrepreneurs, the exception being finance, which they rated as the least serious constraint. The higher scores of the Japanese group no doubt reflect the effects of prolonged recession and deflation in Japan, and the more favorable economic conditions in the UK.

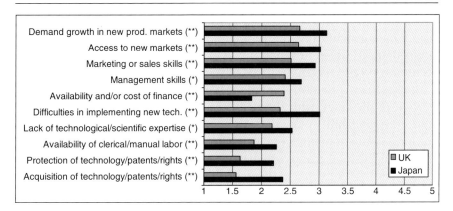

Figure 5.2 Limitations

Note: ** differences significant at .01; * differences significant at .05

Once again, four of the five top items were the same in both countries. The top two – growth in demand in main product markets and access to new markets – were external. The other two – availability of management skills and sales and marketing skills – were internal limitations, although clearly linked to the external constraints, preventing the businesses from addressing them. Together, they reflect the disadvantage small businesses often have in both product and labor markets.

But what about financial markets? This was the fifth most serious constraint for the UK entrepreneurs, but tenth in Japan. In the UK there has been much debate about finance as a constraint of small business growth. Cambridge CBR surveys show that availability and cost of finance remains a problem, especially for growing and innovating businesses, but it diminished as a constraint between 1991 and 2004 (while management, marketing, and other skill constraints became more severe; Cosh and Hughes, 2007*a*, 2007*b*). Despite the fact that Japan was in the midst of a bad loan crisis, which supposedly made banks less willing to roll over or extend new loans, Japanese entrepreneurs rated this as their least serious impediment. This may be related to their limited growth objectives, or to the wider range of financing options that exists for small businesses in Japan, including some government banks specifically for SMEs. They clearly thought their key problems were elsewhere, in product markets, as well as innovation, and implementation of new technology. (Moreover, interest rates were much lower than in the UK.)

Once again, technology figured prominently in Japan. Difficulties in implementing new technology were the third most serious limitation there, compared with number six in the UK. Acquisition of new technology or patent rights and lack of technological or scientific expertise were deemed more serious limitations as well. These differences reflect the technology – and internal – focus of the Japanese entrepreneurs.

Discriminant function analysis classified the country correctly in 70 percent of the cases, with the strongest discriminators being IPR acquisition, cost/availability of finance, implementation of new technology, and the availability of manual or clerical labor. Factor analysis produced three factors for the total group, which were exactly the same as for the Japanese group. The first consisted of the two market items together with marketing skills, and implementation of new technology. This "technology and new markets" growth factor might prevent forward-looking entrepreneurs from moving to the next level. The second – "input limitations" – consisted of the various skills (technological/scientific expertise, management skills, and manual/clerical labor) as well as cost/availability of finance and the third consisted of the two IPR items by themselves. Thus growth was limited by the ability to access new markets as well as internal competences, exacerbated by difficulties in recruiting able people. IPR was a separate, minor issue.

In the UK there were four factors. The first – "growth and innovation" – consisted of four items. Implementation of new technology, and interestingly, availability/cost of finance were joined by the two IPR items. The second – "expertise/skills" – consisted of management, technological, and marketing skills. Manual/clerical skills were a separate factor. While the Japanese participants expressed frustration about being able to recruit any kind of skills, in the UK a distinction, possibly a traditional one, was made. The final factor – "markets" – combined access to new markets and growth in demand. While they were not as serious as for the Japanese entrepreneurs, then, the UK entrepreneurs felt limitations in innovation, markets, and securing (stratified) skills.

It is tough with Sterling as it is. I could not go back to all my suppliers and employees and say Sterling is 30% overvalued, do you mind if I pay your wages and invoices short. There have been ups and downs, and I thought I would wait until it came down. I waited, and it's still over-valued. (UK8)

I've got 50 employees now, including two who have been with me almost from the beginning. It was really hard going at the beginning. I couldn't even recruit graduates of technical high schools. (J19)

I used to have to get workers through the public employment agency, and they weren't very good. Recently I have people coming from famous universities asking if I will employ them. It's ironic, I can't do it now (because hospital budgets are shrinking). (J6)

High performers

Do high performers face different limitations than non-high performers? Do they face greater limitations because of their higher aspirations, or fewer limitations because of their superior competitive advantages or competences? In the UK, non-high performers on average registered greater limitations on all the items except implementation of new technology, but only management skills and growth in demand were significantly different. In Japan, the high performers scored higher on five items, and the non-high performers scored higher on five. The high performers scored significantly higher on availability of manual/clerical labor while, as in the UK, the non-high performers scored significantly higher on growth of demand. Non-high performers were more likely to attribute their limitations to external demand conditions, while high performers were more likely to feel constrained by difficulties in securing inputs, including recruiting manual and clerical labor.

Table 5.5 Limitations: high performer and non-high performer factors

	High performers	Non-high performers

UK	*Innovation and skills*
	1. Growth and innovation
	   IPR protection, acquisition,
	   implementing new technology, finance
	2. Professional skills
	   management skills, S&T expertise,
	   sales/marketing skills
	3. Input–output markets
	   manual/clerical labor, new markets
	4. Demand growth
	   growth in demand
		Mixed bag
		1. Management and R&D
		   S&T expertise, management skills
		2. Technology
		   IPR protection, acquisition,
		   implementing new technology
		3. Input–output markets 2
		   new markets, growth in demand,
		   manual/clerical labor
		4. Market prerequisites
		   finance, sales/marketing skills

Japan	*Skills and finance*
	1. Input limitations
	   management skills, manual/clerical
	   labor, S&T expertise, finance
	2. Technology and new markets
	   new technology, growth in demand,
	   new markets, sales/marketing skills
	3. IPR
	   IPR protection, acquisition
		Everything
		1. Obstacles
		   growth in demand, sales/marketing
		   skills, implementing new technology,
		   'new markets, management skills, S&T
		   expertise
		2. Finance and labor
		   finance, manual/clerical labor
		3. IPR
		   IPR protection, acquisition

The factor structure of the UK high performers was similar to that of the whole UK group (Table 5.5). The non-high performers reversed the first two factors, with some modifications, combined the third and fourth factors, and placed the other items – finance and sales/marketing skills – in a fourth factor, producing something of a mixed bag. The first and second factors of the overall Japanese group were reversed for the Japanese high performers, giving greater prominence to skills, with finance included. Until they reach a certain size, and establish a reputation, recruiting appears to be a severe constraint on the growth of small, innovative Japanese companies. Technology and markets were also a constraint. For non-high performers almost everything appeared to be an obstacle, with six items lumped into one factor, contributing to almost half the variance explained. The factor encompasses both supply and demand items, and suggests that business was very hard for those in this group.

Concluding comments

In this chapter we have looked at the markets the businesses traded in, their competitive orientations, and limitations on achieving business objectives. The business is the unit of analysis here, but we are relying on the entrepreneurs' interpretations.

First we looked at engagement in subcontracting and reliance on top customers. There was a similar proportion of businesses in both the UK and Japan which did no subcontracting – around a third – but of those that did, there was greater reliance in Japan. Similarly, a small proportion – around 10 percent – relied on their top three customers for less than 10 percent of their turnover, but otherwise reliance was greater in Japan. High performers in the UK were less reliant on subcontracting and top customers than non-high performers, but the high performers in Japan showed similar levels of reliance on subcontracting. Both groups reported relatively small numbers of direct competitors. Most competitors were domestic, although more were overseas in the case of UK businesses, especially high performers. All this suggests that most of the businesses traded in niche markets, but the differences suggest different types of niches, with varying degrees of bespoken-ness, and geographical boundedness. A minority appeared to trade in more open markets.

Competitive advantages as perceived by the entrepreneurs are neatly summarized in Figure 5.1 and Table 5.4. Here we see some interesting differences between the UK and Japanese businesses, as well as between high performers and non-high performers. As could be predicted from previous chapters, the UK entrepreneurs tended to be more externally focused, while the Japanese entrepreneurs were more internally focused. Critically, however, the high performers in the UK were focused on their key customers, whereas the non-high performers exhibited a more general orientation toward the "market," without the focus of the high performers. In Japan, the high performers sought to build up internal competences, addressing today's business while preparing for tomorrow through innovation, while the non-high performers were focused more on today's business, and (current) products. The UK high performers speak to the focused nature of many entrepreneurial high-tech businesses, while the Japanese high performers speak to technology-driven innovativeness. Perhaps a combination is ideal; in reality it is difficult to achieve.

As a group, the Japanese entrepreneurs were less sanguine about their competitive advantages. They were also more pessimistic when it came to growth limitations. They rated nine out of ten limitation items more highly. Like the UK entrepreneurs, they saw the main limitations coming from external markets, but they also felt very constrained in terms of input factors, and internal abilities. The notable exception was finance, which they ranked as the least serious constraint (despite being in a supposedly hostile financial environment).

The UK high performers were relatively clear that their key constraints were in innovation and in professional skills. The non-high performers were less clear about their limitations. The Japanese high performers felt constrained by product markets, but particularly by input limitations, notably their ability to secure a whole range of skills. For the Japanese non-high performers, prospects appeared bleak as everything was an obstacle. This may have reflected their reality, or it may have been symptomatic of their lack of management and broader business experience.

Despite similarities in their orientations to niche markets, then, we see some important differences between the UK and Japanese entrepreneurs, which are sustained or even amplified by the high performers, and which are consistent with the findings of the previous chapters.

6

HRM, Leadership, and Culture

Opportunity and business creation, innovation, competitive orientations, and outcomes are not achieved by entrepreneurs acting alone, or even through founding teams. They are achieved through organization. In developing organizational capabilities, the ability to attract, retain, and motivate the right kinds of employees is crucial. We have already seen (in Chapter 5) that many of the entrepreneurs had difficulties in doing this, and it was a serious limitation for them in trying to achieve their business objectives. But do the problems stem from environments, structural disadvantages of start-ups and small businesses, or from the entrepreneurs themselves? Writing in the 1970s, Kets de Vries had no doubt about the source:

What we frequently encounter in an entrepreneurial organization is an organizational structure and work environment completely dependent and totally dominated by the entrepreneur. . . . We are also faced with an individual who refuses to delegate, is impulsive, lacks any interest in conscious, analytical forms of planning. (Kets de Vries, 1977: 63, cited in Stanworth and Curran, 1989: 160)

Stanworth and Curran (1989: 161) contend that this picture, which includes role ambiguity, role conflict, and low levels of job satisfaction for employees, "has emerged from repeated studies of the small business and must now be regarded as approximating the most 'typical' pattern."[1] Recently, Cosh and Hughes (2007c) found that where CEOs in small firms control both strategic and operating decisions, employees are less likely to be engaged in "high-performance" management and work practices.

---

[1] In studies of employment relations in small firms in the UK, an early positive view (Ingham, 1970; cf. also Bolton Report, 1971) was challenged by a much more negative view (Rainnie, 1989), which was in turn challenged, with more emphasis placed on fraternalism, negotiated paternalism, and plain muddling though (Ram, 1994; Marlow, 2005). In Japan, employment relations in small firms were traditionally seen in a negative light (Whittaker, 1997).

As entrepreneurial businesses grow – in order for them to grow – their employment practices normally become more formalized, standardized, and systematic. This is accompanied by decentralization of authority (e.g., Pugh and Hickson, 1976; more recently, Kotey and Slade, 2005). These practices may be accompanied by "high-commitment" practices, such as single status, family-friendly working arrangements, employee share ownership schemes, and "guaranteed" job security, which are more prevalent in larger workplaces (Cully et al. 1999: 80–2).

There are contrary views. Hornsby and Kuratko studied a sample of 247 small businesses in the US Midwest and found that "the personnel practices of smaller firms are much more sophisticated than the literature leads one to believe," especially in manufacturing (Hornsby and Kuratko, 1990: 16). Moreover the respondents were *concerned* about the same issues, regardless of their size: "The highest ranked issues in all three size categories focus upon the need to obtain and retain a quality workforce" (ibid., p. 17).

How do they believe they should go about obtaining and retaining a quality workforce? What kinds of factors influence their beliefs? And what are the consequences of their beliefs, for instance on their ability to grow and innovate? These are questions addressed in this chapter. If Hornsby and Kuratko are right about sophistication of practices in manufacturing, this is likely to be amplified in high-tech manufacturing, where, in contrast to the low levels of education and managerial skills in the study by Kets de Vries, many entrepreneurs have advanced education, and previous managerial experience.

Baron, Burton, and Hannan (1996) have documented how models of employment relations espoused by founders have a pervasive effect on the development of human resource management within their organizations (cf. also Hannan, Burton, and Baron, 1996). They develop a typology of employment models – star, engineering, commitment, and factory – which show internal consistency, and are particularly influenced by founders' views of attachment and motivation. Our approach is similar, although developed independently. Like Baron and colleagues, too, we explore congruence or fit with the external social environment of the businesses, only in this case we mean the UK and Japan. Are there systematic differences between the UK and Japanese entrepreneurs? Do high performers converge on a set of "best practices," or do they retain or amplify differences, gaining advantage by "best fit"?

We begin by looking at the means the entrepreneurs advocate to recruit, retain, and motivate a quality workforce. We call this "HRM orientations," not assuming that the entrepreneurs had a human resource management *strategy*, but to denote how they thought about securing employee commitment and motivating employees to achieve their business goals (Guest,

1987; Wilkinson, 2000). We explore some potentially counterintuitive findings through the case interviews, and find that these are linked to different styles of entrepreneur engagement in the business, and leadership. This discussion is supported by a brief analysis of company cultures. Finally, we look at high performers.

Securing a quality, motivated workforce

In responses to an open question in the first UK survey (which did not specifically ask about employment relations) there were numerous comments about the importance of people management and creating motivated teams to meet customer needs in specialized niches. Comments like the following were common:

To provide good quality products and service to customers with appropriate rewards to all our staff. . . . Pay as much as can be afforded rather than as little as one can get away with.

To harness the expertise of our team to work in partnership with our clients to provide customers high quality solutions. To ensure that every employee is valued as a real business asset.

The secret of success of any company lies in the quality of their staff, and in this age of fierce competition, customer service should be at the forefront of all their considerations.

Allow people the freedom to use their own creativity for the good of the company. Keep the family atmosphere as far as possible. Delegate and allow people the freedom to make mistakes.

The comments indicated an orientation at odds with that commonly depicted in traditional small firms, and in large firms for that matter. In fact, some of the respondents suggested that their orientations were consciously formed as a reaction to past negative experiences, mostly in large firms.[2] These differences have also been commented on by Scase (2005; cf. also Davis and Scase, 2000) in his studies of creative and professional small firms in the UK. In these businesses,

[w]ork roles tend to be broadly defined with high levels of discretion and responsibility. Professional employees working in these small businesses are assumed to prefer personal autonomy, responsibility and recognition and, indeed, these are

---

[2] "When I was an employee, I saw continual Customer dissatisfaction caused by co-workers who lacked Technical Expertise, and pressure to achieve Unrealistic Objectives," and so on.

typically their motives for moving from employment in large organizations. Staff are encouraged to develop close working relationships with clients so that, in a relatively autonomous manner, they can exercise particular expert, creative and technical skills. (Scase, 2005: 73)

Scase suggests that much of the control and discipline comes from client relations rather than employment relations per se. Internally, work is organized into projects (or "jobs" or "accounts"), with high levels of decentralization. This would fit well with the "client focus" competitive advantage orientation discussed in Chapter 5.

We wanted to find out more about this, and whether there were systematic differences from the Japanese businesses (as one would suspect from the discussion of Chapter 5). To do this, we asked the entrepreneurs to rate ten items on a 1 (not at all) to 5 (crucial) scale in response to the following question: "Some personnel policies are more important than others in recruiting and keeping good personnel. How important are the following for you?" The items listed assumed that the entrepreneurs had at least an implicit theory of motivation, and would stress either intrinsic or job-related items, extrinsic reward items, and/or supporting or environmental items.[3] The results are summarized in Figure 6.1.

The first thing to note is the much wider range of responses from the UK entrepreneurs (with means ranging from 1.92 to 4.06) and the more constrained range of responses from the Japanese entrepreneurs (with means ranging from 2.89 to 3.83). This might indicate an "everything matters" reaction to the question on the part of the Japanese entrepreneurs,

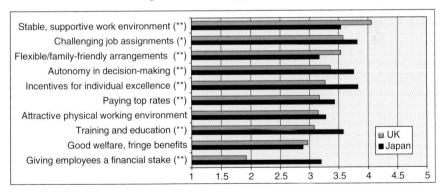

Figure 6.1 HRM orientations

Note: ** differences significant at .01; * differences significant at .05

---

[3] This is similar to Baron et al.'s (1996) "work", "money" and "love", although love is somewhat different from our support, and our work/job items incorporate their (separate) "control" variable.

or that they do not think much about matters in the way we asked.[4] A further preliminary observation concerns "providing incentives for individual excellence." With hindsight, this item is poorly worded, as incentives can be pecuniary or non-pecuniary. UK entrepreneurs may have opted for the former, but the Japanese translation may have nudged the Japanese entrepreneurs toward the latter.

Looking at content, we find some obvious similarities, with four of the five top-ranked items shared, and two of the three bottom-ranked items also shared. Yet the differences are more noticeable than the similarities.[5] Within the top five, challenging job assignments were stressed by both groups, and linked with this, autonomy. Providing a stable and supportive work environment was even more important for the UK entrepreneurs, however, but ranked a middling number five in Japan. Similarly, and linked to a supportive work environment, flexible, family-friendly work arrangements was ranked number three in the UK, but number nine in Japan. On the other hand, providing incentives for individual excellence was stressed more in Japan, but ranked only a middling number five in the UK, while training and education was ranked fourth in Japan, but eighth in the UK. These differences are intriguing, and we will look at them more closely.

Financial incentives did not figure prominently. Paying top rates was ranked sixth in both countries, while giving employees a financial stake in the company, and providing fringe benefit packages, were even more emphatically rejected. The former financial stake rejection is at variance with Scase's (2005) findings in creative and professional services, and with the emphasis on stock options by many Silicon Valley high-tech businesses.[6]

Let us explore these initial findings further through factor analysis. There were two factors for the total group, relating to individuals, and their organizational environments.[7] Separate factor analysis findings are given

---

[4] It could also indicate a tendency of Japanese questionnaire respondents to avoid extremes. Their standard deviations on nine of the ten items were also smaller. However, this tendency does not appear to have shown up in the previous chapters.

[5] Seven of the item means were very significantly different (.01), and one was significantly different (.05).

[6] Only 13 percent of the UK businesses had employee share ownership schemes, 9 percent for key employees, and 4 percent for all full-time employees. They were more common in Japan, where a quarter of businesses reported them, 11 percent for key employees, and 14 percent for all full-time employees. They do not appear to have been stressed as an HRM factor in Japan, however. (There was a higher proportion among our – innovative – case interview businesses.)

[7] The "individual" factor consisted of giving employees a financial stake in the company, encouraging autonomy in decision making, giving challenging job assignments, providing/

Table 6.1 HRM orientation factors

Combined	UK	Japan
SOE	SOE Flexible/family-friendly work arrangements, stable and supportive work environment, attractive physical working environment, good welfare a nd fringe benefit package	SOE 1 Attractive physical working environment, good welfare and fringe benefit package (foreground) SOE 2 Flexible/family-friendly work arrangements, stable and supportive work environment (background)
Individual	Involvement Autonomy in decision-making, challenging job assignments, giving employees a financial stake in the company Incentives and recognition Paying top rates, training and education, incentives for individual excellence	Personal growth Autonomy in decision-making, incentives for individual excellence, training and education, giving employees a financial stake in the company Effort–reward Paying top rates, giving challenging job assignments

Note: SOE = supportive organizational environment

in Table 6.1. This shows three factors in the UK. The first was identical to the supportive organizational environment of the combined group, and two of the items were rated very highly by the UK entrepreneurs. The "individual" factor of the combined group broke into two factors: "involvement" consisted of autonomy, challenging job assignments, and financial stake, while "incentives and recognition" consisted of paying top rates, training and education, and incentives for excellence.

Training and education may seem like an odd fit, but from the case interviews, this is how it was used. More than simply a functional means of gaining skills for necessary work, it signaled to employees that their company was progressive, that expectations were being placed on them to bring back new skills to deploy in their work and teach others, and their potential for doing this was recognized. They were gaining skills which might help them in their future careers at the same time. Overall, the UK picture is of a strong emphasis on providing a supportive work environment, challenging employees to get involved (taking the initiative to respond to and to anticipate customer needs), and to some extent, providing incentives and recognition for this.

facilitating training and education, providing incentives for individual excellence, and paying top rates. The "organizational environment" factor consisted of providing a stable and supportive work environment, offering flexible/family-friendly work arrangements, providing a good welfare and fringe benefit package, and providing an attractive physical working environment.

The Japanese responses broke down into four factors. The individual factor of the combined group also split into two, but differently from the UK group, and so did the supportive organizational environment factor. The first factor contains four items, including three of the top four – autonomy, incentives for individual excellence, training and education, and financial stake. From our interviews, it appears that these were concerned with "raising" or nurturing employees and employee involvement – *ikusei* in Japanese. We have called it "personal growth."

The second and third factors are the supportive organizational environment of the combined group. The Japanese entrepreneurs appeared to distinguish between items which might enable employees to work with "peace of mind" – "background" items for them, but ranked extremely highly by the UK entrepreneurs (third and first, respectively) – and more tangible or visible items of physical working environment and fringe benefit package, which both groups assigned low priority to. The final factor – "effort–reward" – combines challenging job assignments and payment for them. Overall, there is an emphasis on "raising" employees through "challenge" first and foremost, moderate recognition for those who accept their challenges, and a downplaying of environmental factors.

This is what the entrepreneurs believe is important for attracting, retaining, and motivating good employees. We cannot be sure that their practices conform to these beliefs, or that their employees would agree with them. The emphasis on supportive organizational environment items by the UK entrepreneurs and their de-emphasis by the Japanese entrepreneurs, who emphasized autonomy, challenge, and individual excellence, is interesting and counterintuitive from common views of employment in both countries. We cannot explain it from the survey data alone, and for interpretation, we turn to our case interviews.

Leadership and motivation

Flexibility and family friendliness

From the interviews it was clear that for the UK entrepreneurs, motivating employees effectively was crucial to the delivery of their products or services, and they spent quite a lot of time thinking about it and worrying about it. They did not fit Kets de Vries' image of the entrepreneur. Many of the Japanese entrepreneurs, on the other hand, appeared closer to that image, at least superficially. The focus of their discourse was very much on the technology or product, and while they might have spent time thinking and worrying about employee management, it did not figure in their accounts nearly as much, and when it did, it figured differently.

Both groups seemed to be looking for broadly similar employees. Fit with the organization – and the entrepreneur or entrepreneurial team – was crucial. This meant hiring people with a "positive" attitude, people who were not nine-to-five clock watchers. They were looking for people enthusiastic about work, willing to learn, and willing to take initiative. Subsequently, however, paths diverged. The UK entrepreneurs sought to recruit the above people, and to integrate them into a team of like-minded employees, creating a strong *esprit de corps*. Employees sometimes had to go the extra mile, to spend long hours working before a deadline, for instance. Willingness to do this could not be taken for granted, or forced. It had to be voluntarily offered. To ensure that discretionary effort was forthcoming, a trade-off was made. In return for such discretionary effort, which could be expected to have a negative impact on the employee's private life, flexibility was offered. The employee could take time off to attend to family matters, go to a daughter or son's sports day at school, for example. There was give and take on the issue, as long as there was not an imbalance toward the take.[8] This helps to explain the importance of supportive organizational environment items, especially flexible, family-friendly work arrangements, as the following quotes illustrate:

These guys are the A team. They will stick with me through thick and thin. We work as a team. Nobody says that's not my job, or I'm too busy with my job to help you with yours. . . . Immense flexibility. If you want to go four hours early today that's no problem, so long as it's not happening constantly. No recording, no clocking in and out. . . . Also we often need to meet a deadline, say for a large order for Australia. We've had them working all night, have worked through till four in the morning, then I will go out and get a big pile of pizzas and a crate of beer. (UK8)

We're really flexible about hours of working. We've got one person who travels here from Edinburgh every day. He'd have to come through the rush hour so he works from 10:00 to 6:00 and that makes a huge difference to his working day. It cuts about two hours off his travelling time. Certainly when we were larger there were one or two people who abused the system, but most didn't and we could very much take on trust most people. (UK9)

---

[8] This give and take was different from the "negotiation of order" depicted in many UK workplace studies. We might add, however, that employees who did not achieve "fit" with what the entrepreneur was seeking – who were seen as taking more than they were giving – were "let go."

I take an interest in their lives and they respond by doing the same with me and the company.... You know, it's a serious employee, has been here a long time, done a good job, has a problem – they get paid, you know, whatever their condition is and exceptional absences from work. (UK7)

We know everyone's family, and we network and have events like picnics, evenings out with families. Whatever this company does in terms of entertainment, we always involve families... We have some very dedicated people and it's to thank them for allowing their husband or wife to work so hard. (UK10)

The Japanese entrepreneurs, on the other hand, needed to make no such trade-off. They wanted to recruit similar people, and they had the same needs as far as Friday evening or weekend work went. But this was *expected* of their employees. What they were expected to offer their employees – and their families – in return was first and foremost stable employment, which they appeared to see largely in terms of personal responsibility rather than an HRM orientation, and then average or better wages and conditions and opportunities for growth through work – incentives for individual excellence and challenging job assignments, as we also saw in some of our quotes in Chapter 4.

To some extent, of course, this reflects the different labor-market conditions in both countries. Greater fluidity in the UK presumably presses entrepreneurs to be sensitive to employee needs for flexibility. But it was more than that. It reflected different social or family relationships as well. The UK employee could not be expected to give all when this created family tensions. The potential for family tensions was considerable, judging from the complicated family arrangements recounted by some of the entrepreneurs. This explains their attempts to create goodwill in the families themselves through family events. In effect, employees' families were part of the implicit contract. There had to be give and take for them as well.

The Japanese entrepreneurs could not necessarily assume that employees would not leave them – turnover in small businesses is much higher than in large businesses, and poaching allegedly happened – but they could more easily assume acquiescence on the part of their employees' families. Certainly they knew about their employees' families, and sometimes if there were tensions at home, but offering flexibility to deal with it happened at the margins. "Mature" employees should not only go the extra mile for the development of the company, which would benefit everyone including themselves, but in doing so should not let family matters impinge on their work.

The comparison highlights a neglected dimension of environmental "fit." It is not just the competitive environment that the entrepreneurs must be mindful of, or even the institutional (labor-market) environment, but the social environment as well. This impacts on the company most visibly through the employment relationship. The UK entrepreneurs were well aware of this need for fit from *their own* family lives, moreover. The stability in their social environment, on the other hand, allowed the Japanese entrepreneurs to take this for granted, and to interpret dedication to the company in terms of individual commitment and maturity. Quite a few of the Japanese entrepreneurs, in fact, prided themselves on the fact that they worked harder and longer hours than anyone else, hardly grounds for sympathy in terms of family–work balance from their employees, if it was sought.

Specialization and delegation

A second set of observations also calls for qualification to the autocratic entrepreneur and chaotic employment relations pictures, again with divergence mainly on the part of the British entrepreneurs. It also calls for caution if not qualification to the many studies which see HRM practices in entrepreneurial businesses as emerging gradually from a state of chaos and high informality toward greater formalization, specialization, and systematization, accompanied by delegation as the company grows. As Marlow (2005) argues, informality and formalization are not necessarily polar opposites; they coexist in various combinations.

We saw in Chapter 3 that many of the UK entrepreneurs started their business with a small team of colleagues from a former business. From the inception there appeared to be a specialization, and while there was a CEO, his role appeared to be – or was presented as – more of a team leader than someone with absolute authority. This was reinforced by a sense of shared enthusiasm and partnership in a new adventure at the time of founding. It seemed that this ethos and division of labor more easily led to a division of labor and delegation when employees were recruited. The backgrounds of many of the entrepreneurs, especially experience in a variety of companies and in a variety of management positions, also seemed to facilitate early delegation and a division of labor.

I try not to interfere. My old boss used to do it and it was very annoying. I don't get involved in the technical side. People ask my opinion and I make a contribution but that's their responsibility. Same with sales where I came from, the guys have got responsibility. If they want to go and do a show in Timbuktu then fine, they can go, as long as they can show there is a reason for them to go. (UK5)

Many of the recruits were highly qualified and expected to have challenging work delegated to them from an early stage, moreover.[9] If they were not promised it, they would not join the company, and if they did not get it, they would quit. High levels of qualifications seemed to enhance collegiality and delegation. In this environment, the entrepreneur was like a *conductor*.

In Japan, however, there was a different set of dynamics. Quite a few of the entrepreneurs had felt frustrated at aspects of HRM at their previous large company – seniority in promotions and work assignments, lack of opportunities to develop individual creativity, and so on – which instilled a desire to give their employees opportunities for individual excellence and challenging job assignments.

Old established companies like M have lots of graduates from the top universities. I was not one of them, so even though I had the most patents, they were reluctant to take up my ideas. From that, I felt the importance of individual creativity, bringing it out and applying it. I try not to impose my ideas on others, but to encourage them to come up with suggestions, and to experience the joy of inventing. (J1)

I was quick in doing my work, but the others did a lot of overtime. I was seen as half-hearted, and they were seen as loyal. I didn't think rewards should be based on time worked. And the differences were so small – just a few thousand yen after several years. I believe pay should be based on performance, not on years of experience, education or gender. (J4)

These convictions, on the other hand, were tempered in practice by pressing business needs, which the president (not CEO) felt acutely, but thought that not all employees did likewise. He did not see himself as a conductor so much as a *locomotive*, pulling along a train which frequently threatened to go off the rails.[10] As we saw, often he had started the business by himself, or with family members or former colleagues, or a right-hand man, generally in subordinate positions. His years of work in R&D in a large company, or R&D and sales, and his focus on technology as the core of the business, both gave him confidence that he knew best how to develop the company, and put pressure on him to control many activities as well. This made it more difficult to delegate, especially when there

---

[9] Twelve percent (15 percent) of the UK (Japanese) entrepreneurs reported that 50 percent or more of their full-time employees were university graduates, 43 percent (61 percent) that 10 percent or more were graduates, and 22 percent (18 percent) that none were graduates. The figure was higher in the interview companies, and some of these included a significant number of Ph.D.s, especially in the UK.

[10] Two or three of the interviewees themselves used similes of locomotives or railway tracks.

was still a risk of staff turnover. The fact that he relied on a small number of clients initially, whom sometimes he alone had personal relations with, further reinforced this tendency.

There was often a difficulty in recruiting (and retaining – large companies poached good engineers) employees of the caliber seen as necessary, and hence these raw recruits required "raising." Even if postgraduates with high technical skills could be recruited, moreover, they were seen as apt to allow technology fascination to override commercial sense. Mid-career hires, too, needed to be integrated into the corporate culture, which took time.

Work has to be enjoyable, but it also has to make money. It shouldn't just be enjoyable by yourself, but for those around, and customers. (J1)

For the first 10 years I had to do everything – lay the rails to go on. . . . Japanese school education nowadays is very problematic. It promotes a funny kind of egalitarianism – no losers. But in business there are only gold medals – nothing else. You either get the order or you don't. This year's keyword is "tatakai" (fight). It's in the notebook, look. I check how each of my employees are doing – 30 minutes each per month. The critical thing is to get values aligned. (J13)

Thus the early years were spent with the president and perhaps a "right-hand man" battling to establish the business, and the next years when employees were hired to "raising them" to create a viable company core. This was reflected in the emphasis on building internal competences, seen in Chapter 5. It might involve providing incentives for individual excellence, challenging job assignments, and autonomy, but the autonomy was in fact within prescribed bounds, and only gradually increased. The president was still firmly in control (and not initially interested in relinquishing it). In fact, some of the entrepreneurs indicated that their preferred company size was small:

That's because I can oversee it all. If it gets to be above 30 employees the best idea would probably be to split off another company. If the business is growing, I think the most difficult time would be when there are 100 employees. You can't oversee them all, and energy levels go down. You get people going along for the ride. If there are three people like this in a company of ten, the company won't make it. With 100, you might get half the employees becoming like this. (J5)

Similar sentiments about size and "baggage employees" were expressed elsewhere.[11] In those companies which *did* grow beyond twenty to thirty

---

[11] Twenty employees is often cited as a cut-off or plateau figure for many (UK) businesses as it is at this stage that the limits of informality begin to become apparent: Roberts et al. (1992: 255).

employees, it was only when the company got to have about sixty to eighty employees that the president started thinking seriously about systematic organization, formalization, and delegation. In some cases, at that point the company had established a strong competitive base, and was poised for substantial growth. The "raising" had been accomplished, potential leaders identified, values aligned, and employees were ready for new challenges through product diversification. Challenging job assignments and autonomy took on a different meaning at this stage.

Training and education

It appears, then, that many of the Japanese businesses were closer to the orthodox view of the evolution of HRM practices, sometimes in slow motion. Our third observation relates to education and training. The UK entrepreneurs were more likely to see their employees as independent actors, and to take on-job training (OJT) for granted in their accounts (which is not to say it did not happen). They encouraged their employees to go on courses, however, and sometimes set aside a fixed portion of turnover, or established target hours for them to do this, hoping that they would gain new insights and motivation, and that they would diffuse the knowledge they gained within the company.

Some Japanese entrepreneurs encouraged their employees to go on external courses, too, but in most instances emphasis was placed on OJT. This is hardly surprising, since the entrepreneur was the locomotive, and the direction of knowledge or skill transfer was from him. "Raising" employees through OJT, moreover, was not just about skills, but about acculturation, which was seen to take place slowly. (It took place through doing – *praxis* – rather than cognitively, through the head, which appeared to characterize learning in the UK.) Thus the meaning of education and training was very different.

While the qualitative differences were striking, it is unclear to what extent there were quantitative differences, as training and education costs are difficult to calculate. In terms of itemized, budgeted expenditure, it seems as if the UK entrepreneurs spent more, given the extent of external courses. This would contradict functionalist theories of human capital which hold that employers are reluctant to invest if they cannot be certain of recouping their investments – where external labor markets are developed. The interviews suggest that training and education considerations are part of more complex calculations, which differ in the two countries, involving autonomy and motivation and the implicit contract of the employment relationship in the UK, and "raising" employees gradually or at least pulling them along by the entrepreneur in Japan.

We did not set out to explore leadership formally, but these interpretations do suggest different leadership styles. On an autocratic–democratic leader scale, UK entrepreneurs would appear to be (or see themselves as) closer to the democratic end, or closer toward the distributed leadership end of a shared leadership spectrum (Jackson and Parry, 2008), than their Japanese counterparts. We retain the similes leader-as-conductor and leader-as-locomotive here. The conductor is more willing and able to delegate earlier on, creating a managerial function. The locomotive needs followers as extensions of himself initially, and the transition to a delegated structure takes longer. Whether the extent of formalization corresponded with these differences is difficult to say. In the UK the entrepreneurs relied on a mixture of formalization and informality, using informality to nurture an *esprit de corps* with their highly educated employees.[12] The Japanese entrepreneurs had formal expectations of their employees in terms of work practices and to some extent the functional division of labor, but many were cautious about delegating authority prematurely.

Company culture

Further evidence for these views comes from responses to a question on company culture. The entrepreneurs were asked how accurately a number of statements depicted their business, again on a 1 (strongly disagree) to 5 (strongly agree) scale. The results are shown in Figure 6.2. Although there were some similarities, three of the five means were very significantly different. The marked contrast between the means of "My business is a personal place; it's like an extended family" signals its positive meaning for the UK entrepreneurs, and a negative meaning for Japanese entrepreneurs. This negative reaction has probably been intensified by long years of small firm advisers and commentators who condemn Japanese small-firm owners for mixing family and business, and the association of family-like business as backward.

---

[12] "(S)taff can resent the imposition of procedures through which they are compelled to communicate with managers and/or proprietors. As they perceive it, hierarchical and impersonal systems erect boundaries between the managerial and operational functions of the business. The imposition of rational monitoring mechanisms designed to measure output and productivity may, in fact, lead to demotivation" (Scase, 2005: 80).

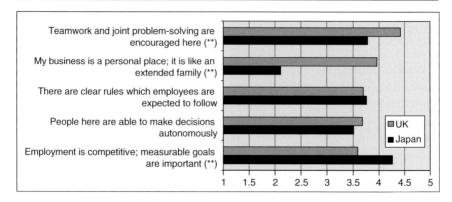

Figure 6.2 Company culture
Note: ** differences significant at .01

Teamwork and joint problem-solving were ranked highly by both groups, but in the UK this meant teamwork with specialization and to some extent devolved authority (ideally, at least), while in Japan it generally appeared to mean teamwork under supervision. "Measurable goals" were even more strongly supported by the Japanese entrepreneurs, and figured in their attempts to create discipline, keep employees on their toes and "raise" them by establishing tangible goals to work toward. In the UK these concerns were overlaid with concern to create a friendly working environment, blurring formal authority.

The high performers

Finally, do the differences we have outlined so far also apply to "high performers"? The means of the high performers for the HRM orientations are given in Figure 6.3. Comparing these results with Figure 6.1, we see that the basic scores and rankings are similar. For the UK group, however, offering flexible/family-friendly work arrangements was even more important (rank three to second equal), as were training and education and physical work environment (marginally moving from seventh and eighth respectively to sixth equal). Thus the changes were minor, but if anything, the UK tendencies were strengthened rather than diluted or changed.

With the Japanese high performers, too, the order of the first- and second-ranked items was reversed, but the original difference was tiny. Likewise the order of the fifth- and sixth-ranked variables was reversed, as

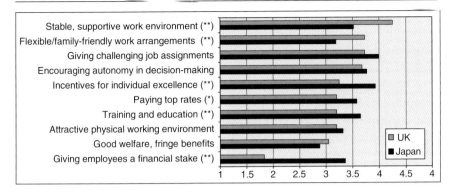

Figure 6.3 HRM orientations of high performers
Note: ** differences significant at .01; * differences significant at .05

was that of the seventh- and eighth-ranked variables. The result is that the variables of the two "individual" factors – growth and stretch – were given somewhat more priority, and organization/environment variables were given somewhat less. The overall effect, if anything, is to strengthen the Japanese tendencies, and to heighten the contrast between the UK and Japanese entrepreneurs in terms of espoused HRM orientations.

Concluding discussion

Before we analyzed our data, we expected that the UK entrepreneurs would score higher on extrinsic motivation items, and Japanese entrepreneurs would give more weight to the environment items. We did not expect extrinsic motivation orientations to be rated quite so low by both groups, or the environmental factors to be rated so high by the UK entrepreneurs, or so low by the Japanese entrepreneurs. To explain this puzzle, we turned to our case interviews, and found plausible explanations. We also saw, as suggested by the factor analysis, that the same item sometimes took on a very different meaning through its relationship with other items, and in a different social context.

Employment relations and HRM issues figured more prominently in the UK entrepreneurs' accounts. They particularly emphasized fitting in, motivation, and retention. In the Japanese entrepreneurs' accounts HRM issues were more likely to arise in the context of hiring difficulties, and of "raising" employees. Both groups were looking for similar kinds of employees, and emphasized challenging job assignments and autonomy, but challenge and autonomy meant different things. The UK entrepreneurs, however, stressed a supportive organizational environment, in part to blur authority lines and create a "team" ethos, but also because they needed to create a "give-and-take" culture to get the most from their employees.

Much has been written in recent years about the "new employment relationship" and "high-performance" or "high-commitment" work practices. To some extent there have been attempts to introduce these practices into small, progressive businesses (cf. Wilkinson, 2000). Here the focus is on challenging work, flexibility, quality, teamwork, with compensation systems reflecting these emphases, and "strong" cultures to balance autonomy.[13] Our findings suggest a further dimension, in the form of "give and take" over work and flexibility to fit in personal and family arrangements outside the workplace in the UK. This was used to engender trust relations which could then impact positively on relations with customers. Relative homogeneity in terms of education levels facilitated this, as did that fact that most of these businesses were not engaged in routine or volume manufacturing. It was notable that businesses in which entrepreneurs emphasized control, and concerns about trust or employee willingness to exert discretionary effort, were often businesses which included rather traditional manufacturing operations.

In Japan there was also an emphasis on challenging jobs, derived from entrepreneurs' own experiences in employment, as well as their quest to secure elusive recruits who were less willing to tolerate tedious jobs than in the past. But employment relations also appeared to be more "traditional," which is not surprising given that many of the businesses were older, and some had diversified into high-tech industries from traditional manufacturing. The social environment was also more stable, and the entrepreneurs did not have to factor this into their employee relations in the same way as the UK entrepreneurs. If we recall, moreover, that the Japanese entrepreneurs were concerned about building their internal competences, their emphasis on internal nurturing makes sense. Employment relations, leadership and company cultures, therefore, were very different.

---

[13] In our survey 56 percent of the businesses reported some form of profit-related pay in the UK – either group or individual, for key employees only, or for all full-time employees. These practices often included variable, performance-related pay. The figure rose to 73 percent for high performers. High performers were also somewhat more likely to have employee share ownership schemes. In Japan some 86 percent of businesses reported some form of profit–related pay, with 25 percent having share ownership schemes, and again somewhat higher figures for high performers (96 percent with performance related pay; 32 percent with share ownership schemes). These data, too, are context-dependent, and a full analysis is beyond our scope here.

7

Interfirm Collaboration

No company is an island, entire of itself, and when it comes to innovation and new business development in smaller businesses, the need to complement limited internal resources and capabilities can be acute. In fact, a large body of research from the past two decades shows that firms are increasingly reliant on external knowledge (Howells, 2000) and use external collaboration to supplement or complement their own internal innovation activities in the face of intensification of innovation (Dodgson, 1993) and the increasing importance of scientific knowledge. Innovators do this more than non-innovators (Tether, 2002).

Approaches to studying interfirm collaboration range from transaction costs, through resource-based and strategic views, to more sociological perspectives stressing social capital and legitimacy enhancement. Collaboration differs by industry, age, and size of a business, but is not necessarily determined by these (e.g., Hagedoorn, 1993, 2002). Hence an important entrepreneurial task is the initiation, development, maintenance, and termination of collaborative relations (Lorenzoni and Lipparini, 1999). These efforts often fail to achieve their initial strategic objectives, but there can still be significant reputation or legitimacy-enhancing benefits, especially for young or small firms collaborating with established businesses (Stuart, 2000). Conversely, however, small firms may find it difficult to enter into such arrangements, even with expertise, because they lack legitimacy.

As some of the initial interest in collaborations was inspired by interfirm relations and subcontracting in Japan,[1] we might expect collaboration to be particularly widespread there. On the other hand, if managing collaborations are an important managerial skill, we might expect them to be

---

[1] Cf. Dore (1983), Asanuma (1989), Nishiguchi (1992), Sako (1992).

common – or more successful – in the UK, given the differences in entrepreneurs' backgrounds (Chapter 2), and given their more outward-looking competitive orientations (Chapter 5). This chapter looks at interfirm – or interorganizational – collaborations, specifically at how extensively the entrepreneurs collaborated, with whom, and for what reasons. The first section provides an overview. The second section focuses on private–public collaborations, especially relations with universities, since these have become increasingly important for science-based technological innovation, and a focus of policy promotion in both countries in recent years. Finally, we examine differences between high performers and non-high performers. Some of our expectations are confirmed, but there are some surprises as well.

Interfirm collaborations

Our second survey asked: "Has your business entered into formal or informal collaborative or partnership arrangements with any other organization in the *last two years*?" It then went on to ask: "If 'yes' what were those organizations, and where were they located? And what was the main purpose of the collaborative or partnership arrangements?"[2] Existing research, based on the European CIS surveys, for instance, suggests that customers and suppliers are the most common and important sources of information for innovation (DeBresson et al. 1998; see also Cosh, Hughes, and Lester, 2006, for the UK and the USA, based on a separate survey; and Hughes, 2007, for Australian data) as well as for collaboration (Drejer and Jorgensen, 2005). Reasons for collaborating will depend on the type of partner, industry, technological maturity, and so on.

Essentially our findings, summarized in Tables 7.1 and 7.2, concur with this research. First of all, Table 7.1 suggests that collaborations are common, but far from universal (cf. Tether, 2002). Just over half the entrepreneurs collaborated; 59 percent in the UK and 49 percent in Japan. The higher figure for the UK might seem surprising given depictions of Japan as a country of "alliance capitalism" (Gerlach, 1992), and indeed given widespread participation of small businesses in cooperative associations (Momose, 1989; Whittaker, 1997). It is possible that this participation,

---

[2] "Collaborative or partnership arrangements" and "formal or informal arrangements" are open to subjective interpretation, of course, but the list of possible partners and reasons should have reduced the scope for major or systematic differences.

Table 7.1 Extent of collaboration and type of partner

	UK	Japan
Extent of collaboration	59.3	49.3
Type of collaborating organization		
Suppliers	44.2	36.6
Customers	42.5	34.7
Firms in your line of business	38.7	17.3
Higher education institutions	30.3	13.5
Distributors	29.2	18.5
Medical or research institutions	20.7	16.7
Other	4.2	9.1
No. of types of organizations collaborated with		
1	35.8	39.6
2	23.9	28.3
3	26.9	18.9
4 +	13.5	13.2

which tends to be ongoing, did not register as "collaboration." Certainly there were numerous instances of prototype and other development work for customers among our case interviews which might be considered – and *were* considered by the UK entrepreneurs – collaboration. Another possibility is that the UK entrepreneurs were more attuned to increasing trends toward collaboration (in Europe), were more outward-oriented anyway, and had greater management experience to draw upon for creating and managing collaborations.[3] We should also note, however, that the differences were only significant at the 0.1 level. Differences in the number of types of organizations collaborated with were also modest.

Table 7.1 also shows, unsurprisingly, a greater propensity to collaborate with upstream suppliers and downstream customers than with other partners in both countries. They were easily the most important partners in Japan. In the UK, however, firms in the same line of business were almost as common, some of them no doubt competitors (cf. Dodgson, 1993; Cosh, Hughes, and Lester, 2006, show that this is much more common in the UK than in the USA). We found in our interviews that such collaborations were often a precursor to, or accompanied, capital ties or mergers and acquisitions:

There's a company called L. We are looking at a potential merger with them in the future. If you take a long term hard view there are too many competitors in the business, and if we don't do something I suspect they will go under. . . . We swap

---

[3] The 2004 Cambridge CBR survey found collaborations in 37.6 percent of manufacturing businesses, 51.3 percent of innovators, and 57.1 percent of fast growth businesses (Cosh and Hughes, 2007*a*: 24). Our figures are high in comparison but not aberrant.

Table 7.2 Purpose of collaborations

	UK	Japan
Main purpose of collaboration		
Expand range of products/services	51.6	30.1
Provide access to new markets	45.1	10.7
Develop products/services required by current		
customers	41.6	34.7
Share R&D activity	39.2	31.9
Improve financial and market credibility	23.7	8.4
Access or spread costs of new equipment or		
information sources	15.1	19.3
Assist in management and staff development	6.3	13.5
Number of types of purposes		
1	14.3	17.9
2	16.1	12.3
3	15.2	13.7
4 +	14.3	5.2

balance sheet information at the moment, so we know exactly what's happening in each other's company. (UK3)

We are in talks with our main competitor and are definitely going to start collaborating. We have strengths and they have strengths and we are going to remove each other's weaknesses. We will make synergy. That's a definite. I suspect that we will eventually merge. (UK8)

This was much less common in Japan.[4] Likewise, differences in distributors as partners are very significant, and noteworthy given the important role distributors play in many industries in Japan, and their declining role in the UK.[5] Part of the explanation for the differences might lie in the location of these partners. In the UK many of the collaborating distributors and to a lesser extent firms in the same line of business were located overseas, and the collaborations were attempts to expand business abroad. In Japan most of the collaborating distributors were not just domestic, but local. Firms in the same line of business were more widely distributed, but still mostly domestic, reflecting the large domestic manufacturing base, as well as limited business horizons.[6]

[4] It is possible, too, that the Japanese entrepreneurs interpreted "firms in the same line of business" more narrowly, with large firms in the same line of business whom they subcontracted for classed as "customers."

[5] See, for example, Miyamoto and Whittaker (2005) on the book publishing industry in the UK and Japan.

[6] As reported in Chapter 5, a higher proportion of UK business turnover was generated abroad – almost a third (31 percent) on average, compared with just 12 percent of the Japanese businesses. The difference between high performers was even greater – 43 percent, compared with just 13 percent.

Finally, UK entrepreneurs were more likely to collaborate with universities. These links have been growing over the past two decades, but in Japan the distance between universities and businesses in general, and small businesses in particular, has only recently begun to shrink with concerted policy efforts in the early 2000s.[7] The differences with other research institutions were much smaller, no doubt reflecting their greater prevalence in Japan. We shall return to university–industry relations below.

A small company like us has to collaborate or die. Most of our collaboration is with US companies. That is where the technology is. (UK10)

Turning to purposes of collaboration, the most common purposes reflect relations with these partners. In the UK the top purposes were to "expand (our) range of products/services," "provide access to new markets," and "develop services/products required by current customers," followed closely by "share R&D activity."[8] The first two suggest innovation for expansion, and R&D collaboration suggests future innovation. Three of the top four UK purposes were also the top purposes in Japan, although here, significantly, the top purpose was to develop products for existing customers, presumably key customers. Access to new markets was ranked conspicuously down, along with improving financial and market credibility – legitimacy – also necessary for moving into new markets. Here we see more limited growth aspirations of the Japanese entrepreneurs, as well as long-term relations with major customers. The two items the Japanese entrepreneurs scored higher on – "access or spread costs of new equipment or information sources" and "assist in management and staff development" – were less central to innovation, and are sometimes functions of cooperative or small business associations, as well as relations with key customers or suppliers.

Overall, the UK picture is one of collaboration for innovation and expansion as much as servicing existing customers. The Japanese picture, when combined with the results of Chapter 4 showing high levels of (diverse kinds of) innovation, suggests more emphasis on internal innovation, or innovation in collaboration with key customers and suppliers while maintaining long-term relationships. Finally, while not the

---

[7] University–industry relations were closer in pre-World War II Japan, but the discrediting of such links as an element of militaristic mobilization, and subsequent postwar underfunding of universities during the 1960s expansion, coupled with an expansion of large corporate R&D meant that such links were downgraded (cf. Kobayashi, 1997).

[8] The 2004 CBR survey shows similar partners, and reasons for collaboration, with slightly different orderings (Cosh and Hughes, 2007a: 25–6).

most common partners for collaboration, universities were relatively more important when it came to R&D collaboration in both the UK and Japan.

High performers

Does the picture change when we focus on high performers? In the UK there were significantly higher levels of collaboration on the part of high performers than non-high performers – 70 percent versus 50 percent. High performers also reported more collaborations, and more kinds of collaboration. The overall pattern of collaborating partners was maintained, but at a higher level. Suppliers were the most frequently cited, by almost 60 percent, falling to just under half with other firms in the same line of business. Higher education institutions (HEIs) and other research institutions trailed at 43 percent and 33 percent. As for the purposes of collaboration, accessing new markets came top, followed by expanding the range of products/services, indicating a growth and expansion orientation. In third place, moreover, was sharing R&D activity, ahead of developing services/products required by current customers. Improving financial and market credibility was cited by over one-third of high performers.

With the UK *non*-high performers, the ordering of partners was similar, except that distributor collaborations were less common, indicating a less aggressive stance toward overseas expansion. The ordering of reasons was the same as for the total UK subsample, only at a slightly lower level. Comparing the UK high performers and non-high performers, it seems that there are clear benefits to collaboration, although the direction of causation is unclear. Collaboration might help entrepreneurs to innovate, but innovation might make it easier to engage in collaboration (through reputation, and expertise in innovation).

In view of these findings, and the widely cited benefits of collaboration, a surprising picture presents itself when we turn to Japan. Here we find the opposite situation. Only 44 percent of high performers reported collaborations in the past two years, compared with 56 percent of non-high performers. And there were fewer collaborations per participant! Japanese high performers collaborated mostly with customers (32 percent) and suppliers (30 percent), and trailing by a large margin were distributors (16 percent) and HEIs (11 percent).

With non-high performers, the ordering of the partners was similar, at higher levels, except that firms in the same line of business and other research institutes came third equal at 25 percent. Non-high performers were four times more likely to report collaborations with firms in the same line of business than high performers, and six times as likely to report collaborations with other research institutions! This offers some clues to the apparent paradox. Many non-high performer collaborations appeared to be with other small businesses, offering limited network advantages, and limited benefits for innovation, expansion, and access to new markets. Other research institutions might refer to public testing facilities which smaller businesses find important, but which more successful growing businesses "graduate" from.

There were more surprises when it came to the purposes of collaboration. The ordering by the non-high performers was basically the same as by the overall Japanese group, but both developing services/products required by current customers and sharing R&D activity were substantially higher (45 percent and 39 percent respectively), which means that they were substantially lower for the high performers (25 percent and 26 percent). The most commonly cited purpose by the high performers was expanding the range of products/services, followed by these two choices. This also means that, apart from assisting in management and staff development, the high performers in the UK were almost twice as likely to collaborate with the respective partners as the Japanese high performers, with a similar gap for most purposes. In fact, the UK high performers were seven times as likely as their Japanese counterparts to collaborate for the purpose of access to new markets.

What accounts for the reversal of high performers and non-high performers in Japan, and the large differences between the high performers in both countries? It would be consistent with the picture we have painted so far if the strong internal focus and the slow accumulation of internal competences, as well as the centrality of the entrepreneur in this process, meant that those who succeeded in this approach were more likely to eschew external collaborations. When the entrepreneurs started out, it was often through collaborations with customers (as a junior partner) that they found an initial niche. As they developed their own technology and products, however, they began to pursue self-determined R&D. By this stage they had developed sufficiently to be able to recruit engineers with graduate degrees to work on this R&D, which from our interviews often involved a related second or third core technology which could become the basis for future expansion. When developing their own technologies, collaborating with large (Japanese) companies could be seen as counterproductive.

This (opto-electronic) technology is absorbing most of my time these days. The potential market is very big, but we have to bring the price down. This requires large investment and mass production, and a market. The government can't help, and it's no good going to a company like S – they would just eat us up. I'm actually investigating the possibility of tie-ups in the US or Europe. (J1)

We now have multiple technologies, and want to build our strength by making products combining them. The head of our lasers was the head of (M Inc.) lasers before, so he knows what he's doing. We have three Ph.Ds working in R&D. Nowadays universities come to us to ask if they can do U-I [presumably to get grants]. We can make a 5 micron hole in a diamond. (J13)

I encourage my employees to think about the science that underlies technology. It takes several years. Of course you can't eat science, and you need to make profits, but that's where a lot of our energy is concentrated. Five of my employees have quit to become university professors. (J7)

Such comments appear to indicate a "closed-innovation" orientation (Chesbrough, 2003), driven partly out of fear of losing the benefits of the core technologies they were building up, which were so central to their future development plans. The more competitive the technology, the greater the fear of such loss. The potential predators in most cases were large domestic companies. It seemed that this was a *phase* such technology-oriented companies went through, and that this phase was eventually succeeded by a new phase in which the company's reputation was established, and it became easier to enter into new, more speculative technology collaborations, including collaborations with large companies, without fear that their technologies would be appropriated unfairly.[9]

Smaller, newer, less-established companies, by contrast, might enter into such collaborations before their technology base and reputation were secure, hoping to enhance these. They would do so, however, on less favorable terms, and risked being caught in the "swamp" we referred to in Chapter 2. Non-high performers, without a real strategic focus and beset with growth limitations (Chapter 5) appeared to enter into collaborations from a weak position, with insufficient resources or expertise, and unable to benefit from them.

The UK non-high performers, in fact, had similar levels of collaboration to the Japanese non-high performers. Without a strong strategic customer focus, they may have fared little better. One or two mentioned a reluctance to collaborate with competitors until they had a stronger hand to play. The benefits of collaboration, not surprisingly, are conditional.

[9] Similar observations are made by Ibata-Arens (2005) of innovative, entrepreneurial businesses in Japan avoiding becoming caught up in *keiretsu* (enterprise groups) of large enterprises.

University–industry collaboration

One explanation for the lower levels of collaboration with universities and other research institutes compared with customers and suppliers is that they – university collaborations, at least – are limited to explorations of fundamentally new technologies, or "new science." Another explanation is that they are very different types of organizations, speaking different "languages." Small firms, in particular, have limited ability to absorb knowledge generated by universities (Drejer and Jorgensen, 2005). Nonetheless, almost one-third of the UK entrepreneurs reported collaborations with universities in the past two years, and a fifth with other research institutions. The main purposes were sharing R&D activity, expanding the range of products/services and developing services/products required by current customers. We might assume that these were primarily novel innovations. As we have seen, the Japanese figures were lower, and the main purposes cited were sharing R&D activity and developing products/ services required by current customers.

Relations with universities were more complex than these figures alone suggest, however. First, in a quarter of both the UK and Japanese businesses, at least one member of the founding team had worked full time at some point in a higher education, medical, or research institution. Some had kept or developed faculty, advisory, or guest lecturer links, and were semi-insiders in such institutions. In such businesses, not surprisingly, the propensity to collaborate with universities was quite high, though not universal.

Second, there was a wide range of interactions, not necessarily captured by the notion of "collaboration." For example, universities provided participants in both countries with human resources:

At the moment we have a master's student, a Ph.D student, a TCS (Teaching Company Scheme) student and a major European Framework project, all linking us in with local universities. (UK4)

In Japan, internships were less frequent, but university links were cultivated to secure full-time employee recruits. In both countries universities were sometimes the recipients of corporate expertise.

Their second year students have an annual design project that they run with us and we mentor. (UK18)

We are in a project to develop an artificial heart. It's not business for us – we won't get a product out of it, but we are helping the doctor. (J19)

While in some sense most of the relationships could be described as strategic for the participants, they were frequently the result of personal relationships – colleagues of siblings, friends of friends, and so on. Thus there was a personal element in the relationships. Geographically, too, the links were spread; there were more nonlocal than local collaborations in both countries.[10] This sometimes reflected strategic partner choice, but again it was also the result of contacts moving, introductions by friends, and so on:

Technology transfer is a "body contact sport." It's about people, not about places. (UK4)

It all just comes through personal relationships. . . . The connection at Oxford – that all came through me. And the connection at Essex came because some of the people I knew at Oxford moved on to Essex. (UK12)

The university links on our web site? Well, the one at Iwate is a person who quit his job and joined Iwate University. Tokyo Institute of Technology – a professor introduced me to that person. And Gifu – that was introduced by a customer. (J5)

While some of the relationships were delivering what the participants hoped, a good number were not. In fact, in Japan, the majority of evaluations were negative, so much so that they frequently did not get off the ground:

D. University's engineering faculty is nearby. I asked if there was anyone who might collaborate in laser work. I was told they aren't here to help companies with their current needs, they were interested in future-oriented work. Well, that's a waste of time. (J16)

Our joint project is not working because the development speed is different. I need products out within half a year; they can't help with that. (J19)

We have a problem because the students aren't taught to be sensitive about non-disclosure. If they go to a big company they won't get exposed to secrets, but in small businesses it's right in front of them, and they aren't taught about confidentiality. (J10)

These representative comments might explain why such collaborations were not more widespread in Japan. Some entrepreneurs, too, complained about bureaucracy and red tape adding to the drag and slowness of getting collaborations moving. This was also a UK bugbear.

I'd licensed products before, but this was just horrendous. I've never seen so much paper work. They probably spent more on their solicitors than they got out of me for the royalty. (UK3)

---

[10] Many of these aspects of partner selection were found by Karlson (2006) in a study of science-based start-ups and universities in Denmark and New Zealand.

In addition, there was a perception gap about intellectual property. One entrepreneur summed it up neatly:

People from universities think they've finished when they've got a working model. But that's a long way from something that we can sell.... The gap between making the thing work and putting it into a product which is commercially viable is still very much underestimated. (UK9)

The multidimensional nature of university–industry relations and difficulties endemic in collaboration have been widely noted, but downplayed in the university-originating model of technology transfer and spinouts which has become fashionable in policy circles in both countries, perhaps more crudely so in Japan. In the words of the UK Council for Industry and Higher Education, the focus has been "too narrow.... It ignores many of the mechanisms through which universities and business together influence innovation and business performance."[11]

Cosh, Hughes, and Lester (2006) emphasize the multifaceted role of universities, which includes education and recruits, and "public space" for social interaction (cf. Lester and Piore, 2004) through entrepreneurship centers, meetings, and conferences, and alumni networks, increasing the stock of codified knowledge, and problem-solving through contract research and consulting. Discussing these results, and recent responses by leading US universities, Hughes (2007: 18) remarks: "If the 'US model' is to guide innovation policy elsewhere it is as well that the current evolving model rather than the 'old' one is a reference point and the full range of interactions is recognized." We shall return to this in Chapter 9.

Concluding comments

Internal innovation is increasingly supported or complemented by external sources of knowledge and collaborations. Partner choice naturally depends on the purpose, but most common are collaborations with customers and suppliers, to expand product offerings required by current or potential customers. Collaboration partners can also include direct

---

[11] 2008 report, cited in *Times Higher Education*, June 5, 2008, p. 16. Cathy Garner, chief executive of Manchester: Knowledge Capital comments: "[W]e need to understand this breath and stop counting things like patents, which may not be driving the right behaviour. The way we have modeled ourselves, on a paradigm that came out of the US, is not actually recognizing the way that businesses are embracing innovation" (ibid.).

competitors, however, as well as universities and other institutions associated with the research base, which have received most attention.

The first surprising finding – for us, although some of the findings of previous chapters have pointed in this direction – was the somewhat higher proportion of collaborations reported in the UK, notably with other customers, suppliers, and firms in the same line of business, but also with distributors.[12] The emphases were also different: Japanese collaborations largely took place in the context of existing business relations, while the UK emphasis appeared to be more on accessing new markets and customers.

The second surprise was that the high performers accentuated these differences. (Indeed they accounted for them – the non-high performers had similar levels of collaboration.) The UK high performers were more likely to collaborate, with an emphasis on accessing new markets, growth, and expansion. The Japanese high performers were *less* likely to collaborate, and when they did, it was even more strongly in the context of existing business relations. This no doubt reflects long-term relations common in Japan, but the lower propensity for high performers to collaborate, in stark contrast with the UK high performers, needed explanation.

We proposed that high-potential entrepreneurial businesses in Japan, developing innovative technologies, risked collaborating under unfavorable terms when they were small, and that this led them to focus their energies on building up internal competences, including technological innovation, to improve their base for growth, and potential future engagement on more favorable terms. This was consistent with some of our case interviews, findings on innovation and competitive orientations, and HRM orientations. It suggests that the inward focus of many of the Japanese entrepreneurs was not simply a product of their backgrounds. We will look at this in more detail in Chapter 8.

Finally, in a quarter of the businesses in both countries at least one member of the founding team had been employed full time in the research base, most commonly in a university. Links were fluid, and diverse, but recent policy initiatives aimed at furthering and formalizing university–industry relations, for instance through technology transfer or licensing offices, were frequently criticized in both countries for increasing bureaucracy, and indeed creating barriers to collaboration. (Some Japanese

---

[12] The differences may have been more apparent than real, depending on respective interpretations of "collaboration," but Cosh, Hughes, and Lester (2006), too, found a somewhat higher propensity to seek external information from a wider range of sources in the UK compared to the USA.

entrepreneurs also reported an increasing tendency to be approached by universities to submit joint bids for government funding, to satisfy funding requirements.) In spite of such complaints, collaborative relations between the entrepreneurial businesses and universities appeared to be on the rise in both countries.

8

Entrepreneurship and Markets

Our analysis of entrepreneurs and their businesses in the UK and Japan has highlighted some significant similarities, and differences. To some extent these are artifacts of the analysis itself. We did not explore thoroughly different lines of division – younger versus older entrepreneurs or businesses, differences by industry, or region – but concentrated primarily on country-based analysis. We did this, however, because the country division seemed most compelling; industry, regional, and other divisions could not explain our data in the way that countries did. We have seen this in our comparisons of high performers and non-high performers.

We stand by our approach to the analysis, then, but we have yet to *integrate* and *explain* the findings. Chapters 8 and 9 take up this task. We acknowledge some important, broad similarities between the entrepreneurs in both countries in terms of the importance of prior work experience, "soft" starts, founding with others, and balancing control with complementary resources, personal business orientations and business principles, and so on. The fundamental processes of entrepreneurship were similar. But the differences were also striking, particularly in technology emphases, competitive orientations, growing the business, innovation emphases, extent of collaboration, and overall orientations to the business, and these are what we want to explain. This means addressing the contexts of entrepreneurship. How we do this has important theoretical implications.

We might try to explain the differences primarily in terms of the social networks of the entrepreneurs in both countries. In the UK, ties were "weak" enough (Granovetter, 1983) to enable recombinations to occur relatively easily, with colleagues splitting off together to create a new business, sometimes to pursue a new opportunity, sometimes to preserve and advance the work they had been doing in employment, as a kind of a project, which could then be subject to recombination later. With stronger ties in Japan, and pressure from those around not to chop and change, a project approach was less viable, and entrepreneurs were forced into a committed form of entrepreneurship which evolving network relations further locked them into. They might not have started out as lifework/commitment entrepreneurs, but they were progressively forced into a lifework orientation.

Immediate social networks can explain some of the differences, but there were important institutional influences which were not generated by these networks, but which were the result of broader social, political, and historical processes, influencing both these networks and entrepreneurial processes. Hence we must consider culture and institutions.[1] Our selective focus is on the latter, and especially on markets. We have already referred to labor markets at various points, as shaping entrepreneurs' backgrounds, influencing the timing and terms of spinning out from employment, influencing HRM orientations, and so on. We have not discussed capital markets much; they appear less critical in terms of explaining *differences* than labor markets, but they are important and we will return to them in Chapter 9. In this chapter we will concentrate on markets for products and services, as well as for businesses themselves. Markets may not be sufficient to explain all the differences between entrepreneurs and entrepreneurship in the two countries, but they are an important and necessary part of the explanation.

Drawing on Polanyi (1944), some writers see markets as institutionally embedded in coordinated market economies (CMEs) like Germany and Japan, and disembedded in liberal market economies (LMEs) like the UK and the USA. Crouch and Streeck (1997: 3) note of such writing: "Some national economies were found to be more institutional than others, in that they subjected a wider range of economic governance mechanisms other than and in addition to market exchange and managerial prerogative, while typically also modifying the two through various forms of social intervention."[2] These comments may be particularly relevant to the niche markets of entrepreneurs, discussed in Chapter 5.

More or less embedded markets or the extent of marketization can certainly explain some of our differences, but the *nature* – rather than level – of embeddedness is also important. As some economic sociologists have pointed out, markets are always embedded, but in different ways, including ideological (Block, 2003; Fligstein, 2001; Somers and Block, 2005). Following

---

[1] As Crouch (2005: 18) puts it, rather strongly: "Institutions exist; their origins may have nothing to do with the uses to which current actors are trying to put them. Individuals and groups inherit them, not necessarily willingly or even consciously; they encounter them and have to shape their lives and projects in relation to them. These institutions both constrain and facilitate; they can often be adjusted; but they should not be expected to be fully subject to human will."

[2] Cited in Krippner and Alvarez (2007), who provide a useful review of the concept of "embeddedness." See also Hall and Soskice (2001), Dore (2000), Yamamura and Streeck (2003).

133

a number of economic sociologists (beginning with Weber, 1922/1978), we will look at two stages of the market process, namely competition between producers (or production markets) and exchange itself (exchange markets).

We begin the chapter with a brief review of similarities and differences from Chapters 2 to 7 which need explanation. We then proceed to a discussion of how these differences force us to construct a picture of market differences, as in a "wasgij," and we attempt to construct the respective "wasgijs." A further dimension of this explanation – time orientations – is introduced in Chapter 9.

Project and lifework entrepreneurship: summing up

We begin by acknowledging important similarities in entrepreneurship in the UK and Japan. These can be categorized as (*a*) similarities in core processes of entrepreneurship; and (*b*) similarities due to liabilities of newness (Stinchcombe, 1965; Aldrich and Fiol, 1994) and also liabilities of smallness (Freeman, Carrol, and Hannan, 1983). Let us start with core processes. Most founders only started thinking about starting their own business after working for several years. Whilst in employment, they gained skills, their motivations were shaped, and many perceived opportunities, as well as lessons for managing their business. The average age of founding their current business was 37 (with all the implications described by Liles, 1974). In the process of starting their business, moreover, a significant proportion (one-third) had received help from their former employer.

The majority started their business with others in a formal, ownership sense, as well as informally. Co-owners were mostly internal. Here the desire for control was balanced by the desire for both trust and support, and complementary resources. The entrepreneurs started with vague perceptions of where they were going and the type of business they might construct. They did not start as radical innovators, with well-defined concepts or business plans. They started "soft," and generally went on to develop products over a period of time, although some got stuck at the "soft" stage. Many were engaged in subcontracting, for instance.

In terms of personal business objectives, their overriding concern was to establish a viable and trusted business on a platform of basic "principles." Both groups were gradualists in their approach to business development, and most advocated taking only calculated risks. They operated in niche markets, with a limited number of competitors and customers, and their perceived competitive advantages – personal attention/responsiveness to customer needs, speed, quality, etc. – reflected these. Thus there were strong similarities, especially in terms of how opportunity and business creation were intertwined, which reflected the desire to reduce risk while pursuing multiple goals (securing an income, establishing a business, pursuing an opportunity).

There were subsequent similarities as well, related to the liabilities of newness and smallness. External market conditions were seen as the biggest limitations, but there were constraints in terms of inputs as well, especially the ability to secure key skills, and internally in terms of management capabilities. By and large, the entrepreneurs were looking for broadly similar types of people to develop the business, and their external collaborations were mainly with customers and suppliers, to strengthen their competitive position in their niche markets. Relations with universities were diverse, and sometimes frustrating, despite links in the founding teams in some cases.

The two groups of similarities are worth noting because they do not necessarily fit common images of entrepreneurship, or policy emphases, in the two countries. In these images, the importance of prior experience is downplayed; rational and formal planning, big hits and funding from venture capital are emphasized, as well as links with universities focused on technology transfer. We will consider the implications of the gap between our findings and these images and policy emphases in Chapter 9.

If there were broad similarities, however, there were striking differences as well. First, as we saw in Chapter 2, the entrepreneurs' backgrounds were significantly different, with the UK entrepreneurs having broader functional experience, more management experience, and more experience of job changing than the Japanese entrepreneurs, many of whose careers were rooted in production and/or R&D. The UK founders had started more businesses, either in parallel or serially, and more were directors of other businesses. The Japanese founders had most often started a single business, and were less involved in other businesses, unless – as happened occasionally – they had acquired a stake in them. In founding motivations there was stronger emphasis in the UK on personal advancement and seeking opportunities to use skills more fully, and in Japan on pursuing technology opportunities – technology (ad)venture – and in gaining a more satisfactory working life, and work–life balance. The UK entrepreneurs on the whole appeared to be more sensitive to market opportunities, while the Japanese entrepreneurs tended to emphasize technological opportunities (although many of our innovative interviewees sought a balance). Thus backgrounds appeared to influence opportunity and business creation.

Significantly, UK entrepreneurs tended to approach their business as if it were a "project," which might be modified, and commitment adjusted or even withdrawn if career or life priorities moved elsewhere. The Japanese entrepreneurs, by contrast, approached their business as if it were a "lifework," something which required their full commitment not just in the first few years, but further into the future as well. *If* their life priorities changed, they were likely to pursue them within the context of the business they had founded, or at least create some link with it to demonstrate continuity. These differences may have been largely latent at the point of leaving employment and starting the new business, but circumstances sharpened them over time.

Social relations and networks were important, in different ways. In the UK internal cofounders on average owned a larger share of the capital, and were seen to have contributed more key resources. They were often former colleagues, and were more likely to constitute a "team." In Japan there was more likely to be a single dominant entrepreneur, cofounders were more likely to be family members, or former subordinates. In a number of cases, teams of an earlier business had fractured. Project entrepreneurship in the UK thus appeared to be collegial, with owner control downplayed, while lifework entrepreneurship in Japan had a clear, dominant founder.

"Principles" were important in both countries, but the top personal business objectives in the UK reflected a "stakeholder" orientation, or a concern for "citizenship," whereas the top Japanese objectives were more concerned with the relationship of the entrepreneur to the business, which we interpreted as a desire to build a business which could be passed on. This fits with the notion of a "lifework." The UK entrepreneurs sought more growth than the Japanese entrepreneurs, although growth preferences reflected recent experiences of growth and the business environment. Both groups were cautious about risk, but the UK entrepreneurs appeared to see risk as something they could increase or decrease as part of their business strategy. Many Japanese entrepreneurs seemed to see being in business as a risk in itself, creating a need for a platform for steady growth to minimize that risk.

This approach was compatible with concerted innovation. Levels of product innovation were similar, but the Japanese entrepreneurs were more engaged in process and other kinds of innovation as well. Overall, these differences are consistent with a more market-oriented (or market-aware) approach to business in the UK, and a more technological orientation in Japan.

Of those who did subcontracting – a similar proportion in both countries did none – there was heavier reliance on it in Japan, and similarly, heavier reliance on major customers. The number of serious competitors tended to be small, but almost twice as many UK entrepreneurs reported six or more, with more of them overseas. Japanese businesses were more domestically oriented.

Factor analysis of perceived competitive advantages also showed an outward-directed focus in the UK and an inward-directed focus in Japan. High performers in the UK were focused on satisfying the needs of specific customers, but non-high performers had a general "market" orientation. The Japanese entrepreneurs were the mirror image of this. High performers were focused on building up competences, while the non-high performers were preoccupied with "today's" products.

The UK entrepreneurs rated most limitations as less serious, with the notable exception of cost and availability of finance. The Japanese entrepreneurs rated technology impediments as relatively more serious, again reflecting their technological and internal orientations. And while a number of the UK entrepreneurs found it difficult to recruit people with certain professional or management skills, the Japanese entrepreneurs, especially the high performers (who were growing), struggled to secure all categories of skills.

In terms of HRM orientations, there was a strong emphasis on providing a supportive organizational environment in the UK. This was much less important for the Japanese entrepreneurs, who professed to emphasize challenging work. These differences reflected an "implicit contract" – flexibility in return for sustained and extra commitment when needed in the UK, and loyalty or hard work for job security, and perhaps challenging work in Japan, with the entrepreneur setting the terms of engagement. These HRM orientations were related to labor markets and broader social relations of course, but also to the role that the entrepreneurs perceived of themselves in relation to their businesses, or leadership. We used the similes of entrepreneur-as-conductor and entrepreneur-as-locomotive respectively, which amplify the differences in founding teams and the greater emphasis on control in Japan, and collegiality in the UK.

Finally, the UK entrepreneurs were engaged in more collaborations, with more partners (including some in the same line of business), than the Japanese entrepreneurs. The differences came mostly from the high performers, whose propensity to collaborate differed sharply, and amplified the external and collegial orientations of the UK entrepreneurs, and the internal competence building and technological orientations of the Japanese entrepreneurs. The UK entrepreneurs collaborated for innovation and expansion as much as servicing current customers, moreover, while the Japanese collaborations took place more in the context of relationships with key customers and other long-term partners.

Table 8.1 summarizes key empirical differences.

Table 8.1 Summary of empirical UK–Japan differences

Chapter	Issue	UK	Japan
2	Backgrounds	Managerial	Technical
	No. of businesses founded	Sometimes multiple, some MBO	Mostly single, or successor
	Reasons for founding	Personal advancement and skill deployment	Technology (ad)venture better, independent working life
	Opportunity creation	Market-pull – balance	Technology-push – balance
	Fundamental orientation	Project	Lifework
3	Founding team	Colleagues (complementary assets)	Family (trust, supplementary assets)
	Founding resources	Team	Individual founder
4	Entrepreneurial objectives	Entrepreneurial "citizenship"	Entrepreneurial existence
	Risk orientation	Elective, personal preference	Involuntary, inherent in doing business
	Innovation	Product innovation focus	Product and process, logistics
5	Subcontracting	Less reliance (those that subcontracted)	More reliance (those that subcontracted)
	Competitors	More serious competitors perceived, more overseas	Fewer serious competitors perceived, fewer overseas
	Competitive advantages	"Outward-oriented" (customer focus, market orientation)	"Inward oriented" (competences, products)
	Limitations	Fewer (innovation, professional skills)	More (technology, markets, all skills)
6	Leadership	Entrepreneur as conductor/team leader	Entrepreneur as locomotive
	Employment relationship	"Give-and-take" employment relationship	Implicitly hard work and loyalty for security and challenge
	Education and training	Cognitive, implicitly egalitarian	Through *praxis*, implicitly hierarchical
	Culture	Espoused culture of teamwork, mutual support	Espoused culture of goals and challenge
7	Collaborations	More collaborations, more partners	Fewer collaborations, fewer partners
	Purposes of collaboration	(Innovation and expansion)	(Maintaining, improving long-term relationships)

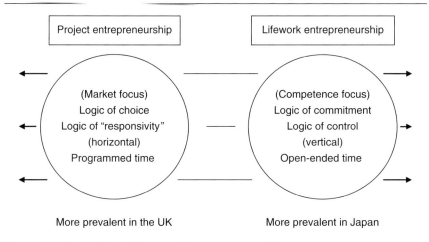

Figure 8.1 Underlying differences in entrepreneurship

Note: Differences maintained or even accentuated by high performers

Underlying these are some more fundamental differences, which we have summarized in Figure 8.1. We have already elaborated on the relative market focus of the UK entrepreneurs and the technology of competence focus of the Japanese entrepreneurs. We will elaborate on the "logic of choice" and the "logic of commitment" in chapter 9. The "logic of control" that we saw at various points in the study – from founding teams to innovation practices and competitive orientations, HRM orientations and (limited) propensity to collaborate – emphasizes the centrality of the entrepreneur and vertical coordination. It may reflect a "traditional" entrepreneurship orientation, but may also be seen as integrally connected with the logic of commitment, and both of these with a lifework approach to entrepreneurship. This approach was more prevalent in Japan. Conversely, the logic of "responsivity," seen through the same phenomena of founding teams, etc. emphasizes an orientation to leveraging complementary assets and horizontal coordination. The obverse of the logic of control, it may reflect a new, "open" entrepreneurship orientation, but may also be seen as linked to the logic of choice and openness to market exchange on the basis of utility. The logics of choice and "responsivity" infuse project entrepreneurship. This approach was more prevalent in the UK.

Environments, niches, and markets

How do we explain these differences? Some might be explained by the current respective environments; a more benign environment in the UK (and export markets) which fostered optimism and external orientation, and a much less benign environment in Japan which forced entrepreneurs to batten down the hatches and build up capabilities to survive, if not for the future. This would be a partial and superficial explanation, however. Most of the differences were upheld – or amplified – by the high performers, and we would not expect to see many of the differences reversed in a different economic climate.

Some of the differences might boil down to the backgrounds of the entrepreneurs. The broader professional skill base of the UK entrepreneurs may have equipped them with a greater understanding of the importance of networks, complementary resources, strategic ordering of multiple goals, organization building, and markets. The more technical backgrounds of the Japanese entrepreneurs, by contrast, may have encouraged them to focus more on technology itself, as well as competences needed to build a technological base for the business, and to think about markets in terms of technological potential. But where do these differences come from? From labor markets in part, of course, or more generally from the environments of the entrepreneurs, and interactions between the entrepreneurs and their respective environments.

Population ecology offers some useful insights here. First, and despite the current economic climate, the more specialized, technological aspirations of the Japanese entrepreneurs might reflect a historically more stable business environment, and the more generalized aspirations of the UK entrepreneurs might reflect greater instability (Hannan and Freeman, 1977). Relatedly, given the larger, more stable population of manufacturing businesses in Japan, the Japanese entrepreneurs appear to be K-strategists, efficient at exploiting narrow niches in a stable population. With greater turbulence and restructuring in the UK, entrepreneurs there appear to be r-strategists, who exploit opportunities in new, disturbed, or transitory environments.

Second, a "liability of newness" appears to apply to start-ups everywhere, as does the liability of "smallness,"[3] but they appear to weigh

[3] In the USA: "Many (businesses and institutions) are putting their new small suppliers through a far more rigorous inspection process than in the past before deciding whether to buy from them. Among other things, they are consulting industry research firms to vet the start-up's financials and are talking with other customers to see how the start-up responds to problems" (*Wall Street Journal*, May 22, 2007).

particularly heavily in Japan. Some UK entrepreneurs we interviewed ranked the USA as the most tolerant of newness, and Continental European countries as much less tolerant, with the UK in between. In Japan, some entrepreneurs had to go to the USA to secure their first customers, before any major Japanese company would consider doing business with them. It is no surprise, then, that the transition from employment to independence, the "soft" start, is often marked by subcontracting in Japan, and that this is often for the former employer. Sometimes the entrepreneurs were given trial prototype work during this soft start, and they gradually built their reputation and legitimacy from there.

The liabilities of newness and smallness, and questions of legitimacy, also appeared to weigh more heavily on the Japanese entrepreneurs in input markets, particularly for labor, reinforcing their gradualist approach to business development. They even weighed at home; spouse opposition to leaving secure employment to start a new business was not uncommon. Family resistance in the UK appears to have been more easily overcome, at least where the house did not have to be offered as security to launch the business. Colleagues, too, were more easily persuaded. In Japan we suspect that entrepreneurs made less effort to persuade colleagues because they knew that legitimacy problems would mean a tough road ahead.

Environments and liabilities of newness and smallness, and legitimacy, offer some explanation for Table 8.1, generally speaking, but we need to move beyond generalizations. In fact, we need to look more carefully at markets. Differences in backgrounds that we noted at the beginning of this section might be explained in terms of respective labor markets and skill formation (cf. also Baker, Gedajlovic, and Lubatkin, 2005). These would also influence team composition, employment relations, and internal HRM dynamics. There is a considerable body of research on differences between the UK and Japan in terms of employment and industrial relations, which points to a more market-oriented approach in the UK and a more organization-oriented approach in Japan (cf. Dore, 1973; Whittaker, 1990). Moreover, studies of buyer supplier relations in the UK and Japan (Sako, 1992; Dore, 1983) point to similar differences in product and service markets, with more (spot) market-oriented transactions in the former, and "relational contracting" in the latter.

We propose to delve further into differences in markets, as an explanation of differences in entrepreneurship, by asking three fundamental questions: (*a*) What can be brought to the market? (*b*) Who can participate in the market? and (*c*) What are the terms of participation and exchange? These questions do not arise in most economic treatments of "the market," but similar questions have been asked by economic sociologists from Weber (especially 1922) and more recently White (1981) and others.

Utility and relational markets

What can be brought to the market?

Let us begin with what may be brought to the market, or marketization. Polanyi (1944) and others have emphasized that, far from being universal and natural products of human activity, markets are in fact carefully constructed artifacts. For Polanyi, this took place through "disembedding" of exchange from social relations, while for others markets are always embedded in actor relations and institutions (cf. Block, 2003). As Callon (1998: 8) suggests:

> The actors engaged in the construction and functioning of concrete markets are legion. All the usual suspects are there: firms, consumers and their organizations, researchers from private enterprises or government labs (natural or life sciences), technological engineers, lawyers, accountants, civil servants who draw up regulations, consultancies, patent offices, etc. – and economists. There is no reason to shorten or close this list.

Varieties of capitalism writing suggest that LMEs, including the UK, have been more active in marketization than CMEs, including Japan, especially over the past two decades. This helps to explain differences in what may be brought to the market and what may not.

If it is difficult for entrepreneurs in Japan to find initial customers, it is generally even more difficult for them to sell their business, or pieces of their business like their customer list, or other intangible assets (cf. Furuse, 2005). It is not impossible, but the basic principles for doing so are less established, supported, or accepted. This situation, we contend, reinforces a lifework or commitment approach. In the UK, a market for these has been established, partly with the addition of appropriate actors and their respective tools, and company and customer list sales are reasonably common. A project entrepreneur can realistically expect to exit his project through a market transaction. The general lack of a market for (private, but even, it might be said, public) companies in Japan is not simply because of a lack of actors – in fact banks can and do act as brokers – but due to difficulties in passing one set of social relations, such as customers and especially co-owners, employees, and suppliers, from one owner to another.[4]

Who can participate in the market?

Not only is the extent of marketization different in the two countries, but markets themselves seem to be constructed differently. Let us depict them temporally, recalling that in our entrepreneurs' markets, the numbers of both producers and customers are limited – they are typically niche markets. In the Japanese market or *agora*, there are different categories of "member," and membership is not easily gained. A lower category can be obtained by recommendations from existing members, but is not granted straightaway to strangers. Strangers are not necessarily barred; they are allowed to bring their wares, but because they are not members, they may be offered lower prices than would otherwise be offered to a full member. There is a way to membership without patronage or even prior reputation. The stranger must demonstrate that he is not going to upset the rules, and is worthy of membership. This is most easily demonstrated by hard work and commitment, in addition to sound products. Over time this shows that the newcomer is not going to create havoc in the market place, and may result in progressive acceptance.

In the UK market or *agora*, there is greater openness to strangers. What matters is what they bring to the market. By and large there is a norm – ideology even – that anyone should be able to trade, provided they are not deceitful and accept some basic rules of mutuality. Furthermore, the exchange price should depend on utility, not on who is selling. A wider range of goods is traded, and there are daily changes in terms of offerings and people offering them.

We will call the latter "utility markets," and the former "relational markets" after Dore's (1983) "relational contracting." These markets seem to us to be the wasgij pictures or mirror of project and lifework/commitment entrepreneurship, and can help to explain and integrate a number of phenomena depicted in Table 8.1. Even the comments by the Japanese entrepreneurs about working harder or longer than anyone else, and not taking days off for years on end, on the face of it are about a personal investment in their business, but they also appeared to point to a means of gaining

---

[4] In other words, they are strongly embedded in Granovetter's (1985) sense, in immediate social relations or networks. Conversely, greater "marketization" in the UK means a greater acceptance of transferability.

legitimacy, particularly vis-à-vis those buying their products, but by other possible stakeholders as well. Comments by entrepreneurs of not only having to go abroad to find initial customers, but of wildly different valuations put on their innovations by different parties, with those of large Japanese companies typically lowest, also make sense. It is little wonder that high performers in these cases withdrew from collaborations until they could participate on more favorable terms.

Terms of participation, and changing ideologies

Economic sociologists have distinguished between two types of markets or two stages of the market process, namely production markets, which are characterized by competition between producers, and exchange markets, where there is "civilized conflict" between buyer and seller (Swedberg, 2003). Weber (1922) saw "struggle" in both, while others like White (1981), who was mainly interested in production markets, emphasized the importance of monitoring, signaling, and roles. Fligstein's (2001) "political-cultural" markets, too, are dominated by incumbents, who set the rules for interaction:

The tactics we observe in business are oriented toward producing stable social relations, particularly between competitors. These relationships define fields. Once in place, firms signal one another about their price and product tactics. The relationships define how the market works, what a given firm's place is, and how actors should interpret one another's actions. Incumbent firms use the power of their position to undertake strategies that reinforce that position. To survive, challenger firms must find a place in the existing set of social relationships. (Fligstein, 2001: 18)[5]

This depiction seems particularly apt for Japan, where there has been a greater propensity for large firms or their group subsidiaries to move into emerging markets. In fact, some of our interviewees referred to tiers in (production) markets, and one or two with pride at how they had now come to compete with "tier one" companies much bigger and more established than them. Most, however, avoided such competition, and competed with smaller businesses in lower tiers in smaller markets.

Fligstein's depiction appears less apt for the UK, however, where there typically appeared to be greater fluidity and fewer dominant competitors who created the rules and relationships that challengers had to adapt

[5] Cf. Bourdieu (1977); also White's (1981) view of the market as a "self-reproducing role structure of producers."

to. This might, of course, reflect the greater predominance of "other manufacturing" businesses in the UK. It might also reflect the aftermath of 1980s and 1990s restructuring. In the absence of dominant competitors, it was not clear how order was created in these markets. As we have seen, companies tended to keep a close eye on each other, with a view to mergers and acquisitions to establish an "appropriate" level of competition for the size of the industry. There did not appear to be a concept of tiers as such. On the contrary, there appeared to be an ideological de-emphasis on who the seller was, in favor of judging what was being sold.

Where might such an ideology come from? There are various possibilities. The seeds might have been planted by dissenters' egalitarianism in the UK, or the "bourgeois revolution" (in the sense used by Moore, 1966), the rise of Polanyi's "market society," or the rise of neoliberalism combined with economic restructuring from the 1980s. Regarding the last of these, we do note a comment from the Bolton Report which stressed difficulties of challengers as a factor in the precipitous decline of UK small businesses up to the end of the 1960s:

> We believe that the health of the economy requires the birth of new enterprises in substantial numbers and the growth of some to a position from which they are able to challenge and supplant the existing leaders of industry. . . . We cannot assume that the ordinary working of market forces will necessarily preserve a small firm sector large enough to perform this function in the future. (Cited in Stanworth and Gray, 1991: 1)

With an already receptive foundation, the subsequent ideological swing toward "freeing up" markets in the UK, or more accurately, marketization, in tandem with the growth of new actors propelling this, and the large-scale restructuring of large firms, could have produced changes in production and exchange markets, accentuating the difference. From a trough at the time of the Bolton Report small business numbers began to revive; by the late 1980s they had reached levels – in terms of employment share in manufacturing – of the 1940s (Stanworth and Gray, 1991: 3–7).

The nature of the 1980s transformation in the UK is and will continue to be disputed. We are sympathetic to the view of some who emphasize the role of ideas – and ideology – which is not reducible to interests (Blyth, 2002; Hay, 2006), but corporate and industrial restructuring also changed the structure, and potentially participation rules, of markets in the UK.

Japan also experienced a crisis – or several – in the 1990s and early 2000s, which produced several ideologically conflicting responses. On the one hand, there was an attempt to revive productionism (Tsai, 2006) as well as technology management (Cole and Whittaker, 2006), modifying but not fundamentally altering relational markets and participation norms. On the other hand, there was a succession of new laws promoting "global standards" in accounting, corporate governance, and to some extent competition, with an underlying push toward marketization and financialization (Dore, 2000). Laws changed and new market-creating actors appeared, either locally or from the USA. However, the impact on niche entrepreneurial markets was muted, at least until the 2000s. In other words, it appears that in Japan patterned social relations that frame markets (and benefit incumbents) have been stronger, and legitimized by several decades of postwar economic growth. Attempts to delegitimize these have only been partly successful, and have not produced the enormous number of start-ups that marked the post-"restoration" Meiji period, or the post-World War II turmoil and subsequent high growth period.

Price mechanism

The differences we have just outlined for production markets (or stages) apply also to exchange markets (or stages), in the process of price determination. If the number of competitors is typically small, as we saw in Chapter 5, the number of customers is also limited. Relations between the buyer and seller are frequently ongoing, in both countries, and there appears to be scope for price negotiation.

Our sense is that who is selling the goods matters in both countries, but it matters more in Japan, on the grounds given by the purchasing manager to justify purchase in his company, for example. Moreover, this consideration is brought into the price bargaining more aggressively. Here the liability of newness (or smallness) means the less known or established an entrepreneur, the greater the discount expected to offset the uncertainty. Or more generally, a newcomer or small player will have more to gain from the transaction, so the price will reflect this. There is likely to be some discount in the UK as well, but ideologically, this appears more difficult to justify. In fact, a discount may be built into the norms of purchasing in Japan, at least on the part of the purchasing manager, which is ultimately a reflection of a power difference in a social relationship.[6] For an entrepreneur proud of an

---

[6] There are exceptions, based on individual circumstances, but so well is this known that there are laws aiming at preventing late payment by large customers to small suppliers (a form of enforced discount) – the size categories are defined – and other means of abusing differences in market power. The laws are not known for being particularly effective. Similar but more tentative measures were debated in the UK after widely reported "subby bashing" in the recession of the early 1990s, but were abandoned.

innovative product, it is not easy to swallow these conditions, which can apply to collaborations as well as sales.[7]

In brief, in terms of what can be brought to the market – marketization – as well as who may participate, and the terms of participation and exchange, there appear to be subtle but important differences in the markets for goods and services in the UK and Japan, and these appear to reinforce if not cause many of the differences in entrepreneurship in the two countries. These differences are incorporated in the concepts of "utility" and "relational" markets, respectively. Utility markets are the result, first of disembedding of exchange norms from immediate social relations or networks, and second of their embedding in markets constructed by a variety of actors, institutions, and an ideology emphasizing what is brought to the market rather than who is bringing it. In relational markets, on the other hand, the initial disembedding is weaker, the ideology of utility is also weaker, and entrepreneurial businesses often need to make extra efforts to overcome their liabilities of newness and smallness.

Concluding comments

We began this chapter by summarizing the similarities and differences between entrepreneurship in the UK and Japan. We will not repeat these here. It was important to note the similarities in how the entrepreneurs pursued opportunities and started their businesses, as well as their basic approaches to business, as these contrast not only with some of the popular images of entrepreneurship, but also the policy approach pursued in the UK and Japan, and indeed many other countries (see Chapter 9). Our main focus in this chapter, however, was on explaining the differences. Here we noted the importance of social and cultural factors, but emphasized the nature of markets, focusing on markets for products, services, and businesses. Our findings, we argued, could not be explained convincingly without exploring these. This view is consistent with the "varieties of capitalism" perspective, which sees a big difference between the role of markets in LMEs and CMEs, if not in their characteristics as well.

We looked at what could be traded, who could trade, and the terms of participation and exchange. In the UK more things could be traded,

---

[7] In "relational contracting" on the other hand, norms distributing the benefits of collaboration and contracting may be spelled out.

including businesses themselves. The option of exit in this way was a powerful reinforcer of project entrepreneurship, and its difficulty – not impossibility – in Japan conversely reinforced the lifework approach. As for "who," we argued that market membership and participation was more conditional in Japan. Newcomers might be allowed to bring their wares, but if they were not members, they would be offered lower prices. Gaining full membership was a gradual process. Some steps might be gained by reputation as a scientist or engineer, or by patronage, but the newcomer had to demonstrate that he was not going to upset the rules, and was worthy of membership. This was most easily demonstrated by hard work, and a commitment to furthering that market, a metaphorical preparedness to sweep down the market square after the market.

The liability of newness in the UK was real, but (*a*) there appeared to be fewer dominant players, at least domestically, and (*b*) an ideological acceptance that in principle, at least, participation in markets should be open, and worthiness to participate should not depend on who the entrepreneur was, but on what they were offering. This applied not only in production markets or stages, but in exchange markets as well.

The starting point in the UK and Japan was not the same, but changes from the 1980s were influential in the UK. In Japan large firms have proved more resilient and innovative, which has blunted appeals to elevate the social status of start-ups and small businesses. While pursued in legal reforms recently, neoliberalism, financialization, and marketization have not achieved the same level of dominance by any means, at least in production and exchange markets the entrepreneurs participated in. These differences fed the respective approaches of entrepreneurship, intensifying the differences.

9

Entrepreneurship, Rationality, and Time

Max Weber held that markets are the "archetype of all rational social action" (Weber, 1922/1978: 635). Rational social action requires tools of calculation, which he saw as being particularly well developed in modern accounting methods. These methods can help to calculate expected returns of alternative actions over time. But if project and lifework entrepreneurship are linked to different types of market orientation or embeddedness, as we saw in Chapter 8, they are also linked to different orientations to time. Here we will explore this proposition and its implications for innovation and entrepreneurship policy.

In essence, the argument is as follows. As direct social relations embed market transactions more strongly in lifework entrepreneurship, they appear to influence time orientations in a similar way. Time is, in a sense, embedded in direct social relations. In project entrepreneurship, however, it becomes disembedded from them, to the extent that social relations become organized around "programmed time." Weber's tools of calculation were used to bring about this inversion, which in parallel with "marketization," came to the fore with "projectification" in the UK from the 1980s.

We argued in Chapter 8 that marketization has had limited impact on entrepreneurial markets in Japan to date, despite some rather aggressive governmental promotion of a new institutional environment. We have the same question regarding projectification, potentially another lever of change. More generally, we ask whether the differences between project and lifework entrepreneurship are essentially the differences of era – postindustrial UK versus industrial Japan – and whether Japan will move toward project entrepreneurship with its postindustrial transition.

Innovation and entrepreneurship policy in both the UK and Japan have been strongly influenced by the USA, especially (certain interpretations of) the successes of Silicon Valley. Will the project entrepreneur (not necessarily the UK variant) eventually come to dominate the Japanese entrepreneurial landscape? Is the UK caught between the project entrepreneurship of Silicon Valley and lifework entrepreneurship? Should policy aim to promote such project entrepreneurship? Here we enter a debate which has featured in varieties of capitalism writing, namely institutional convergence, but from an entrepreneurship perspective. We do not dismiss the policy emphases of the UK and Japan, but we argue for a more nuanced approach which also recognizes the potential contribution of existing approaches to entrepreneurship.

Rationality, time, and "projectification"

The concepts of "project" and "lifework" entrepreneurship encompass another underlying difference, which has remained implicit in our analysis so far, namely different orientations to time. The time frame of project entrepreneurship, it will already be clear, is shorter than that of lifework entrepreneurship with regards the entrepreneurs' involvement in their business, and potentially in the development of the business itself. "Short-term" and "long-term" do not fully capture the differences, however.

We argued in Chapter 8 that lifework entrepreneurship takes place in markets which are more strongly embedded in direct social relations than project entrepreneurship, whose markets are "disembedded" from direct social relations, though still embedded in a different way. We believe we can make a similar argument regarding time; the orientation toward time in lifework entrepreneurship is strongly influenced by social relations, whereas in project entrepreneurship this influence is minimized. In an extreme form the reverse is the case – social relations are consciously nurtured and organized in an orientation to time which is calculative and rational in an instrumental way.

This latter orientation assigns a monetary evaluation to time, through tools like net present value. While the (spot) market is seen as a means of ensuring the most efficient allocation of resources at a particular point in time, these tools extend the quest for efficiency over time, or efficiency which is not time-dependent. While project entrepreneurs do not necessarily use them in a formal sense, it is no surprise that such techniques – including the spread of quarterly accounting – accelerated with the marketization and financialization from the 1980s.

In addition, we can identify further related developments, including the growth of "project-based organizations" (Lundin and Söderholm, 1995; Sydow, Lindkvist, and DeFillippi, 2004), "project-led organizations" (Davies and Hobday, 2005), "projectification of the firm" (Midler, 1995), and indeed the "projectification of society" (Lundin and Söderholm, 1998; Ekstedt et al. 1999). According to Hodgson (2007: 222):

It is also in relatively recent years – particularly since the 1980s – that the tools, techniques and principles of project management have been promoted and utilized in sectors beyond the traditional engineering and construction base of the discipline. Projects have been promoted as universally applicable templates for the deliberate integration of diverse specialisms, enabling the organization of flexible, autonomous and knowledgeable individuals into temporary teams for the timely, efficient and effective accomplishment of defined goals.

These industries include the creative arts, health care, IT, and many others. As an indicator of "projectification," the Project Management Institute, formulator of PMBOK® (Project Management Body of Knowledge) saw its membership surge from less than 10,000 in the late 1980s to 220,000 by 2004, with almost two-thirds of members reporting project management to be their "primary profession" (Hodgson, 2007). Project management can, of course, be developed in the context of long-term relationships and resource commitments (as can net present value, and indeed market transactions). As "projectification," however, it becomes not only a quest to enhance efficiency in the deployment of resources, but an ideological belief that long-term commitments threaten to undermine this efficiency.

"Projectification" has accelerated the spread of "nonstandard" employment practices, and the rise of the "portfolio," project-based career, or in Heckscher's (1995) terms the replacement of "communities of loyalty" with "communities of purpose." Thus project entrepreneurship may be part of a broader set of transformations which have been called "projectification," a feature of which is not simply a short time frame, but the positioning of time as an instrument to calculate the merits of allocating resources to one project relative to another. This is the very calculativeness referred to by Weber.

A further related trend is the rise of audits. In *The Audit Society*, Power (1997) argues that the rise of auditing in the 1980s was linked to political demands for accountability and control. It began with privatization and growing private sector participation in markets in which the government was the direct or ultimate customer, and then spread throughout society:

During the late 1980s and early 1990s, the word "audit" began to be used in Britain with growing frequency in a wide variety of contexts. In addition to the regulation of private company accounting by financial audit, practices of environmental audit, value for money audit, management audit, forensic audit, data audit, intellectual property audit ... emerged, and to varying degrees, acquired a degree of institutional stability and acceptance. Increasing numbers of individuals and organizations found themselves subject to new or more intensive accounting and audit requirements. (Power, 1997: 3)

Audits, of course, have the goal of ensuring efficient deployment of resources as well, and value for money over a specific time period. Like quarterly accounting, audits seek – very imperfectly, according to Power – to promote transparency, so that those with resources to invest or deploy can make informed decisions to go ahead or switch them to where they will get better returns. Power is right to stress demands for accountability and control in audits. However, we would argue that an underlying and common theme across all these developments, including audits, is *choice*.

The connection with project entrepreneurship should be clear. The entrepreneur's decision to switch jobs, change careers, start a business, or advise a portfolio of businesses is the result of a series of choices which one is *expected* to make in order to satisfy preferences which are personal and may change over time. Decisions, such as that to start a business, are kept under review.[1] Failure to do so is, well, a failure.

When people start a business with others, or hire an employee, it will be in the expectation that they are exercising – and will continue to exercise – their own choice, and will do so through periodic monitoring and review. Rather than building up too many resources in-house, moreover, ad hoc collaboration, a part of which is projectification, offers an attractive alternative, including the advantage of cheap experimentation. If it does not work out, alternatives can be pursued. This might be one factor in differences in collaboration, which we looked at in Chapter 7.

And what of the lifework entrepreneurs? Here there is clearly a different orientation to time. The unit of evaluation is much longer, because of a different logic; time is embedded in social relations, and social relations determine how time is used. In small businesses this is often seen in heroic

---

[1] We should note, moreover, that part of the review was whether the business was still "fun." In their open responses to the first survey, quite a few of the UK entrepreneurs commented on the importance of this.

efforts to fill an order despite unforeseen problems, or in efforts to produce a new product after a public commitment to do so by a certain time. The use of time in such instances takes place in the context of ongoing social relations, and is quite different from attempts to promote allocative efficiency through disembedding, thus allowing choice to be exercised.

Project management has spread in Japan, of course, as have audits and performance management. Despite attempts to use the latter as instruments of efficiency and choice in the public sector and the interstices of the public and private sector, however such practices tend to clash with another logic, namely that of *commitment*, which is ultimately the logic of lifework entrepreneurship. Here choice is exercised at certain points (such as joining a company or, in the case of our entrepreneurs, leaving such a company), but to a large extent social approval rests not on a process of constant monitoring and reevaluation to enable choice, but in the way commitments are adhered to and carried out. There is a strong echo of Weber's concept of vocation, which is freely chosen and adhered to, ultimately as an end in itself.

As mentioned in Chapter 8, one way for an entrepreneur to gain acceptance in the marketplace is to appear strongly committed to a chosen path, through discipline and very hard work. There is considerable flexibility within these parameters; if that path is ultimately blocked by technological obsolescence or a dramatic recession, for instance, a radical change in direction is condoned, or even applauded. But the circumstances tend to be external, and not simply a product of personal choice.

What triggered the change was the Kobe earthquake. The factories and machines were all destroyed, but I didn't lose any employees. I felt I was really lucky and I wanted to help people, and so I began this new business. I was just reading a book about OTEC [ocean thermal energy conversion] at the time by a professor at Saga University and thought that's what I want to do. (J25)

We aim to be a marathon runner, not a sprinter. I'm 58 now and I will think about retirement soon. My successor will be chosen from the six directors. They are in their 30s; I appointed them two years ago....IPO to sell the company is an American way of doing business. (J21)

These interpretations are intended to express *relative tendencies*, and not to imply that all the UK entrepreneurs were constantly reevaluating their choices, while all the Japanese entrepreneurs were doggedly pursuing their commitments. Rather, there was a tendency in the UK toward periodic reevaluation as to whether their activities were meeting the entrepreneurs' own personal goals, and in Japan toward the exercise of choice *within* the development of their business. No doubt there was overlap between the two groups, and movements along the scale depending on circumstances. During founding and initial opportunity pursuit, in particular, the differences might not have been very great, as a good deal of commitment was required on the one hand, and many choices needed to be made on the other. Over time, however, the entrepreneurs appeared to diverge, moving toward a project or lifework orientation, respectively.

Time orientations and venture capital

As with markets, we can think of time as a continuum, with "programmed time" at one end and "open-ended time" at the other. Location on this continuum has important implications for financing, particularly in the form of venture capital. Unsurprisingly, few of the Japanese entrepreneurs sought venture capital, either at start-up or subsequently (6.8 percent sought and got it, 4.1 percent sought and did not get it; for high performers the figures were 7.6 percent and 5.2 percent). With venture capital, time-based goals for exit and milestones to get there are paramount; time is programmed and social relations are arranged around achieving the milestones. This sharply contradicts the tendency for commitment, and embeddedness of time in social relations. In fact, as some of the Japanese case recipients of venture funding commented, it was the nature of venture funding which had been changed rather than their own orientation to time:

At the beginning I had most of the shares. My older brother had some, and a couple of others as well. In 1983 the president of JAFCO came to visit . . . They invested ¥27 million, which gave them a 20 percent stake. They still have these shares but the stake is now worth less than 10 percent. I said I wasn't interested in an investment consortium they were putting together because these are wound up in 10 years, and I wasn't confident that I would be able to IPO by then. This is a manufacturing business. . . . I can't say this too openly yet, but I'm hoping to IPO by late 2005, or 2006 at the latest. (J1, interview in September 2004)

In 1985 or 86, S. Bank Lease Capital invested ¥10 million. Now they are the biggest shareholder, with ¥15 million, and I am next, followed by S. (J4, also interviewed in September 2004)[2]

---

[2] Japanese venture capital companies typically acquire 10 percent or less of the capital of the firms they invest in as well, so have little influence over the management of the businesses. They may exit through IPO – seldom M&A – but it can take a long time to get there (Kutsuna, 2002).

Perhaps surprisingly, few of the UK entrepreneurs had sought venture capital funding, either (10 percent sought and got it, 7.5 percent sought and did not get it; for high performers the figures were 11.5 percent and 12.4 percent). It is not surprising, however, if we recall the emergent way they went about creating opportunities and businesses. It appears that relatively few fitted the typical requirements of venture capital, and some that did could not accept the terms, either for stakeholders, or themselves:

So we put together a business plan and the VC said yes, we've got a deal here. I'm a little concerned about the lack of experience you've got on the Board, so we'll put a Chairman in place. And we said fine. And they said what we will aim to do is in about three years time we'll sell the business and we'll all be very rich. And we stopped the meeting and said what do you mean? They said our exit strategy is about three years and because of the shares you'll have you'll be very rich, and we'll move on. We said who will you sell the business to? It doesn't matter they said. And we said we've done a lot of research into this and the only people who would buy this business would be a hostile bid from our competitors. Well yes, fine, as long as they pay the money. Well no we said because any hostile bid would probably buy it for its assets, products and goodwill and close the business down. Yep they said, they would pay the redundancy. No we said, we have an allegiance and responsibility to our employees who we are going to take this business forward with. And we walked out of the meeting.... It was a mismatch of exit strategies. (UK18)

In fact, it is possible to imagine more extreme – extended – positions on *both sides* of the continuum. Toward the programmed-time pole is a focused pursuit of opportunity, rapid growth, and exit with large capital gains (in theory). This might entail "24/7" working, with the hope of switching to a less frantic lifestyle in the future. Even further, we might envisage entrepreneurs engaged in arbitrage or trading-related activities. Toward the open-ended time pole, we might envisage types of entrepreneurship in which choices and commitments are made not just in the light of an immediate social network, but to parents or ancestors of previous generations on the one hand, and future generations on the other, as might be the case in indigenous entrepreneurship. In other words, time could be embedded across generations.[3]

---

[3] Of Maori entrepreneurship in New Zealand, Tapsell and Woods (2008: 18) write: "[T]he challenge...is to balance the individual desire to be entrepreneurial (autonomy) with the need and desire to contribute to the enhancement of Maori (connectivity) be it with whanau (family), hapu (subtribe) or iwi (tribe). To ensure that connectivity and avoid the perils of autonomy and the crises of the colonisation, Maori entrepreneurial models cannot focus solely on the opportunity-seeking potiki; they must successfully integrate the genealogical check and balance of the potiki, namely the elder-rangatira."

Another way of looking at the respective logics of choice and commitment underpinning project and lifework entrepreneurship, and their different orientations to time, is to see them as two logics inherent in entrepreneurship itself. In other words, we could see entrepreneurship as embodying both choices and commitments, with tensions and trade-offs between them. In some contexts – for example, countries at specific times – there will be greater pressures to emphasize choices, and in others, commitments. If the context changes, so might the relative emphases.

Different eras?

In 2005, a hostile takeover bid was played out in and by the mass media in Japan; upstart internet business Livedoor attempted to take over established media company Nippon Broadcasting System in what was cast as a battle of the "new" versus the "old" Japan. In 1996, Tokyo University student Takafumi Horie founded the internet advertising/home page company On the Edge. Becoming Cyber Click in 1998, it listed on the Mothers Exchange in 2000, acquired the free internet provider Livedoor in 2002, and adopted that name in 2004. Livedoor pursued ambitious growth by a succession of acquisitions using frequent stock splits, becoming an investment company with IT constituting a minor part of its business (Iwasaki, 2006).

The t-shirted president Horie and other directors were flamboyant and courted media attention. Their goals, ways of doing business, employment relations, and personal lives were quite different from those of firms founded in the postwar high-growth period, and appeared to be in tune with the dreams of at least some of the younger generation. They were helped by – and in turn pushed – changes in Japanese law regarding the establishment of holding companies, new financial instruments, and mergers and acquisitions and takeovers. Indeed, many saw the IT, financial services and consulting entrepreneurs of Roppongi Hills as harbingers of a new type of business in Japan, focused on rapid growth, financial gain, temporary business structures, and shifting short-term commitments.

Perhaps some of the differences between the two countries are the result of comparing postindustrial UK with industrial Japan. Indeed, responses to the open questions of the first survey portrayed the Japanese entrepreneurs as struggling to break into a relatively stable postwar industrial order dominated by large players. By contrast, the UK responses painted a picture of entrepreneurs navigating turbulence, corporate restructuring, deregulation, and increasing openness. Japan began to experience some of this around the turn of the century, but we cannot assume it influenced the behavior of established entrepreneurs and their businesses, or even new businesses in old industries.

Stinchcombe (1965) held that organizations are formed in ways that broader social relations allow them to be formed, and that once formed, they continue to embody the social relations of that time into the future.[4] Thus, textiles businesses founded in the nineteenth century had different structures from automobile companies founded in the twentieth century. In Japan, Dore (1973) argued, late development meant that the time lag between the emergence of modern textile mills and automobile plants was much smaller, and hence textiles moved more quickly into the twentieth-century pattern of organization and social relations. The upheavals and reshaping of social relations after World War II, moreover, further reduced the differences. The characteristics of Japanese entrepreneurship we have described are likely to have been shaped by Japan's postwar manufacturing experience, and the social relations of that time.

But what about newer industries, like financial services, IT, and biotechnology? Does Livedoor symbolize a change going on in Japan as well?[5] There is some evidence pointing to institutional change in venture capital, and business listing on Japan's new exchanges (cf. Sako, 2007). Moreover, our limited interviews in biotechnology start-ups and spinouts suggest founding and management styles shaped by the high education levels of founders and employees, with project-based working and greater employee fluidity than in most of our *UK* sample.

We originally intended to compare manufacturing with nonmanufacturing high-tech entrepreneurs and their businesses in both countries, with the expectation of finding differences between computer and IT services on the one hand, and manufacturing on the other. Unfortunately, we cannot do this convincingly, and differences can only be suggestive.[6] In

---

[4] "Organizations which have purposes that can be efficiently reached with the socially possible organizational forms tend to be founded during the period in which they become possible. Then, both because they can function effectively with those organizational forms, and because the forms tend to become institutionalized, the basic structure of the organization tends to remain relatively stable" (Stinchcombe, 1965: 153).

[5] Or is such a change being suppressed? Horie and his colleagues were arrested on charges of reporting irregularities. Their fall from grace was seen by some as a reassertion of "old" business values, although it did nothing to stop the spread of takeover bids.

[6] First, there was an average difference of only eight years between the founding of the manufacturing and non-manufacturing businesses in both countries. (The mean and median founding dates for the UK high-tech nonmanufacturing businesses were 1988 and 1989 respectively, compared with 1980 and 1982 for manufacturing. For the Japanese businesses they were 1980 and 1982, and 1972 and 1973, respectively.) Second, and more critically,

terms of personal business objectives, for instance, "build a business which will continue to exist without me" was significantly less important for non-manufacturing entrepreneurs in Japan, but public listing was significantly more important (and might mean something different). UK nonmanufacturing entrepreneurs, too, were less concerned about building a business to exist without them, and were even less concerned with contributions to science and technology or society. There was slightly more emphasis on financial objectives (and financial incentives for employees) in both countries.

That said, differences between the countries again stood out. Japanese entrepreneurs rated public listing and contribution to science and technology significantly higher, for instance. Perceived competitive advantages and limitations, too, were very different; the UK entrepreneurs rated established reputation, quality, design, and speed much higher, while the Japanese entrepreneurs rated implementation of new technology, acquisition and protection of IPR, and availability of manual and clerical labor much higher. These figures replicate those of the manufacturers.

Evidence of change is thus anecdotal. There does seem to have been change in both countries, but there also appears to be continuity in terms of social relations as well, particularly in Japan.

The shadow(s) of Silicon Valley

Governments in many countries have become aware of the contribution of small businesses to economic and social well-being, and have introduced policies to promote these contributions (Storey, 2003). In many cases these policies envisage a particular kind of entrepreneurship, directly or indirectly linked to the Silicon Valley phenomenon. But if entrepreneurship is embedded as we have described it, what are the prospects of such policies achieving their goals? If context does matter, should entrepreneurship policy seek to change the context or change to fit the context? This is the inherent dilemma of entrepreneurship policy.

Complementing their view of the emergence of the entrepreneurial economy (see Chapter 1), Audretsch and Beckmann (2007) describe the emergence of "entrepreneurship policy," which they distinguish from traditional small-firm policy. Public policy in the large-firm "Solow economy," they argue, tried to resolve tensions between the benefits and costs of scale and economic concentration. Small firms were seen either as

eighty-two nonmanufacturing high-tech businesses in the UK satisfied all the requirements of founding date, industry and size, but only twenty-four in Japan did so. This severely limits what we can do with the data, especially given the diversity of services represented.

expendable or in need of protection and support. They see a transition period in which public policy shifted to R&D or "knowledge investments," which produced poor returns, before swinging behind entrepreneurship in the 1990s: "These new policies are not designed to support existing businesses, as was the case with previous small business policies, or just to invest in the creation of knowledge. Instead, the new entrepreneurship policies focus on knowledge commercialization; that is, they support the creation of business ideas" (Audretsch and Beckmann, 2007: 42). Enabling policies at the state, regional or even local level have become more important, with a focus on creating a context or ecosystem for entrepreneurship, as well as entrepreneurship itself. A primary example of this is cluster policies (Audretsch, 2005).

Lundström and Stevenson (2002, 2005) also contrast traditional small-firm or SME policy and entrepreneurship policy. The former, they argue, emphasizes existing firms and is generally the province of a single government agency. The latter emphasizes individuals, as well as the contexts which influence individuals' skills, motivations, and opportunities. Rather than belonging to a single government agency, policies are pursued across agencies, in central, regional, and local governments.

In their comparative study of entrepreneurship policy in thirteen countries, Lundström and Stevenson found that some countries have simply added entrepreneurship policy to existing small business policy, some have pursued "niche" policies for specific groups such as ethnic minorities or entrepreneurs with technological experience, some have emphasized new firm creation, and some have pursued entrepreneurship policy "holistically," attempting to strengthen entrepreneurship culture and capacity. The UK falls into the "holistic" category, along with the Netherlands and Finland, but other countries are moving in this direction as well.[7]

Such policies have not been created *ex nihilo*. Indeed a remarkable feature has been attempts by both industrialized and developing countries to learn from exemplars. Given its resurgence in the 1990s, these tend to be located in the USA, with none more imposing than Silicon Valley.[8] Intel founder Moore caricatures the recipe as:

---

[7] As Storey (2003: 477) notes, Margaret Thatcher's "enterprise culture" was aimed at all individuals in the UK, while many Continental European countries targeted groups like young people. Japan was not part of Lundström and Stevenson's study, but could probably be seen as combining elements of the first three types.

[8] Other US exemplars include North Carolina's Research Triangle, and Austin, Texas (cf. Smilor, Gibson, and Kozmetsky, 1989).

Combine liberal amounts of

Technology
Entrepreneurs
Capital, and
Sunshine

Add one (1)

University
Stir vigorously.[9]

In Japan there have been significant legal changes, premised on promoting a new type of entrepreneur and entrepreneurial business – fleet-footed, responsive, flexible, independent, providing attractive employment conditions, and participating in networks which power regional economies. This image is depicted in a publication by the SME Agency (Chusho kigyocho, 1999), for example, explaining and defending the passage of the new SME Basic Law. The passage of the revised SME Basic Law through the "SME and Venture Parliament" in 1999 itself capped a decade of new legislation to encourage such business.[10] It was followed by further legislation aimed at reforming Japan's national innovation system, including METI's Industrial Cluster Plan and MEXT's Knowledge Cluster Plan. Entrepreneurship has clearly arrived in Japan's central ministries, both as a target of promotion and as a policy mindset. Inspiration has been drawn from the USA and the UK.

The images of old and new are cogently captured by Sano and Kitachi (2000), whose "past entrepreneurial businesses" – readily recognizable from this study – grow gradually to sales of ¥3–10 billion after twenty to thirty years, are niche-oriented, closed, rely on bank finance, and are dependent on the entrepreneurs' total commitment.[11] "21st century

---

[9] Moore and Davis (2004: 9). This caricature is preceded by a criticism of such policies: "What 'works' right now in this dynamic, regional, high-technology economy tells us little of how precisely Silicon Valley came to be just such a place, or how any such place comes into being. The potential disaster lies in the fact that these static, descriptive efforts culminate in policy recommendations and analytical tomes that resemble recipes or magic potions."

[10] For example, the New Business Law (1989), the Temporary Law for Smooth Movement of SMEs into New Business Areas (1993; 1995), Law to Promote Creative SME Activities (1995), tax reforms for angel investors (1997), University, etc. Technology Transfer Promotion Law (1998), New Business Creation Promotion Law (1998), the SME Management Innovation Law (1999), and the Industry Revitalization Law (1999): cf. Hamada and Asai (2000).

[11] They have little good to say about the "old" type. Whether it be a corporate spinout or a self-started business, there are multiple and conflicting objectives, reliance on hustle, and development of a business plan only under duress. Second-generation successors are even more unfocused, they believe.

entrepreneurial businesses," by contrast, will grow to 5–10 billion after three to five years, will be open, global, shareholder-centered, performance-based, project-oriented and led by "producer" entrepreneurs. They will begin with a business concept, which is developed into a business plan, and only then will a company be constructed. The business plan will enable others to buy into the project, speeding the accumulation of resources. Needless to say, the plan will have clear milestones and rapid growth will allow investors to exit through IPO or M&A. Risk is dealt with by the growth of risk capital. No empirical evidence is offered for this shift, but the vision appears to be strongly influenced by the USA.

It would seem that small businesses and the majority of entrepreneurs have emerged from the shadow of large firms only to fall under another shadow – that of Silicon Valley. In fact, there appear to be two shadows; partial interpretations of what has made Silicon Valley such a dynamic incubator of new businesses and technologies, and the shadow these interpretations cast as they find their way into academic and media discourse in other countries, and especially into policy. Those who fall under these shadows and do not fit the image are either ignored, derided as being "old," or criticized for their poverty of ambition.

There are at least two dangers in this. The first, general danger is its partialness, summed up by Hughes (2007), who likens recent EU innovation policy to a "cargo cult." He particularly criticizes the emphases on R&D-intensive high-tech sectors, spin-offs from the science base, start-ups, and private sector venture capital, as misrepresenting the sources of US knowledge-led productivity growth. Rather, he suggests, we should be looking more at the influence of ICT in user sectors, contributions, and transformations of existing firms, the interplay between large and small firms, the diverse role of universities including their "public space function" (cf. Chapter 7), the role of other sources of capital (especially internal, angel, and government sources) and the role of government procurement in "soft" starts.

The second, specific danger is the type of entrepreneurial business implicitly or explicitly promoted. It is typically closer to the project pole and programmed time pole than most of our UK entrepreneurs, let alone the Japanese entrepreneurs. It tends to be agnostic with regards to previous work experience; stresses a clear business concept with a formal business plan, and a narrowing of goals and hence motivations; focuses almost entirely on new start-ups; promotes rapid growth in a short time frame and the organization of social relations to achieve this; favors a home-run product or service; and as a result, encourages a contingent relation to the business of the entrepreneur herself or himself. This is quite different from the type of entrepreneurship we have encountered in Japan and the UK in this book.[12]

Should the aim of policy be to encourage such entrepreneurship, changing the context to do so (as might be the case in "holistic" entrepreneurship policy)? Or should policy be modified to fit the existing context? This is the crucial dilemma of entrepreneurship policy.

On the one hand, there is no reason to suppose that what already exists is the best that can exist or can be aspired to. The Silicon Valley-inspired models favored by policy should be recognized as a distinct type of (project) entrepreneurship. In this type the increasingly contingent relationship of the entrepreneur to the business is counterbalanced by ongoing institutions in which it develops, from universities to funding institutions and legal and business services. Continuity consists of the entrepreneurial concept and the context; the business is the temporary vehicle. Seen as a separate type, there is a case to be made for pluralism, and for nurturing it.[13]

On the other hand, there will be costs – beyond high monetary costs – of promoting a specific type of entrepreneurship and innovation which fails to build on what already exists. Rather than positive sum pluralism, the result could be increasing churning of ideas and businesses, with little substantial contribution to economic growth and well-being. There are also potential opportunity costs in *not* promoting entrepreneurship which *does* match the environment, by failing to capitalize on mutually reinforcing interaction between entrepreneur and environment. In this case, however, the strengths and weaknesses of the particular type of entrepreneurship must still be recognized.

Japan's lifework entrepreneurship has some obvious strengths. It results in the buildup of technological competences which can help support a broad manufacturing base, as well as the ongoing livelihoods of those working in the businesses. Its weaknesses are frequently a lack of focus, over-reliance on heroic efforts of the entrepreneur, and limited market

---

[12] It also appears to be different from the majority of entrepreneurial businesses in the USA itself. The proportion of early stage technology development funded by venture capital in the USA is estimated at about 2.3 percent, compared with internal funds of 47.2 percent, 23.9 percent by angels, 3.9 percent by universities and 22.7 percent by federal and state governments (Hughes, 2007, citing Branscomb and Auerswald, 2002).

[13] As Brown and Linden (2008) note in their global semiconductor industry study: "In both the United States and Japan, major semiconductor and electronics producers undertake a great deal of R&D, but less than half of the ideas generated internally are developed further. Startups can be an important vehicle for exploiting ideas that industry leaders overlook, but Japan's startup environment is weak, particularly in the semiconductor industry."

recognition and access. Supportive entrepreneurship policy here could include public procurement to aid innovative "soft" starts and encouragement of flexible and diverse interaction with universities, including entrepreneur, successor, and employee education and training.

Strengths of the UK variety of project entrepreneurship include a sensitivity to potential market opportunities, relative nimbleness in achieving new combinations, allocative efficiency, and facilitation of choice. Its weaknesses are the mirror image; growth can be shallow, volatile, and difficult to sustain over the long term. Almost one in five of the 2002 Cambridge CBR survey respondents were no longer around in 2004, just two years later. Half of those which had disappeared – younger and smaller businesses – had failed or closed, and half – growth-oriented, innovating, middle-sized businesses – had been acquired (Cosh and Hughes, 2007c: 16).[14] Policy in this case might also include public procurement to facilitate "soft" starts and reduce early closures, the encouragement of nonproduct innovation, reexamination of the availability of "patient" capital for growth and innovation, and perhaps even (founding team) partner "counseling," as suggested by Quince (1998).

In both cases, existing businesses can provide a platform for significant growth and innovation, since entrepreneurs can concentrate on opportunity creation without worrying about business creation (although the difficulties of reconfiguring an existing business may be considerable) and an immediate income stream. This is a potential strength which could be leveraged, in addition to encouraging start-ups.

Can either country produce truly radical innovations through their respective styles of entrepreneurship? Instinctively, we would say "why not?" But we would also question whether there is too much emphasis on radical innovation, and too little recognition of the importance of incremental innovation. This is less glamorous to policy-makers, however, who are themselves coming under pressure to establish entrepreneurial credentials, to perform in project conditions, and to demonstrate that they have absorbed "global standard" best-practice concepts from abroad. As a result, tensions in innovation and entrepreneurship policy are almost inevitable.

---

[14] Likewise Garnsey and Cannon-Brookes (1993) examined the fate of 342 "Cambridge Phenomenon" businesses identified by Segal, Quince, and Wickstead (1985), and found that while failure rates were low (3.7 percent per year on average), few had grown beyond fifty employees. By 2002 one-third had become subsidiaries, often of foreign enterprises. Mergers and acquisitions might bring benefits of scale and access to new resources and markets, but they may also reduce competition, mask underlying weaknesses, or – with post-acquisition integration problems – create new ones.

Concluding comments

This chapter began by considering orientations to time in approaches to entrepreneurship. In parallel with our discussion of the embeddedness of markets, we recognized the embeddedness of time, or "programmed time" in project entrepreneurship, and "open-ended time" in lifework entrepreneurship. The former was linked to developments in the UK in the 1980s. We then considered another sense of time – eras – and whether the types of entrepreneurship were in fact differences between postindustrial Britain, and industrial Japan. Unfortunately, our data did not allow us to explore emerging industries adequately, but evidence of change in Japan was partial. In fact, a counterargument could be made, for continuity in newer industries, reinforced by entry through diversification of existing businesses.

Policy attempts to change entrepreneurship and innovation in the UK and Japan have been inspired directly or indirectly by the USA. We referred to "shadows of Silicon Valley" cast on entrepreneurs in both countries. In a positive scenario, this might nurture pluralism in entrepreneurship types. However, it might also result in frustration, wasted resources, and churning with little economic or social gain.

It is one thing to envisage pockets of "Silicon Valley" entrepreneurship developing in supportive institutional environments – or clusters – but it is quite another to see this becoming the mainstream of entrepreneurship. We do not see this happening in the near future, either in Japan or the UK (or even the USA). Routes to entrepreneurship will remain varied, and most entrepreneurs will start out toward the "imitator" end of the spectrum, with "soft" starts and multiple objectives, and learning by doing. Most entrepreneurs will not want to see themselves as a contingent part of their project or lifework from the outset because it is an expression of them. For better or worse then, many entrepreneurs in both Japan and the UK will go about creating opportunities and businesses outside the limelight. Many of the differences we have described between UK and Japanese entrepreneurship will persist, moreover. We may legitimately talk about "varieties of entrepreneurship," just as we do about "varieties of capitalism."

Final observations

In the introduction of this book we asked a number of questions, including: Are entrepreneurs the same everywhere? Do they strive for the same things? Are the processes of entrepreneurship similar? Are they equally collaborative? Or are all of these shaped by their environments? If so, how?

We have seen that entrepreneurs are not the same everywhere. Some of the things they strive for are the same, some are different. Likewise, some of the broad processes of entrepreneurship are similar, particularly in initial opportunity and business creation, and in constructing a principles-based platform for business, but many of the processes – including founding team relations, competitive advantage emphases, HRM, and leadership, and the extent of collaboration – are quite different. These reflect different underlying logics – of "responsivity" versus "control" and "choice" versus "commitment" – and orientations – ultimately "project" versus "lifework." Entrepreneurship undoubtedly is shaped by its environment, and we have paid particular attention to social relations, institutions – especially markets – and time. But have we gone too far in emphasizing the importance of (national) contexts? Perhaps, but then again, this might be a necessary corrective to a pendulum swing which places great emphasis on freedom of action, along with universality of entrepreneurship processes, especially in policy debates.

In their discussion of institutions and entrepreneurship, Hwang and Powell (2005: 203) note how entrepreneurship, once associated with marginal groups, has now become not only accepted, but actively encouraged. "This transformation, in which the concept and practice of entrepreneurship is enshrined with virtuous status is a potent act of institutionalization." Institutionalization includes the phenomenal growth in the teaching of entrepreneurship in business schools, research commercialization activities, supporting services and policy promotion, not to mention writing about entrepreneurship. They add:

Critical to this growth and celebration of entrepreneurship is the reframing of all manner of activities as entrepreneurial. . . . (A) diverse array of activities that have long been regarded as "tilting at windmills" have been redefined as entrepreneurial. Indeed the very notion that research on institutions, things we tend to regard as relatively fixed, durable, and potent, can inform the study of entrepreneurship is further evidence of this expansion. We find some considerable irony in the growth in usage in the scholarly literature of the term "institutional entrepreneur." (Hwang and Powell, 2005: 204)

This raises the profile and expectations of individual agency. The entrepreneur comes in from the shadowy fringes, to claim center stage. As this happens, we must be careful not to forget some of the systemic forces which shape entrepreneurship in different countries.

We have been cautious in our assessment of whether entrepreneurship in Japan will become projectified. In some pockets such as financial services this may already be happening, but as we saw with venture capital, projectification itself may well be accommodated to lifework entrepreneurship. Varieties of entrepreneurship are real, and are likely to be durable.

DESIGN, METHODS, ANALYSIS, AND INTERPRETATION: AN ACT OF SENSEMAKING

Appendix 1 sets out the research design, methods, analysis, and interpretation. The first section simply outlines the design and data set, the second section examines some methodological issues relating to the analysis and interpretation, and the third section briefly looks at our sense of balance between "agency" and "structure," or entrepreneurs and their environments. Overall, we set out some of the distinctive features of this research, as well as common ground with other research on entrepreneurship and comparative organization.

Research design and data set

This research was originally stimulated by a survey by Momose and Morishita in Japan in 1996, published in 1997. It was sent to the CEOs of 2314 "entrepreneurial businesses" selected from the *1996 nen ban Nikkei bencha bijinesu nenkan* (Nikkei Entrepreneurial Business Annual, 1996), and Toyo keizai's *Kaisha shikiho jojo, tento kaisha ban'96* (Listed and Over-the-Counter Company Quarterly 1996) and *Kaisha shikiho mijojo kaisha ban'96* (Quarterly Unlisted Company Edition 1996). Criteria were: businesses founded since 1965; innovative, distinctive businesses; growth orientation espoused by the owner-founder; and customer-oriented. Most were independent of business group affiliation, but a small number of group companies which met all the other criteria were included. The questionnaire for this survey was constructed without a view to international comparisons. The valid response rate was 13.3 percent.

Discussions between Whittaker and Momose led to an interest in a UK comparison. The problem of identifying a matching sample in the UK, where there was no similar category of "entrepreneurial (*bencha*) business," led us to focus on CEOs of businesses in "high-tech" industries, where innovative, entrepreneurial behavior was likely to be widespread. We used the definition of "high-tech" industries created by Butchart (1987), which had been applied successfully in a number of other studies (such as Hughes and Moore, 1998). It includes industries with high R&D intensity, and a high proportion of scientists, professional engineers, and technicians in the workforce (Table A1.1).

The UK sample was selected from single-site, independent businesses in these industries which were listed on the Dun and Bradstreet database in January 1998. Half were in manufacturing, a quarter in computer services, and a quarter in "other services." A quarter had fewer than 20 employees, half had 20–99, and a quarter had 100–199. The UK questionnaire was sent to the CEOs of 2000 businesses who were asked to fill in the questionnaire themselves, as in the Japanese survey. The response rate was 28.6 percent, but some returns were subsequently excluded because their activities did not match their database industry code.

The Japanese survey had a higher proportion of larger businesses. And although the broad sectoral compositions (manufacturing, computer services, and other services) were reasonably similar, at an industry level the match was less tight. In the end, as a result of returns to the second survey (see below), we decided to focus on high-tech *manufacturing*. Further, some of the questions in the UK survey had been modified in the light of analysis of the Japanese survey, and to ensure

Table A1.1 High-tech industries

1992 SIC code	Activity
Manufacturing	
24.16	Plastics in primary forms
24.17	Synthetic rubber in primary forms
24.41	Basic pharmaceutical products
24.42	Pharmaceutical preparations
30.01	Office machinery
30.02	Computers and other information processing equipment
31.10	Electric motors, generators, and transformers
31.20	Electricity distribution and control apparatus
32.10	Electronic valves, tubes, and other electronic components
32.20	Telephone and telegraph apparatus and equipment, and radio and electronic capital goods
33.10	Medical and surgical equipment and orthopaedic appliances
33.20	Instruments and appliances for measuring, checking, testing, navigating, and other purposes
33.30	Industrial process control equipment
33.40/2	Optical precision instruments
33.40/3	Photographic and cinematographic equipment
35.30	Aircraft and spacecraft
Services	
64.20	Telecommunications
72.10	Hardware consultancy
72.20	Software consultancy and supply
72.30	Data processing
72.40	Database activities
72.60	Other computer-related activities
73.10	Research and development on natural sciences and engineering
73.20	Research and development on social services and humanities

Note: SIC = standard industrial classification
Source: Modified from Butchart (1987)

questions were relevant and meaningful to UK entrepreneurs. Overall, this limited our ability to use the first survey for comparative purposes, and we decided to focus our analysis of this survey on founders' backgrounds and the founding process. This includes age, education, work experience, management experience, and job-changing experience – why they left their former business, help from their former business, motivations for starting their new business, and how and with whom they started their business, resources for starting the business, and so on. Here the data are largely comparable, and some of it is presented in Chapter 2 and part of Chapter 3. The final data set for the "Founders and Founding" survey consisted of 148 UK and 90 Japanese high-tech manufacturing founder-CEOs (Table A1.2).

The first survey raised almost as many questions as it answered. It seemed from the UK responses, for example, and particularly from the open questions, that the entrepreneurs adopted a very cautious approach to growing their businesses, yet we had not asked them specifically what their growth objectives were. The majority said they started their businesses with others, but we did not know with whom. They appeared to be innovative, with high aspirations in terms of quality, and dedicated to serving clients in niche markets, but we lacked data on innovativeness and competitive orientations. And they claimed they were dedicated to achieving niche-market excellence through teams of highly motivated and highly educated employees, but we lacked concrete data on how they recruited and retained employees.

To obtain fuller and more convincing data, we decided to do a follow-up survey, and to construct it with a comparison in mind. We reversed the order, with the UK survey carried out in December 2000–January 2001, and the Japanese survey carried out a year later. To better facilitate comparison, and to accommodate recent growth of high-tech activity, the "high-tech" industry selection was modified slightly, after Hecker (1999).[1] The UK sample included roughly 400 traceable,

Table A1.2 Characteristics of businesses (first survey, final selection)

		UK % (*n* = 148)	Japan % (*n* = 90)
Size	1–19	27.0	28.2
(employees)	20–49	57.4	31.4
	50–199	15.5	38.4
Founding	1945–79	46.3	68.6
date	1980–9	38.1	22.1
	1990–	15.6	9.3
Founder %		100	100
Average age		53.1	57.2

[1] The most important activities encompassed by Hecker's broader definition were, in manufacturing, "other non-pharmaceutical chemicals," "ordnance and armaments," and certain parts of industrial process and machine tool manufacture, and among services, "architectural, engineering and related technical consultancies" (although architects per se were not included) and "technical testing and analysis."

suitable respondents from the first survey, together with the same number of additional businesses. The latter comprised roughly 200 businesses founded before January 1997, biased toward larger businesses and drawn from activities under-represented or not included in the previous study, and 200 founded since 1997. Again, these were drawn from the Dun and Bradstreet database. The effective response rate from the previous respondents was 42.4 percent, and for the new group 24.9 percent, giving 34.2 percent (237 responses) overall.

The second Japanese survey was conducted in February–March 2002, with some appropriate businesses from the first survey, but mostly new businesses selected from Toyo Keizai's *Nihon no kaisha 78000* (Japanese Companies, 78000) 2001 edition. The response rate was fairly low, at 9.4 percent, but as the sample was large, there were 349 valid responses. However, this again included a high propor-tion of large businesses, and it was heavily skewed toward manufacturing. In order to construct comparable and statistically robust groups for the UK and Japan, we decided to concentrate on manufacturing businesses with fewer than 200 employ-ees, founded since World War II. That left 113 valid responses in the UK and 223 in Japan. The decision to retain nonfounders was based on our definition of entre-preneurship, discussed in Chapter 1.

Within manufacturing there were three broad groups: instruments; computers and electronic equipment; and "other" manufacturing (including other machin-ery, aerospace, and other transport equipment, medical devices as well as pharma-ceuticals). The ratio of the three groups is given in Table A1.3. Electronics was overrepresented in Japan, and "other" manufacturing in the UK, where "other" included a relatively high number of medical device manufacturers. In addition, the UK businesses were on average smaller, and somewhat younger. The final selection was made without eliminating these differences, but tests were conducted for their significance where necessary.

The research design utilized combined methods. We wanted the statistical evi-dence that surveys could provide, but we knew we would miss a lot of contextual

Table A1.3 Characteristics of businesses and CEOs (second survey final selection)

		UK % ($n = 113$)	Japan % ($n = 223$)
Size	1–19	26.5	20.2
(employees)	20–49	45.1	30.5
	50–199	28.3	49.3
Sector	Instruments	45.1	52.0
	Electronics, computers	25.7	39.0
	Other manufacturing	29.2	8.9
Founding	1945–79	43.4	65.9
date	1980–9	28.3	21.5
	1990–	28.3	12.6
Founder %		82.3	49.8
Average age		52.8	57.0

clues to interpreting the data and providing a nuanced picture if we did not have qualitative data as well. Creswell and Plano Clark (2007) categorize mixed quantitative and qualitative research into four types: triangulation, in which both types are given equal weighting in interpretation; embedded design, where one is incorporated into the other as a secondary feature; explanatory, in which qualitative research follows quantitative research; and exploratory research, which reverses the order.[2] Our qualitative phase followed the quantitative phase, but was done before analysis was carried out, and was originally designed as triangulation. When the analysis and interpretation were actually carried out, however, there was a shift toward explanatory use (see below).

From second survey respondents willing to be interviewed, twenty-five case CEOs/businesses were selected in each country. Selection criteria in the UK included indications of innovative activity, collaborative activity, geographic spread, and sectoral balance. Selection of the Japanese interviewees was carried out with a view to comparison with the UK cases, while ensuring sufficient coverage of electronics, which were strongly represented in the Japanese survey responses. A relatively high proportion of interviewees came from the Kyoto and Kansai areas, with a view to possible comparison with Cambridge and the south-east of the UK, where we had carried out pilot, case, and additional interviews.

The interviews were carried out at the entrepreneur's business, and lasted between an hour and two and a half hours. In some cases further clarifications were sought by telephone. The interviews started with a request for the entrepreneur to tell us about his (most were men) background, including where he came from, and about his career prior to starting his current business. They then moved on to founding (or MBO, succession, etc.) circumstances, and post-founding opportunity and business evolution and future aspirations. These were typically difficult to figure out from the questionnaire. The narrative which most entrepreneurs offered with relatively little prompting was supplemented with requests for clarification, as well as extra questions.

Given the way the samples were selected, the comparative data sets were created, and the interviewees were chosen, of course we cannot make any claims about representativeness. This was not our intent, although we believe that we are not misrepresenting UK and Japanese high-tech manufacturing CEOs and their businesses. Comparing manufacturing with nonmanufacturing within both countries would have enhanced our understanding of within-country differences, but due to data limitations we decided to concentrate our analysis on manufacturing, which promised to be a challenging task in itself. We did, however, make some tentative observations about nonmanufacturing in Chapter 9.

Figure A1.1 shows the research process, and gives some details of the composition of the data set.

---

[2] Cf. also Mason (2006).

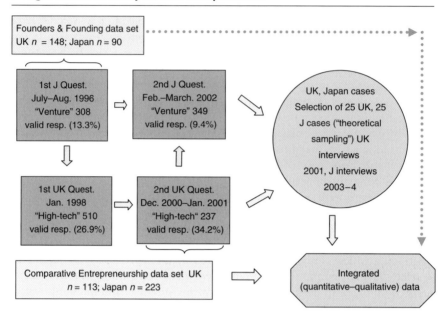

Figure A1.1 Research design and data set

Use of data

Our explanation of the research design and data set may have raised eyebrows as well as interest. Our research appears to be largely curiosity-driven, rather than the theory-driven research called for by Low and MacMillan (1988) and others seeking to define the field of entrepreneurship. We have essentially done cross-sectional research when many are calling for longitudinal research. We have studied survivors, and relied on recollections of the past, which we know to be imperfect. Our choice of countries, sector, and participants may even be questioned. We freely admit that our design and data set are far from perfect from a planning and design perspective. Our study involved processes similar to Sarasvathy's (2001, 2008) effectuation, and now we are engaged in an act of "sensemaking" (Weick, 1979). This sensemaking, however, reassures us that our approach is not without merit, and that it is broadly compatible with some contemporary currents in entrepreneurship (and organization) research.

In the ten years between the beginning of the project and writing this book, the field of entrepreneurship research has developed tremendously. As a very broad generalization, until the late 1980s much of the research focus was on the entrepreneur, and how he or she differed from other categories of people like managers, administrators, or small firm owners. Gartner (1988) famously attacked this focus (and implicitly Liles' [1974] question) by claiming that "'Who is an entrepreneur?' is the wrong question." Low and MacMillan (1988) called for greater rigor, an appreciation of context, and the pursuit of causality. Aldrich and Wiedenmayer (1993) supported a shift from "traits to rates." Despite ongoing debates as to whether the focus should now be on opportunities or business creation, there was general agreement that more attention should be paid to entrepreneurship as a process.

Some subsequently heeded Low and MacMillan's admonition to pursue causality more aggressively (see Chandler and Lyon, 2001, for a review), while others have followed a different path. Drawing on Mohr (1982), for instance, Aldrich (2001) contrasted outcome-driven process research, and event-driven process research. The former selects an outcome as the dependent variable, and works backward to identify independent variables which might have caused it, typically using quantitative methods.[3] The latter, in which his main interest lies, starts with events, and tries to follow their outcomes over time. "Problems arise," he suggests, "when researchers forget that their underlying goal is to build event-driven explanations for outcomes, rather than to celebrate the outcomes" (p. 119). Despite arguing that "we need dynamic and event-oriented designs that leave room for unexpected historical conjunctures, blind alleys and dead ends" (p. 120), however, he concedes that constraints mean the longitudinal research which this implies is seldom undertaken.[4]

Similarly, Van de Ven and Engleman (2004: 348) criticize the dominance of quantitative, outcome-oriented, causal model research, which they attribute to doctoral training programs and journal preferences: "Variables are defined and carefully distinguished from one another both in theory and in the operations used to measure them, and the character of the variables themselves is assumed to remain constant over time. Any unexplained variance is assumed to result either from misspecification . . . or from random error." By contrast, they argue: "*Events* are the natural units of the social process; events are what central subjects do or what happens to them. The process perspective explicitly focuses on events rather than variables because of the inherent complexity of the developmental processes" (p. 352, emphasis in original).

The former approach is better, they suggest, for the question: What are the antecedents or consequences of entrepreneurship? The latter approach is appropriate for the question: How does the entrepreneurial process unfold over time? While both approaches are needed to understand the inputs, processes, and outputs of entrepreneurship, they propose more focus on the second question, which "includes the role of human agency in change and development" (p. 356).

---

[3] Many recent Japanese studies of entrepreneurship fit this type, by taking growth rates as the dependent variable, and seeking to explain them in terms of various entrepreneur attributes, such as education (Honjo, 2003), experience in industry, self-finance (Genda, 2001), youth/age, etc. (Harada, 2003; Honjo, 2004). Yamada and Eshima (2003) and Eshima (2006) take survival as the dependent variable, and test it against a range of entrepreneur attributes, family and non-family management, and notably a range of strategies.

[4] "Junior people could justifiably look at us and say, 'Why didn't you do this stuff when you had the chance? If you didn't do it, why do you expect us to do it?' I recognize this contradiction" (Aldrich, 2001: 123).

Further, they argue that this involves the use of narrative, a view also espoused by Gartner (2007). Gartner's distinction is between paradigmatic and narrative approaches, and while recognizing the usefulness of both, he argues for more emphasis on narrative. This forces the researcher to pay attention to who is relating the narrative, to whom, why, what is left out, as well as what is included, and contexts. In addressing these questions, the researcher becomes involved in the creation of a further narrative of explanation, which ultimately involves the use of creativity, and indeed fiction. Where there are gaps in "facts as given," the researcher is obliged to supply plausible "facts as made" (p. 623). This of course must be done with caution.

We conducted two questionnaire-based surveys. These are standard tools of outcome-driven, variable-specifying, quantitative research. We did debate using our data to try to create a formal model, or at least partial models using multivariate analysis to clarify causal relationships. We did not pursue this path, for a number of reasons. First, there were some potentially important variables which we had insufficient data for. Second, some of the data represented relatively objective phenomena, but others were highly perceptual. Most importantly, however, we doubted whether the analysis would have done justice to the nuanced and contextualized relationships that evidently lay behind the responses and emerged in the open questions. And when we reflected on how we were actually making sense of our data, we decided that an alternative approach was called for.

To some extent, we have used our surveys as narrative rather than variable tools. The second survey was primarily designed as a result of open question responses of the first survey, which were unexpectedly rich and detailed. In the second survey, participants were typically asked to rank a number of items according to their importance for them, and the means were compared, followed by factor analysis. We did not treat the responses as reflections of empirical reality, but we questioned why the respective emphases were given. In the question about recruiting and keeping good personnel, for instance, on the whole UK entrepreneurs rated environment and support items highly, while Japanese entrepreneurs emphasized individual challenge. Explaining such responses was a challenge, as they appeared to fly in the face of cultural stereotypes. We could not look for the explanation in other variables used in the survey. Nor could we dismiss them as irrelevant, or the result of a flawed questionnaire. Instead, we looked to our case interviews, which provided contextual information for interpretation of the individual snapshots, or "frames" provided by each main question. These roughly correspond to individual chapters.

We were then faced with a further challenge – how to link these separate "frames" into a bigger, consistent, and coherent narrative picture. To do this, we again turned to the case interviews. What were the interviewees saying (or not saying, or assuming), which might help to construct the bigger picture? From these questions emerged the concepts of lifework and project entrepreneurship, and the different relationships between entrepreneur and business that these imply. As we constructed the picture, we traveled close to the line between "facts as given" and "facts as made." No doubt we crossed over the line a number of times. And we drew on other narratives, reflections, and theories to do this.

We could have given greater prominence to other aspects of the data, such as regional or industry contexts, technology-push versus market-pull approaches, or innovation versus imitation.[5] We did not go down these paths because, for us, the national differences were the most compelling. Moving from data to analysis to interpretation and presentation, choices have to be made which typically involve simplification, even in process-driven, event-based – or in our case, linked "frame" – approaches.

An outcome-driven approach would have started differently, with different questions. Most likely we would have followed the well-worn trail of looking at either start-up rates or growth rates. We would have sought quantifiable independent variables, such as "culture" (as defined by Hofstede, for example), institutional variables, "entrepreneurial orientations," network resources and/or market orientations, and tried to create a formal model which could explain differences between the UK and Japan. Although this kind of research can surface interesting correlations and influences, its limitations were a motivation to design and conduct a different study in the first place. Culture, for example, for us is simply not reducible to a few dimensions which are context-independent; using it in this way essentially negates the concept of agency which is central to entrepreneurship. At the same time, we retained the survey instrument to surface correlations and evidence of patterns which would have been difficult to obtain from case interviews alone.

Langley (1999: 693) recognizes that it is very difficult, and not necessarily productive, to separate variables and events, because they are intertwined, and "eclectic." She identifies seven strategies for making sense of such eclectic data: narrative, quantification, alternative templates, grounded theory, visual mapping, temporal bracketing, and synthetic. Our strategy, in these terms, would be closest to "synthetic" with elements of "quantification." With Weick (1989), she recognizes that there is inevitably a jump between analysis and interpretation, and that theory making proceeds through a combination of induction, deduction, and interpretation. While this does not mean that anything goes, she ends with a plea: "Sensemaking is the objective. Let us make sense whatever way we can" (Langley, 1999: 708).

We have done so. Our combined-method approach shifted from triangulation to explanatory, based on the magnitude of the task, and on our successes in using qualitative data to interpret the puzzles from the quantitative data we initially analyzed. The result is broadly compatible with the admonitions of Gartner, Aldrich, Van de Ven and Engleman, and others for entrepreneurship research. It is partly a reaction to output-driven approaches, and partly a response to the challenge of linking and explaining complex frames and narratives. Our linked frame approach is depicted in Figure A1.2.

[5] See Quince and Whittaker (2004) for a locational analysis of the second UK survey data, comparing rural and urban businesses, and weak and strong involvement in clusters.

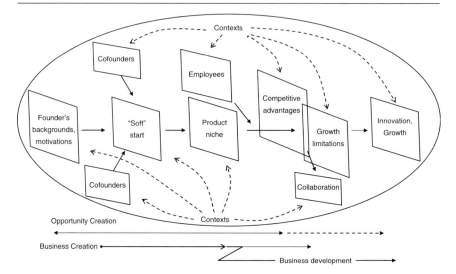

Figure A1.2 Linked "frames" of analysis and interpretation

Bringing the entrepreneur back in

The retreat from traits from the late 1980s, and the new emphasis on process, has other implications for entrepreneurship research. Baumol's (1968: 66) lament – "The theoretical firm is entrepreneurless – the Prince of Denmark has been expunged from the discussion of Hamlet" – echoes beyond mainstream economics; by the early 2000s the entrepreneur was in danger of disappearing from entrepreneurship research as well (cf. Davidsson, 2005)! Often there was a nose, a toe or hair, but not a whole figure. Gartner's (2001) elephant in entrepreneurship research is a coherent theoretical approach, but another elephant may in fact be the entrepreneur.

On the other hand, as we noted, Van de Ven and Engleman advocate an approach which "includes the role of human agency in change and development" – in other words, an approach which includes the entrepreneur. There is some danger, however, that by following the road they point to, we will end up back where we started, only with a narrative entrepreneur replacing the traits entrepreneur:

The possible urge to equal the entrepreneurial event with the story and the story with the one telling the story would be big and in my view problematic. The interest to study and analyze stories lays them in the fact that they give access to the world of the entrepreneur (in a similar vein as personality tests once did). The underlying concern I have is that with applying narrative approaches and methods to entrepreneurship research we might through this narrative backdoor re-introduce the individual entrepreneur to the foreground of our analysis, and in an ironic sense, reinforce what we already had dismissed: we are then not analyzing the stories and storytelling, we are listening to the entrepreneur telling "his" or "her" personal story. (Steyaert, 2007: 735)

So, how much should the entrepreneur be in the foreground, and how are we to depict "agency"? At one extreme are the "larger-than-life and seemingly unique individuals who single-handedly, it often appears, create the organizations that transform both industries and the ways of day-to-day life in a society" (Schoonhoven and Romanelli, 2001: 385). At the other extreme are the cultural or institutional puppets, and phantoms. There are various approaches to depicting the intermediate ground, including Giddens' (1984) structuration theory (cf. Bhowmick, 2007), and Lachmann's (1986) "radical subjectivism" (cf. Chiles, Bluedorn, and Gupta, 2007; Lewis and Runde, 2007). Recently, neo-institutionalists have begun to give more recognition to agency (e.g., "actor-centered" institutionalism: Scharpf, 1997; Mantzavinos, 2001), and this has found its way into comparative organization and governance research (e.g., Aguilera and Jackson, 2003; Crouch, 2005).

While sympathetic to these efforts, our starting point is somewhat different from the latter approaches. Rather than seeking to explain how there is scope for agency in an institutionalist framework, we were interested here in patterns of similarities and differences in attitudes, behaviors, and interactions of entrepreneurs with others. Entrepreneurs are not just influenced by their immediate networks, but by norms and values embedded in institutions which have been created by actors in other networks, at other times, and which they have done little to create (such as laws and market exchange norms). But in pursuing opportunity and business creation, they can maneuver, negotiate, and act creatively to secure preferred outcomes, in turn influencing their environments. Furthermore, we agree with Steyaert that entrepreneurship typically involves cooperation and interaction of multiple individuals, and this interaction itself can be a source of agency (cf. Garud and Karnoe, 2003). It is particularly in this interactional zone, moreover, that the processes of agency and structure (institutions, culture) interact.

At the end of the day, one's approach is not just the result of observation and analysis, but interpretive balance, and this is where creativity comes in. Moving too far in one direction will result in disappearance of the entrepreneur, squashed under the enormous weight of institutions and culture. Moving too far in the other direction will result in entrepreneurial genies, released from a bag of narrative gas. We hope that our research does justice to the delicate balance between an undersocialized and oversocialized treatment of entrepreneurs, which is essential for comparative entrepreneurship. The reader will of course judge the extent to which we have achieved this.

APPENDIX 2

FACTOR ANALYSIS TABLES

Table A2.1 Reasons for starting the business: UK factors

Reason to start	1	2	3	4	5
Be my own boss	**.779**	.048	−.091	.020	.004
Manage a business	**.762**	.380	.030	.021	.022
Get on in the world	**.751**	.095	−.011	.107	−.092
Increase my income	**.730**	−.217	−.028	.215	.126
Do something worthwhile	**.539**	−.018	.336	.105	.105
Use my own management skills	.078	**.870**	.041	−.035	−.072
Use my own marketing skills	.053	**.836**	−.002	.157	.148
Use my own technical skills	.016	**.460**	.111	.395	.204
Development of science & technology	−.052	−.022	**.883**	.012	.003
Something useful for society	.138	.054	**.697**	.077	−.014
Commercialize a new technology	−.097	.077	**.671**	−.097	.311
Enjoy my life	.106	−.013	.104	**.810**	−.115
Happiness of my family	.196	.186	−.118	**.750**	.070
Provide a new service	−.138	.039	.115	−.021	**.821**
Strong future in this work	.240	.089	.060	.024	**.726**
Eigenvalue	3.26	2.13	2.13	1.23	1.13
Variance explained %	21.71	14.19	11.47	8.21	7.55
Cumulative variance explained	21.71	35.90	47.37	55.58	63.13

KMO .677 Bartlett χ^2 421.72 df 105 Sig .000

Table A2.2 Reasons for starting the business: Japan factors

Reason to start	1	2	3	4
Commercialize new technology	.789	.059	.117	−.327
Develop science & technology	.765	−.012	.134	.282
Do something useful for society	.744	.048	.202	.098
Use my own technical skills	.691	.146	.061	−.153
Strong future in this work	.567	−.051	.105	.213
Do something worthwhile	.468	.361	.084	.081
Manage a business	.105	.784	−.067	.111
Increase my income	−.074	.697	.107	.345
Enjoy my life	.418	.677	.000	−.173
Happiness of my family	−.060	.593	.174	.288
Use my own marketing skills	.240	−.076	.825	−.078
Use my own management skills	.029	.145	.824	.115
Provide a new service	.355	.104	.568	−.173
Be my own boss	.102	.139	−.114	.779
Get on in the world	.047	.374	.033	.750
Eigenvalue	3.96	2.52	1.40	1.13
Variance explained %	26.37	16.80	9.35	7.55
Cumulative variance %	26.37	43.17	52.52	60.70

KMO .649 Bartlett χ^2 375.22 df 105 Sig .000

Table A2.3 Personal business objectives: UK factors

Business objective	Principles (UK)	Involve-ment	Social continuation	Financial gain (UK)
Build a business which will continue to exist without me	**.795**	−.144	−.025	−.129
Maintain a balance between work and home life	**.682**	.110	.045	.169
Provide a stable/positive environment for employees	**.659**	.383	.151	.043
Build a business with a reputation for excellence	**.594**	.394	.063	.004
Maximize my enjoyment/satisfaction from work	.074	**.847**	.063	.049
Do business on the basis of fairness and moral integrity	.428	**.640**	.153	−.036
Maintain my involvement in the business	.030	**.615**	−.190	.093
Make a contribution to S&T	.057	−.054	**.843**	.057
Prepare the business for exchange listing	−.014	−.087	**.768**	.132
Contribute to the well-being of society	.256	.425	**.609**	−.057
Maximize current and future returns for owners	.112	.084	−.076	**.866**
Increase the value of the business for potential capital gains	−.057	.017	.262	**.781**
Eigenvalue	3.21	1.77	1.37	1.13
Variance explained %	26.78	14.72	11.43	9.39
Cumulative variance %	26.78	41.50	52.93	62.32

KMO .667 Bartlett χ^2 285.52 df 66 Sig .000

Table A2.4 Personal business objectives: Japan factors

Business objective	Principles (J)	Social continuation (J)	Investment	Financial gain
Provide a stable/positive environment for employees	.774	.027	.234	.010
Build a business with a reputation for excellence	.657	.175	−.073	.161
Build a business which will continue to exist without me	.635	.147	−.102	.167
Provide a stable and positive environment for employees.	.624	.080	.137	−.326
Do business on the basis of fairness and moral integrity	.619	.441	−.083	−.137
Make a contribution to S&T	−.014	.730	−.071	−.058
Prepare the business for exchange listing	−.046	.719	.228	.143
Contribute to the well-being of society	.187	.710	.088	−.160
Maximize my enjoyment/ satisfaction from work	−.023	.516	−.022	.031
Maintain my involvement in the business		−.099	.783	.018
Maximize current and future returns for owners		.376	.701	.002
Increase the value of the business for potential capital gains		−.033	.042	.916
Eigenvalue	3.46	1.50	1.15	1.04
Variance explained %	28.80	12.47	9.59	8.64
Cumulative variance %	28.80	41.27	50.86	59.50

KMO .778 Bartlett χ^2 498.05 df 66 Sig .000

Table A2.5 Competitive advantages: UK factors

Competitive advantage	Innovation	Product line-up	Client focus	Marketing
Technological/scientific expertise	.790	−.044	−.017	.064
Being first in the market with new products/services	.772	.237	−.050	.190
Design of product/service	.619	.227	.127	−.173
Price/cost advantages	−.426	.154	.107	.377
Range of products/services	−.082	.793	−.179	.318
Specialized product/service	.312	.741	.013	−.191
Quality of product/service	.068	.528	.392	−.098
Personal attention and responsiveness to client needs	−.016	−.015	.821	−.087
Speed of service	−.113	−.103	.821	.500
Established reputation	.107	.465	.526	.013
Marketing and promotion	.101	−.030	−.018	.852
Eigenvalue	2.40	1.85	1.27	1.23
Variance explained %	21.83	16.78	11.57	11.21
Cumulative variance %	21.83	38.61	50.18	61.39

KMO .571 Bartlett χ^2 193.57 df 55 Sig .000

Table A2.6 Competitive advantages: Japan factors

Competitive advantage	Superior product	Market presence	Technology base
Being first in the market with new products/services	.749	.087	−.113
Design of product/service	.662	.248	−.121
Quality of product/service	.632	−.088	.066
Specialized product/service	.613	.125	.495
Personal attention and responsiveness to client needs	.371	.136	.033
Marketing and promotion	.025	.813	−.042
Speed of service	.123	.734	−.036
Established reputation	.045	.652	.485
Range of products/services	.377	.550	−.177
Price/cost advantages	.244	.226	−.663
Technological/scientific expertise	.496	.141	.545
Eigenvalue	3.07	1.49	1.22
Variance explained %	27.89	13.50	11.09
Cumulative variance %	27.89	41.39	52.49

KMO .768 Bartlett χ^2 435.94 df 55 Sig .000

Table A2.7 HRM orientations: UK factors

HRM orientation	SOE	Involvement	Incentives & recognition
Offering flexible/family friendly work arrangements	**.746**	.116	−.155
Providing a stable and supportive work environment	**.673**	−.069	.166
Providing an attractive physical working environment	**.496**	.130	.370
Providing a good welfare and fringe benefit package	**.448**	.311	.310
Encouraging autonomy in decision making	.139	**.697**	−.090
Giving challenging job assignments	.398	**.618**	.171
Giving employees a financial stake in the company	−.323	**.601**	.140
Paying top rates	−.138	−.151	**.752**
Providing/facilitating training and education	.248	.199	**.641**
Providing incentives for individual excellence	.307	.306	**.404**
Eigenvalue	1.91	1.52	1.48
Variance Explained %	19.12	15.18	14.80
Cumulative Variance %	19.12	34.31	49.11

KMO .740 Bartlett χ^2 126.56 df 45 Sig .000

Note: SOE = supportive organizational environment

Table A2.8 HRM orientations: Japan factors

HRM orientation	Personal growth	SOE 1	SOE 2	Effort–reward
Encouraging autonomy in decision-making	.773	.074	−.052	.182
Providing incentives for individual excellence	.730	−.204	.276	.072
Providing/facilitating training and education	.691	.115	.059	−.052
Giving employees financial stake in the company	.533	.512	−.152	.189
Providing an attractive physical working environment	.022	.796	.209	−.001
Providing a good welfare and fringe-benefit package	−.014	.778	.211	−.022
Offering flexible/family friendly work arrangements	−.046	.133	.843	.054
Providing a stable and supportive work environment	.187	.248	.779	−.016
Paying top rates	−.023	.052	.069	.913
Giving challenging job assignments	.459	−.050	−.040	.604
Eigenvalue	2.14	1.65	1.52	1.28
Variance explained %	21.39	16.46	15.17	12.79
Cumulative variance %	21.39	35.86	53.02	65.82

KMO .678 Bartlett χ^2 386. df 45 Sig .000

Note: SOE = supportive organizational environment

References

Acs, Z., P. Arenius, M. Hay, and M. Minnuti (2005), *Global Entrepreneurship Monitor: 2004 Executive Report*, London/Babson Park MA: GEM.

Acs. Z. and D. Audretsch (eds.) (2003), *Handbook of Entrepreneurship Research: An Interdisciplinary Survey and Introduction*, New York: Springer.

—— P. Arenius, M. Hay, and M. Minnuti (2005), *Global Entrepreneurship Monitor: 2004 Executive Report*, London/Babson Park, MA: GEM.

Aguilera, R. and G. Jackson (2003), The Cross-national Diversity of Corporate Governance: Dimensions and Determinants, in *Academy of Management Review*, 28/3, pp. 447–65.

Aldrich, H. (1999), *Organizations Evolving*, Thousand Oaks, CA: Sage.

—— (2001), Who Wants to Be an Evolutionary Theorist? in *Journal of Management Inquiry*, 10/2, pp. 115–27.

—— and M. Fiol (1994), Fools Rush In? The Institutional Context of Industry Creation, in *Academy of Management Review*, 19/4, pp. 645–70.

—— and A. Kenworthy (1999), The Accidental Entrepreneur: Campbellian antinomies and organizational foundings in J. Baum and B. McKelvey (eds.), *Variations in Organization Science: In Honor of Donald Campbell*, Newbury Park, CA: Sage.

—— and M. Martinez (2001), Many Are Called, But Few Are Chosen: An Evolutionary Perspective for the Study of Entrepreneurship, in *Entrepreneurship Theory & Practice*, Summer, pp. 41–56.

—— and G. Wiedenmayer (1993), From Traits to Rates: An Ecological Perspective on Organizational Foundings, in J. Katz and R. Brockhaus (eds.), *Advances in Entrepreneurship, Firm Emergence and Growth*, Vol. 1, Greenwich, CT: JAI Press.

Aldrich, H., N. Carter, and M. Ruef (2004), Teams, in W. Gartner et al. (eds.)

Armour, J. and D. Cumming (2005), Bankruptcy Law and Entrepreneurship, CBR Working Paper No. 300, Centre for Business Research: University of Cambridge.

Asanuma, B. (1989), Manufacturer-Supplier Relationships in Japan and the Concept of Relationship-Specific Skill in *Journal of the Japanese & International Economies*, 3/1, pp.1–30.

Audretsch, D. (2005), The Emergence of Entrepreneurship Policy, in D. Audretsch, H. Grimm, and C. Wessner (eds.), *Local Heroes in the Global Village: Globalization and New Entrepreneurship Policies*, New York: Springer.

—— (2007), *The Entrepreneurial Society*, Oxford: Oxford University Press.

—— and I. Beckmann (2007), From Small Business to Entrepreneurship Policy, in D. Audretsch, I. Grilo, and R. Thurik (eds.), *Handbook of Research on Entrepreneurship Policy*, Cheltenham: Edward Elgar.

—— and R. Thurik (2001), What's New About the New Economy? From the Managed to the Entrepreneurial Economy, in *Industrial and Corporate Change*, 10/1, pp. 267–315.

Baker, T., E. Gedajlovic, and M. Lubatkin (2005), A Framework for Comparing Entrepreneurship Processes Across Nations, in *Journal of International Business Studies*, 36, pp. 492–504.

Baron, J., D. Burton, and M. Hannan (1996), The Road Taken: Origins and Evolution of Employment Systems in Emerging Companies, in *Industrial & Corporate Change*, 5/2, pp. 239–74.

Baumol, W. (1968), Entrepreneurship in Economic Theory, in *The American Economic Review*, 58/2, pp. 54–71.

—— (1993), *Entrepreneurship, Management and the Structure of Payoffs*, Cambridge, MA: MIT Press.

Beckman, C. (2006), The Influence of Founding Team Company Affiliations on Firm Behaviour, in *Academy of Management Journal*, 49/4, pp. 741–58.

Berry, M. and J. Taggart (1998), Combining Technology and Corporate Strategy in Small High Tech Firms, in *Research Policy*, 26/7–8, pp. 883–95.

Bhave, M. (1994), A Process Model of Entrepreneurial Venture Creation, in *Journal of Business Venturing*, 9/3, pp. 223–42.

Bhide, A. (1994), How Entrepreneurs Craft Strategies That Work, in *Harvard Business Review*, March–April, pp. 150–161.

—— (2000), *The Origin and Evolution of New Businesses*, Oxford: Oxford University Press.

Bhowmick, S. (2007), Structuration in Entrepreneurial Opportunity: An Exploration, SSRN occasional paper.

Biggadike, R. (1976), Corporate Diversification: Entry, Strategy and Performance in *Harvard Business Review*, 57, May–June, pp. 103–11.

Birch, D. (1979), The Job Generation Process, Report, MIT Program on Neighborhood and Regional Change, MIT.

—— (1981), Who Creates Jobs? in *The Public Interest*, 65 Fall, pp. 3–14.

Birley, S. (1985), The Role of Networks in Entrepreneurial Process in *Journal of Business Venturing*, 1, pp. 107–17.

—— and P. Westhead (1994), A Taxonomy of Business Start-up Reasons and Their Impact on Firm Growth and Size, in *Journal of Business Venturing*, 9, pp. 7–31.

Block, F. (2003), Karl Polanyi and the Writing of *The Great Transformation*, in *Theory & Society*, 32/3, pp. 275–306.

Blyth, M. (2002), *Great Transformations: Economic Ideas and Institutional Change in the Twentieth Century*, Cambridge: Cambridge University Press.

Bolton Committee (Committee of Inquiry on Small Firms) (1971), *Report of the Committee of Inquiry on Small Firms*, London: HMSO.

References

Bourdieu, P. (1977), Le Champ Economique, in *Actes de le Recherche en Sciences Sociales*, 119, pp. 48–66.

Boxall, P. and J. Purcell (2003), *Strategy and Human Resource Management*, Basingstoke: Palgrave Macmillan.

Branscomb, L. and P. Auerswald (2002), Between Invention and Innovation: An Analysis of Funding for Early Stage Technology Development, Washington, DC: US Department of Commerce.

Brockhaus, R. (1982), The Psychology of the Entrepreneur, in C. Kent, D. Sexton, and K. Vesper (eds.), *The Encyclopedia of Entrepreneurship*, Englewood Cliffs, NJ: Prentice Hall.

Brown, C. and G. Linden (2008), *Change is the Only Constant*, book manuscript dated May 12, University of California, Berkeley.

Brown, T., P. Davidsson, and J. Wiklund (2001), An Operationalization of Stevenson's Concept of Entrepreneurship as Opportunity-Based Firm Behaviour, in *Strategic Management Journal*, 22, pp. 953–68.

Brush, C. and T. Manolova (2004), Personal Background, in W. Gartner et al. (eds).

Bullock, M. (1983), *Academic Enterprise, Industrial Innovation and the Development of High Technology Financing in the United States*, London: Brand Bros.

Burchell, B. and A. Hughes (2006), The Stigma of Failure: An International Comparison of Failure Tolerance and Second Chancing, CBR Working Paper No. 334, Centre for Business Research, University of Cambridge.

Busenitz, L., C. Gomez, and J. Spencer (2000), Country Institutional Profiles: Unlocking Entrepreneurial Phenomena, in *Academy of Management Journal*, 43/5, pp. 994–1003.

Butchart, R. (1987), A New UK Definition of the High Technology Industries, in *Economic Trends*, 400, pp. 82–8.

Bygrave, W. and C. Hofer (1991), Theorizing About Entrepreneurship, in *Entrepreneurship Theory & Practice*, 16/2, pp. 13–22.

Callon, M. (ed.) (1998), *The Laws of Markets*, Oxford: Blackwell/The Sociological Review.

Carter, N., W. Gartner, and P. Reynolds (1996), Exploring Start-up Sequence Events, in *Journal of Business Venturing*, 11/3, pp. 151–66.

—— W. Gartner, and K. Shaver (2004), Career Reasons, in W. Gartner et al. (eds.).

—— T. Stearns, P. Reynolds, and B. Miller (1994), New Venture Strategies: Theory Development With An Empirical Base, in *Strategic Management Journal*, 15/1, pp. 21–41.

Casper, S. and R. Whitley (2004), Managing Competencies in Entrepreneurial Technology Firms: A Comparative Institutional Analysis of Germany, Sweden and the UK, in *Research Policy*, 33, pp. 89–106.

—— M. Lehrer, and D. Soskice (1999), Can High-technology Industries Prosper in Germany? Institutional Frameworks and the Evolution of the German Software and Biotechnology Industries, in *Industry and Innovation*, 6/1, pp. 5–24.

Casson, M. (1982), *The Entrepreneur: An Economic Theory*, Oxford: Martin Robertson.

Casson, M. and N. Wadeson (2006), The Discovery of Opportunities: Extending the Economic Theory of the Entrepreneur, Working Paper, University of Reading.

Chaganti, R., R. Chaganti, and V. Mahajan (1989), Profitable Small Business Strategies Under Different Types of Competition, in *Entrepreneurship Theory & Practice*, 13/3, pp. 21–35.

Chandler, G. and D. Lyon (2001), Issues of Research Design and Construct Measurement in Entrepreneurship Research: The Past Decade, in *Entrepreneurship Theory & Practice*, 25/4, pp. 101–13.

Chell, E. (1986), The Entrepreneurial Personality: A Review and Some Theoretical Developments, in J. Curran, J. Stanworth and D. Watkins (eds.), *The Survival of the Small Firm*, Volume 1, Aldershot: Gower.

Chesbrough, H. (2003), *Open Innovation: The New Imperative for Creating and Profiting from Technology*, Boston, CT: Harvard Business School Press.

—— (2006), The Open Innovation Model: Implications for Innovation, in D. H. Whittaker and R. Cole (eds.), *Recovering From Success: Innovation and Technology Management in Japan*, Oxford: Oxford University Press.

Chiles, T., A. Bluedorn, and V. Gupta (2007), Beyond Creative Destruction and Entrepreneurial Discovery: A Radical Austrian Approach to Entrepreneurship, in *Organization Studies*, 28/4, pp. 467–93.

Christensen, P., O. Madsen, and R. Peterson (1994), Conceptualizing Entrepreneurial Opportunity Recognition, in G. Hills (ed.), *Marketing and Entrepreneurship: Research Ideas and Opportunities*, Westport, CT: Quorum Books.

Chusho kigyo cho (ed.) (1999), *Chusho kigyo no aratana tenkai: Chusho kigyo seisaku kenkyukai saishu hokoku yori* (New Developments in SME Policy: From the Final Report of the SME Policy Research Group), Tokyo: Doyukan.

Cole, R. and D. H. Whittaker (2006), Introduction, in D. H. Whittaker and R. Cole (eds.), *Recovering From Success: Innovation and Technology Management in Japan*, Oxford: Oxford University Press.

Collins, O., D. Moore, and D. Unwalla (1964), *The Enterprising Man*, East Lansing, MI: GSB, Michigan State University.

Connell, D. (2004), Exploiting the UK's Science and Technology Base: How to Fill the Gaping Hole in UK Government Policy, TTP Ventures Report: Cambridge.

—— (2006), "Secrets" of the World's Largest Seed Capital Fund, Centre for Business Research Special Report, University of Cambridge.

Cooper, A. and C. Daily (1997), Entrepreneurial Teams, in D. Sexton and R. Smilor (eds.), *Entrepreneurship 2000*, Chicago, IL: Upstart Publishing Co.

Cosh, A. and A. Hughes (2000), Innovation Activity and Performance in UK SMEs, in A. Cosh and A. Hughes (eds.), *British Enterprise in Transition: Growth, Innovation and Public Policy in the Small and Medium-Sized Enterprise Sector, 1994–1999*, Cambridge: Centre for Business Research.

—— —— (2007a), Constraints, Competitiveness and Collaboration, in A. Cosh and A. Hughes (eds.), *British Enterprise: Thriving or Surviving?* Cambridge: Centre for Business Research.

Cosh, A. and A. Hughes (2007*b*), The British SME Sector in 1991–2004, in A. Cosh and A. Hughes (eds.), *British Enterprise: Thriving or Surviving?* Cambridge: Centre for Business Research.

—— —— (2007*c*), Business Formation, Business Leaders and SME Performance, in A. Cosh and A. Hughes (eds.), *British Enterprise: Thriving or Surviving?* Cambridge: Centre for Business Research.

—— —— and R. Lester (2006), *UK Plc: Just How Innovative are We?* Cambridge MIT Institute, University of Cambridge.

Cotis, J.-P (2007), Entrepreneurship as an Engine for Growth: Evidence and Policy Challenges, paper delivered to GEM Forum (Entrepreneurship: Setting the Development Agenda), London, 10–11 January.

Covin, J. and D. Slevin (1989), Strategic Management of Small Firms in Hostile and Benign Environments, in *Strategic Management Journal*, 10/1, pp. 75–87.

Creswell, J. and V. Plano Clark (2007), *Designing and Conducting Mixed Methods Research*, Thousand Oaks, CA: Sage.

Crouch, C. (2005), *Capitalist Diversity and Change: Recombinant Governance and Institutional Entrepreneurs*, New York: Oxford University Press.

—— and W. Streeck (1997), *Political Economy of Modern Capitalism: Mapping Convergence and Diversity*, Thousand Oaks, CA: Sage.

Cully, M., S. Woodland, A. O'Reilly, and G. Dix (1999), *Britain at Work: As Depicted by the 1998 Workplace Employee Relations Survey*, London: Routledge.

Dana, L. and R. Anderson (eds.), *International Handbook of Research on Indigenous Entrepreneurship,* Cheltenham: Edward Elgar.

Davidsson, P. (1991), Continued Entrepreneurship: Ability, Need and Opportunity as Determinants of Small Firm Growth, in *Journal of Business Venturing*, 6, pp. 405–29.

—— (2004), *Researching Entrepreneurship*, New York: Springer.

—— (2005), Paul Reynolds: Entrepreneurship Research Innovator, Coordinator, and Disseminator, in *Small Business Economics*, 24/4, pp. 351–8.

—— and B. Honig (2003), The Role of Human and Social Capital Among Nascent Entrepreneurs, in *Journal of Business Venturing*, 18, pp. 301–31.

—— and J. Wiklund (1997), Values, Beliefs and Regional Variations in New Firm Formation Rates, in *Journal of Economic Psychology*, 18, pp. 179–99.

Davies, A. and M. Hobday (2005), *The Business of Projects*, Cambridge: Cambridge University Press.

Davis, H. and R. Scase (2000), *Managing Creativity: The Dynamics of Work and Organizations*, Milton Keynes: Open University Press.

DeBresson, C., X. Hu, I. Drejer, and B.-A. Lundvall (1998), Innovative Activity in the Learning Economy: A Comparison of Systems in 10 OECD Countries, OECD Draft Report.

Dess, G., G. Lumpkin, and J. Covin (1997), Entrepreneurial Strategy Making and Firm Performance: Test of Contingency and Configurational Models, in *Strategic Management Journal*, 18/9, pp. 677–95.

DiMaggio, P. and W. Powell (1983), The Iron Cage Revisited: Institutional Isomorphism and Collective Rationality in Organizational Fields, in *American Sociological Review*, 48, pp. 147–60.

—— —— (1991), Introduction, in W. Powell and P. DiMaggio (eds.), *The New Institutionalism in Organizational Analysis*, Chicago, IL: Chicago University Press.

Dodgson, M. (1993), *Technological Collaboration in Industry: Strategy, Policy and Internationalization in Innovation*, London: Routledge.

Dore, R. (1973), *British Factory – Japanese Factory: The Origins of National Diversity in Industrial Relations*, London: Allen & Unwin.

—— (1983), Goodwill and the Spirit of Market Capitalism, in *The British Journal of Sociology*, 34/4, pp. 459–82.

—— (2000), *Stock Market Capitalism: Welfare Capitalism: Japan and Germany Versus the Anglo-Saxons*, Oxford: Oxford University Press.

—— (2007), Two Routes to Innovation: Venture Capital and Corporate R&D Compared, paper presented to ITEC-Beijing International Forum: Innovating East Asia, School of Government, Beijing University, 17 March.

Drejer, I. and B. Jorgensen (2005), The Dynamic Creation of Knowledge: Analyzing Public–Private Collaborations, in *Technovation*, 25, pp. 83–94.

Eisenhardt, K. and C. B. Schoonhoven (1990), Organizational Growth: Linking Founding Team, Strategy, Environment and Growth Among US Semiconductor Ventures, 1978–1988, in *Administrative Science Quarterly*, 35/3, pp. 504–29.

Ekstedt, E., R. Lundin, A. Söderholm, and H. Wirdenius (1999), *Neo-industrial Organizing: Renewal by Action and Knowledge Formation in a Project-Intensive Economy*, Routledge: London.

Endres, A. and C. Woods (2006), Modern Theories of Entrepreneurial Behaviour: A Comparison and Appraisal, in *Small Business Economics*, 26/2, pp. 189–202.

Eshima, Y. (2006), Sozoteki chusho kigyo no senryaku taipu to seizonritsu ni kansuru jisho kenkyu (Survival Contrasts Between Strategic Types of Technology-based Small Firms in Japan), Osaka University of Economics Working Papers 2006-4.

Etzioni, A. (1987), Entrepreneurship, Adaptation and Legitimation, in *Journal of Economic Behavior & Organization*, 8, pp. 175–89.

Fligstein, N. (2001), *The Architecture of Markets: An Economic Sociology of Twenty-First-Century Capitalist Societies*, Princeton, NJ: Princeton University Press.

Francis, D. and W. Sandberg (2000), Friendship Within Entrepreneurial Teams and Its Association with Team and Venture Performance, in *Entrepreneurship Theory & Practice*, 25/2, pp. 5–25.

Freeman, J, G. Carrol, and M. Hannan (1983), The Liability of Newness: Age Dependence in Organizational Death Rates, in *American Sociological Review*, 48/5, pp. 692–710.

Furuse, K. (2005), Shijoka shinikui zai no shijo purosesu – chusho kigyo baibai shijo no tokuseiteki chosa (Market Processes of Assets Difficult to Marketize:

Investigation of the characteristics of buying and selling small firms), in *Kigyoka kenkyu*, 2, pp. 1–16.

Galbraith, J. K. (1967), *The New Industrial State*, Boston, MA: Houghton Mifflin.

Garnsey, E. and A. Cannon-Brookes (1993), The "Cambridge Phenomenon" Revisited: Aggregate Change Among Cambridge High-Technology Companies Since 1985, in *Entrepreneurship & Regional Development*, 5, pp. 179–207.

Gartner, W. (1988), Who Is an Entrepreneur? Is the Wrong Question, in *American Journal of Small Business*, 12/4, pp. 11–32.

—— (2001), Is There an Elephant in Entrepreneurship? Blind Assumptions in Theory Development, in *Entrepreneurship Theory & Practice*, 25/4, pp. 27–39.

—— (2007), Entrepreneurial Narrative and a Science of the Imagination, in *Journal of Business Venturing*, 22, pp. 613–27.

—— and N. Carter (2003), Entreprenurial Behavior and Firm Organizing Processes, in Acs and Audretsch (eds.)

—— K. Shaver, N. Carter, and P. Reynolds (eds.) (2004), *Handbook of Entrepreneurial Dynamics: The Process of Business Creation*, Thousand Oaks, CA: Sage.

Garud, R. and P. Karnoe (2003), Bricolage Versus Breakthrough: Distributed and Embedded Agency in Technology Management, in *Research Policy*, 32, pp. 277–300.

Gatewood, E. (2004), Entrepreneurial Expectancies, in W. Gartner et al. (eds.)

Genda, Y. (2001), Dokuritsu no shun: Kaigyo no tame no kyaria keisei (The Time for Independence: Career Formation for Start-up), in *Kokumin kin'yu koko shinki kaigyo no jittai chosa no saibunseki, 1991–2000* (A Re-analysis of the PFC New Startup Survey, 1991–2000), SSJ Data Archive Research Paper Series, 17, pp. 9–21.

Gerlach, M. (1992), *Alliance Capitalism: The Social Organization of Japanese Business*, Berkeley, CA: University of California Press.

Giddens, A. (1984), *The Constitution of Society: Outline of the Theory of Structuration*, Cambridge: Polity Press.

Goel, S. and R. Karri (2006), Entrepreneurs, Effectual Logic, and Over-Trust, in *Entrepreneurship Theory & Practice*, 30/4, pp. 477–93.

Granovetter, M. (1983), The Strength of Weak Ties: A Network Theory Revisited, in *Sociological Theory*, 1, pp. 201–33.

—— (1985), Economic Action and Social Structure: The Problem of Embeddedness, in *American Journal of Sociology*, 91/3, pp. 481–510.

Grilo, I. and R. Thurik (2006), Entrepreneurial Engagement Levels in the European Union, SCALES-paper N200515, EIM, The Netherlands.

Guest, D. (1987), Human Resource Management and Industrial Relations, in *Journal of Management Studies*, 24/5, pp. 503–21.

Hagedoorn, J. (1993), Understanding the Rationale of Strategic Technology Partnering: Interorganizational Modes of Cooperation and Sectoral Differences, in *Strategic Management Journal*, 14, pp. 371–85.

—— (2002), Inter-Firm R&D Partnerships: An Overview of Major Trends and Patterns Since 1960, in *Research Policy*, 31, pp. 477–92.

Hall, P. and D. Soskice (2001), *Varieties of Capitalism: The Institutional Foundations of Comparative Advantage*, Oxford: Oxford University Press.

Hamada, Y. and T. Asai (2000), Bencha e no shien seido (Support System for Entrepreneurial Businesses), in S. Matsuda and WERU (eds.), *Bencha kigyo no keiei to shien* (Management and Support of Entrepreneurial Businesses), Tokyo: Nikkei shinbunsha.

Hannan, M. and J. Freeman (1977), The Population Ecology of Organizations, in *The American Journal of Sociology*, 82/5, pp. 929–64.

—— D. Burton, and J. Baron (1996), Inertia and Change in the Early Years: Employment Relations in Young, High Technology Firms, in *Industrial & Corporate Change*, 5/2, pp. 503–36.

Harada, N. (2003), Who Succeeds as an Entrepreneur? Analysis of the Post-Entry of New Firms in Japan, in *Japan and the World Economy*, 15/2, pp. 211–22.

Hart, S. (1992), An Integrative Framework for Strategy-making Processes, in *Academy of Management Review*, 17, pp. 327–51.

Hay, C. (2006), Constructivist Institutionalism, in R. Rhodes, S. Binder, and B. Rockman (eds.), *The Oxford Handbook of Political Institutions*, Oxford: Oxford University Press.

Hayton, J., G. George, and S. Zahra (2002), National Culture and Entrepreneurship: A Review of Behavioral Research, in *Entrepreneurship Theory & Practice*, 26/4, pp. 33–52.

Hecker, D. (1999), High Technology Employment: A Broader View, in *Monthly Labor Review*, 122/6, pp. 18–28.

Heckscher, C. (1995), *White Collar Blues: Management Loyalties in an Age of Corporate Restructuring*, New York: Basic Books.

Hirata, K. (1999), Bencha kigyo ni okeru sogyo chimu to soshiki seicho (The Start-up Team and Organization Growth in Entrepreneurial Businesses), in *Kodo kagaku kenkyu*, 52, Tokai daigaku shakai kagaku kenkyusho, pp. 109–20.

Hodgson, D. (2007), The New Professionals: Professionalisation and the Struggle for Occupational Control in the Field of Project Management, in D. Muzio, S. Ackroyd, and J.F. Chanlat (eds.), *Redirections in the Study of Expert Labour: Medicine, Law and Management Consultancy*, Basingstoke: Palgrave.

Hofstede, G. (1980), *Culture's Consequences: International Differences in Work-Related Values*, Beverly Hills, CA: Sage.

—— N. Noordchaven, R. Thurik, L. Uhlaner, A. Wennekers, and R. Wildeman (2004), Culture's Role in Entrepreneurship: Self-Employment Out of Dissatisfaction, in T. Brown and J. Ulijn (eds.), *Innovation, Entrepreneurship and Culture: The Interaction Between Technology, Progress and Economic Growth*, Cheltenham: Edward Elgar.

Honjo, Y. (2003), Sutartouppu kigyo no pafomansu (The Performance of Start-ups), in *Shinki kaigyo kenkyukai hokokusho: Kigyoka katsudo ni kansuru kenkyu no shinten oyobi yuko na shien shisutemu no kochiku ni mukete* (Report of the Start-up Research

Group: Developments in Research on Entrepreneurship, and Towards Construct-ing an Effective Support System), Tokyo: Chusho kigyo sogo kenkyukiko.

Honjo, Y. (2004), Growth of New Startup Firms: Evidence from the Japanese Manu-facturing Industry, in *Applied Economics*, 36, pp. 343–55.

Hornsby, J. and D. Kuratko (1990), Human Resource Management in Small Business: Critical Issues for the 1990s, in *Journal of Small Business Management*, 28/3, pp. 9–18.

Howells, J. (2000), Research and Technology Outsourcing and Systems of Innov-ation, in S. Metcalfe and I. Miles (eds.), *Innovation Systems in the Service Economy: Measurement and Case Study Analysis*, Dordrecht: Kluwer.

Hughes, A. (2007), Innovation Policy as Cargo Cult: Myth and Reality in Know-ledge-Led Productivity Growth, CBR Working Paper No. 348, University of Cam-bridge.

—— and B. Moore (1998), High Tech Firms: Market Position, Innovative Perform-ance and Access to Finance, in A. Cosh and A. Hughes (eds.), *Enterprise Britain*, Cambridge: Centre for Business Research.

Hunt, S. and J. Levie (2003), Culture as a Predictor of Entrepreneurial Activity, in *Frontiers of Entrepreneurship Research*, Wellesley, MA: Babson College.

Hwang, H. and W. Powell (2005), Institutions and Entrepreneurship, in S. Alvarez, R. Agarwal and O. Sorenson (eds.), *Handbook of Entrepreneurship Research: Disci-plinary Perspectives*, New York: Springer.

Ibata-Arens, K. (2005), *Innovation and Entrepreneurship in Japan: Politics, Organiza-tions and High Technology Firms*, Cambridge: Cambridge University Press.

Inamura, Y. and M. Nakauchi (2006), Bencha kigyo ni okeru migiude, kanbu shain no yakuwari to sono koka (The Role and Effects of the Right Hand Man and Core Employees in Entrepreneurial Businesses) in *Kigyoka kenkyu*, No. 3, pp. 17–27.

Ingham, G. (1970), *Size of Industrial Organization and Worker Behaviour*, Cambridge: Cambridge University Press.

Inglehart, R. (1990), *Culture Shift in Advanced Industrial Society*, Princeton, NJ: Princeton University Press.

—— (1997), *Modernization and Post-Modernization: Culture, Economic and Political Change in 43 Societies*, Princeton, NJ: Princeton University Press.

Iwasaki, H. (2006), *Livedoor shokku no shinjitsu* (The Truth About the Livedoor Shock), Tokyo: Bunkasha.

Jackson, B. and K. Parry (2008), *A Very Short, Fairly Interesting and Reasonably Cheap Book About Studying Leadership*, London: Sage.

Kamm, J. and A. Nurick (1993), The Stages of Team Venture Formation: A Decision-Making Model, in *Entrepreneurship Theory & Practice*, 17/2, pp. 17–28.

—— J. Shuman, J. Seeger, and A. Nurick (1990), Entrepreneurial Teams in New Venture Creation: A Research Agenda, in *Entrepreneurship Theory & Practice*, 14/4, pp. 7–17.

Karlson, B. (2006), Partner Selection From the Perspective of Small Knowledge-Intensive Firms Seeking Universities as Partners for Innovation: Strategic

Considerations or Behavioural Determination, paper presented to 3rd Asia-Pacific Conference on Knowledge Management, Hong Kong, 11–13 December.

Karlsson, C. and Z. Acs (2002), Introduction to Institutions, Entrepreneurship and Firm Growth: The Case of Sweden, in *Small Business Economics*, 19, pp. 63–7.

Kets de Vries, M. (1977), The Entrepreneurial Personality: A Person at the Cross-roads, in *Journal of Management Studies*, 14/1, pp. 34–57.

Kirchoff, B. (1977), Organzation Effectiveness Measurement and Policy Research, in *Academy of Management Review*, 2/3, pp. 347–55.

Kirzner, I. (1997), Entrepreneurial Discovery and the Competitive Market Process, in *Journal of Economic Literature*, 35, pp. 60–85.

Kitson, M. and F. Wilkinson (2000), Markets, Competition and Collaboration, in A. Hughes and A. Cosh (eds.), *British Enterprise in Transition*, Cambridge University: Centre for Business Research.

Klepper, S. (2001), Employee Startups in High-Tech Industries, in *Industrial and Corporate Change*, 10/3, pp. 639–74.

Kneller, R. (2007), *Bridging Islands: Venture Companies and the Future of Japanese and American Industry*, Oxford: Oxford University Press.

Knight, F. (1921), *Risk, Uncertainty and Profit*, Boston, MA: Hart, Schaffner & Marx; Houghton Mifflin.

Kobayashi, S. (1997), Education System in Raising Human Capital, in Japan Commission on Industrial Performance (ed.), *Made in Japan: Revitalizing Japanese Manufacturing for Economic Growth*, Cambridge, MA: MIT Press.

Kokumin kin'yu koko (ed.) (2002, 2004), *Shinki kaigyo hakusho* (White Paper on Start-ups, 2002; 2004), Tokyo: Chusho kigyo risarchi senta.

Koller, R. (1988), On the Source of Entrepreneurial Ideas, in B. Kirchhoff, W. Long, W. McMullan, K. Vesper, and W. Wetzel Jr. (eds.), *Frontiers of Entrepreneurship Research*, Wellesley, MA: Babson College, pp. 194–207.

Kostova T. (1997), Country Institutional Profiles: Concept and Measurement, in *Academy of Management Best Paper Proceedings*, pp. 180–9.

Kotey, B. and P. Slade (2005), Formal Human Resource Management Practices in Small Growing Firms, in *Journal of Small Business Management*, 43/1, pp. 16–41.

Krippner, G. and A. Alvarez (2007), Embeddedness and the Intellectual Projects of Economic Sociology, in *Annual Review of Sociology*, 33, pp. 219–40.

Kutsuna, K. (2002), Bencha fainansu (Venture Finance), in K. Kanai and R. Tsunoda (eds.), *Bencha kigyo keiei ron* (Views of Entrepreneurial Business Management), Tokyo: Yuhikaku.

Lachmann, L. (1986), *The Market as an Economic Process*, Oxford: Blackwell.

Langley, A. (1999), Strategies for Theorizing From Process Data, in *Academy of Management Review*, 24/4, pp. 691–710.

Leighton, P. and A. Felstead (1992), *The New Entrepreneurs: Self Employment and Small Business in Europe*, London: Kogan Page.

Lester, R. and M. Piore (2004), *Innovation: The Missing Dimension*, Cambridge, MA: Harvard University Press.

References

Lewis, P. and J. Runde (2007), Subjectivism, Social Structure and the Possibility of Socio-Economic Order: The Case of Ludwig Lachmann, in *Journal of Economic Behaviour & Organization*, 62/2, pp. 167–86.

Liles, P. (1974, 1981), Who Are the Entrepreneurs? MSU Business Topics 22/1, reprinted in P. Gorb, P. Dowell and P. Wilson, *Small Business Perspectives*, London: Armstrong.

Liao, J. and H. Welsch (2004), Start-up Resources and Entrepreneurial Discontinuance: An Empirical Investigation of Nascent Entrepreneurs, in *Frontiers of Entrepreneurship Research*, Wellesley, MA: Babson College.

Lorenzoni, G. and A. Lipparini (1999), The Leveraging of Interfirm Relationships as a Distinctive Organizational Capability, in *Strategic Management Journal*, 20, pp. 317–38.

Low, M. and I. MacMillan (1988), Entrepreneurship: Past Research and Future Challenges, in *Journal of Management*, 14/2, pp. 139–61.

Lumpkin, G. and G. Dess (1996), Clarifying the Entrepreneurial Orientation Construct and Linking it to Performance, in *Academy of Management Review* 21/1, pp. 135–72.

Lundin, R. and A. Söderholm (1995), A Theory of the Temporary Organization, in *Scandinavian Journal of Management*, 11/4, pp. 437–55.

—— (1998), Conceptualizing a Projectified Society: Discussion of an Eco-Institutional Approach to a Theory on Temporary Organizations, in R. Lundin and C. Midler (eds.), *Projects as Arenas for Renewal and Learning Processes*, Dordrecht: Kluwer Academic.

Lundström, A. and L. Stevenson (2002), *On the Road to Entrepreneurship Policy*, Stockholm: Swedish Foundation for Small Business Research.

—— (2005), *Entrepreneurship Policy: Theory and Practice*, New York: Springer.

McClelland, D. (1961), *The Achieving Society*, Princeton, NJ: Van Nostrand.

McDougall, P. and R. Robinson (1990), New Venture Strategies: An Empirical Identification of Eight "Archetypes" of Competitive Strategies for Entry, in *Strategic Management Journal*, 11/6, pp. 447–67.

McGrath, R., I. MacMillan, E. Yang, and W. Tsai (1992), Does Culture Endure, or Is It Malleable? in *Journal of Business Venturing*, 7, pp. 441–58.

MacMillan, I. and D. Day (1987), Corporate Ventures into Industrial Markets: Dynamics of Aggressive Entry, in *Journal of Business Venturing*, 2/1, pp. 29–40.

Mantzavinos, C. (2001), *Individuals, Institutions, and Markets*, Cambridge: Cambridge University Press.

Marlow, S. (2005), Introduction, in S. Marlow, D. Patton and M. Ram (eds.), *Managing Labour in Small Firms*, London: Routledge.

Mason, J. (2006), Six Strategies for Mixing Methods and Linking Data in Social Science Research, Real Life Methods Working Paper, University of Manchester, July.

Matsuda, S. (2006), Nihon no shinki jigyo kaigyoritsu wa kyugeki ni uwamuiteiru no dewa naika (Japan's New Business Startup Rate Could be Rising Sharply), in *Nihon bencha gakkaishi*, 8, pp. 3–11.

Midler, C. (1995), "Projectification" of the Firm: The Renault Case, in *Scandanavian Journal of Management*, 11/4, pp. 363–75.

Miller, D. (1983), The Correlates of Entrepreneurship in Three Types of Firms, in *Management Science*, 29/7, pp. 770–91.

—— and P. Friesen (1983), Strategy Making and Environment: The Third Link, in *Strategic Management Journal*, 4/3, pp. 221–35.

Miyamoto, D. and D. H. Whittaker (2005), The Book Publishing Industry in Japan and the UK: Corporate Philosophy/Objectives, Behaviour and Market Structure, ITEC Working Papers 05–10, Doshisha University.

Mohr, L. (1982), *Explaining Organizational Behaviour*, San Francisco, CA: Jossey Bass.

Momose, S. (1989), *Chusho kigyo kumiai no rinen to kasseika* (Principles of SME Associations and Revitalizing Them), Tokyo: Hakuto shobo.

—— and T. Morishita (1997), *Benchagata kigyo no keieishazo* (Profiles of CEOs in Entrepreneurial Businesses), Tokyo: Chuo keizaisha.

Moore, B. (1966), *Social Origins of Dictatorship and Democracy: Lord and Peasant in the Making of the Modern World*, Boston, MA: Beacon Press.

Moore, G. and K. Davis (2004), Learning the Silicon Valley Way, in T. Bresnahan and A. Gambardella (eds.), *Building High Tech Clusters: Silicon Valley and Beyond*, Cambridge: Cambridge University Press.

Naman, J. and D. Slevin (1993), Entrepreneurship and the Concept of Fit: A Model and Empirical Tests, in *Strategic Management Journal*, 14, pp. 137–53.

Nishiguchi, T. (1992), *Strategic Industrial Sourcing*, New York: Oxford University Press.

Parker, S. and M. Robson (2004), Explaining International Variations in Entrepreneurship: Evidence from a Panel of OECD Countries, Durham University Business School research paper.

Piore, M. and C, Sabel (1984), *The Second Industrial Divide: Possibilities for Prosperity*, New York: Basic Books.

Polanyi, K. (1944), *The Great Transformation: The Political and Economic Origins of Our Time*, Boston, MA: Beacon Hill.

Power, M. (1997), *The Audit Society: Rituals of Verification*, Oxford: Oxford University Press.

Pugh, D. and D. Hickson (1976), *Organizational Structure in Its Context: The Aston Programme*, Aldershot: Gower Publishing.

Quince, T. (1998), The Normative Value Orientations of Collaborative Entrepreneurs, Ph.D. dissertation, University of Cambridge.

—— (2001), Entrepreneurial Collaboration: Terms of Endearment or Rules of Engagement? University of Cambridge Centre for Business Research Working Paper No. 207.

—— and D. H. Whittaker (2002), High Tech Businesses in the UK: Performance and Niche Markets, CBR Working Paper No. 234, Centre for Business Research, University of Cambridge.

—— —— (2004), Close Encounters: Evidence of the Potential Benefits of Proximity to Local Industrial Clusters, in W. During, R. Oakey, and S. Kauser (eds.), *New Technology-Based Firms in the New Millenium*, Volume 3, Kidlington: Elsevier.

Rainnie, A. (1989), *Industrial Relations in Small Firms*, London: Routledge.

Ram, M. (1994), *Managing to Survive: Working Lives in Small Firms*, Oxford: Basil Blackwell.

Reynolds, P., W. Bygrave, E. Autio et al. (2004), *Global Entrepreneurship Monitor: 2003 Executive Report*, London and Babson Park, MA: GEM.

Riesman, D. (1950), *The Lonely Crowd: A Study of the Changing American Character*, New Haven, CT: Yale University Press.

Roberts, E. (1991), *Entrepreneurs in High Technology: Lessons from MIT and Beyond*, New York: Oxford University Press.

Roberts, I., D. Sawbridge, and G. Bamber (1992), Employment Relations in Smaller Enterprises, in B. Towers (ed.), *Handbook of Industrial Relations Practice*, London: Kogan Page.

Ronstadt, R. (1988), The Corridor Principle, in *Journal of Business Venturing*, 3, pp. 31–40.

Roper, S. (1999), Under-reporting of R&D in Small Firms, in *Small Business Economics*, 12/2, pp. 131–5.

Ruef, M., H. Aldrich, and N. Carter (2003), The Structure of Founding Teams: Homophily, Strong Ties and Isolation Among US Entrepreneurs, in *American Sociological Review*, 68/2, pp. 195–222.

Sahlman, W., H. Stevenson, M. Roberts, and A. Bhide (1999), Introduction, in W. Sahlman, H. Stevenson, M. Roberts, and A. Bhide (eds.), *The Entrepreneurial Venture*, 2nd edition, Boston, MA: Harvard University Press.

Sako, M. (1992), *Prices, Quality and Trust*, Cambridge: Cambridge University Press.

—— (2007), Organisational Diversity and Institutional Change: Evidence from Financial and Labour Markets, in M. Aoki, G. Jackson and H. Miyajima (eds.), *Corporate Governanace in Japan: Organizational Diversity and Institutional Change*, Oxford: Oxford University Press.

Sano, M. and T. Kitachi (2001), Bencha manejimento no tokusei (Characteristics of Venture Management), in S. Matsuda and WERU (eds.), *Bencha kigyo no keiei to shien* (Management and Support of Entrepreneurial Businesses), Tokyo: Nikkei shinbunsha.

Sarasvathy, S. (2001), Causation and Effectuation: Toward a Theoretical Shift from Economic Inevitability to Entrepreneurial Contingency, in *Academy of Management Review*, 26/2, pp. 243–88.

—— (2008), *Effectuation: Elements of Entrepreneurial Expertise*, Cheltenham, Edward Elgar.

—— and N. Dew (2005), Entrepreneurial Logics for a Technology of Foolishness, in *Scandinavian Journal of Management*, 21, pp. 385–406.

—— —— S. Velamuri, and S. Venkataraman (2003), Three Views of Entrepreneurial Opportunity, in Z. Acs and D. Audretsch (eds.).

Scase, R. (2005), Managerial Strategies in Small Firms, in S. Marlow, D. Patton, and M. Ram (eds.), *Managing Labour in Small Firms*, London: Routledge.

Scharpf, F. (1997), *Games Real Actors Play*, Oxford: Westview Press.

Scheinberg, S. and I. MacMillan (1988), An 11 Country Study of Motivations to Start a Business, in B. Kirchoff, W. Long, W. McMullan, K. Vesper, and W. Wetzel Jnr (eds.), *Frontiers of Entrepreneurship Research*, Wellesley, MA: Babson College.

Schollhammer, H. (1982), Internal Corporate Entrepreneurship, in C. Kent. D. Sexton and K. Vesper (eds.), *Encyclopedia of Entrepreneurship*, Englewood Cliffs, NJ: Prentice Hall.

Schoonhoven, C. and E. Romanelli (2001), Emergent Themes and the Next Wave of Entrepreneurship Research, in C. Schoonhoven and E. Romanelli (eds.), *The Entrepreneurship Dynamic: Origins of Entrepreneurship and the Evolution of Industry*, Stanford, CA: Stanford University Press.

Schumpeter, J. (1934, 1961), *The Theory of Economic Development: An Inquiry into Profits, Capital, Credit, Interest, and the Business Cycle*, New York: Oxford University Press.

—— (1942), *Capitalism, Socialism, and Democracy*, New York: Harper & Brothers.

—— (2000), Entrepreneurship as Innovation, in R. Swedberg (ed.), *Entrepreneurship: The Social Science View*, Oxford: Oxford University Press (extracted from Schumpeter, 1961).

Segal, Quince, and Wickstead (1985), *The Cambridge Phenomenon: The Growth of High Technology Industry in a University Town*, Cambridge: Segal, Quince, and Wickstead.

Sengenberger, W., G. Loveman, and M. Piore (1990), *The Resurgence of Small Enterprises*, Geneva: International Institute for Labour Studies.

Shane, S. (1992), Why Do Some Societies Invent More Than Others? in *Journal of Business Venturing*, 7, pp. 29–46.

—— (1993), Cultural Influences on National Rates of Innovation, in *Journal of Business Venturing*, 8, pp. 59–73.

—— and J. Eckhardt (2003), The Individual-Opportunity Nexus, in Z. Acs and D. Audretsch (eds.)

—— and S. Venkataraman (2000), The Promise of Entrepreneurship as a Field of Research, in *Academy of Management Review*, 26/1, pp. 217–26.

Singh, R. (2000), *Entrepreneurial Opportunity Recognition Through Social Networks*, New York: Garland.

Smilor, R., D. Gibson and G. Kozmetsky (1989), Creating the Technopolis: High Technology Development in Austin, Texas, in *Journal of Business Venturing*, 4/1, pp. 49–67.

Smith, N. (1967), *The Entrepreneur and His Firm: The Relationship Between Type of Man and Type of Company*, East Lansing, MI: Michigan State University Press.

Somers, M. and F. Block (2005), From Poverty to Perversity: Ideas, Markets and Institutions Over 200 Years of Welfare Debate, in *American Sociological Review*, 70/2, pp. 260–87.

Stanworth, J. and J. Curran (1989), Employment Relations in the Small Firm, in P. Burns and J. Dewhurst (eds.), *Small Business and Entrepreneurship*, Basingstoke: Macmillan.

References

Stanworth, J. and C. Gray (eds.) (1991), *Bolton 20 Years On: The Small Firm in the 1990s*, London: Paul Chapman.

Stevenson, H. (1983/1999), A Perspective on Entrepreneurship, HBS Case 384-131, reprinted in W. Sahlman, H. Stevenson, M. Roberts and A. Bhide (eds.), *The Entrepreneurial Venture*, 2nd edition, Boston, MA: Harvard Business School Press.

Steyaert, C. (2007), Of Course That is Not the Whole (Toy) Story: Entrepreneurship and the Cat's Cradle, in *Journal of Business Venturing*, 22, pp. 733–51.

Stinchcombe, A. (1965), Social Structure and Organizations, in J. March (ed.), *Handbook of Organizations*, Chicago, IL: Rand McNally.

Storey, D. (1994), *Understanding the Small Business Sector*, London: Routledge.

—— (2003), Entrepreneurship and Public Policy, in Z. Acs and D. Audretsch (eds.)

Stuart, T. (2000), Interorganizational Alliances and the Performance of Firms: A Study of Growth and Innovation Rates in High-Technology Industry, in *Strategic Management Journal*, 21, pp. 791–811.

Swedburg, R. (2003), *Principles of Economic Sociology*, Princeton, NJ: Princeton University Press.

—— (2005), Markets in Society, in N. Smelser and R. Swedburg (eds.), *The Handbook of Economic Sociology*, 2nd edition, Princeton, NJ: Princeton University Press.

Sydow, J., L. Lindkvist, and R. DeFillippi (2004), Project-Based Organizations, Embeddedness and Repositories of Knowledge: Editorial, in *Organization Studies*, 25/9, pp. 1475–89.

Tan, J. (2002), Culture, Nation and Entrepreneurial Strategic Orientations: Implications for an Emerging Economy, in *Entrepreneurship Theory & Practice*, 26/4, pp. 95–211.

Tapsell, P. and C. Woods (2008), Social Entrepreneurship and Innovation: Self Organization in an Indigenous Context, (forthcoming).

Tether, B. (2002), Who Co-operates for Innovation and Why: An Empirical Analysis, in *Research Policy*, 31, pp. 947–67.

Thelen, K. (2004), *How Institutions Evolve: The Political Economy of Skills in Germany, Britain, the United States and Japan*, Cambridge: Cambridge University Press.

Thomas, A. and S. Mueller (2000), A Case for Comparative Entrepreneurship: Assessing the Relevance of Culture, in *Journal of International Business Studies*, 31/2, pp. 287–301.

Timmons, J. (1990), *New Venture Creation: Getting to the Right Place at the Right Time*, Acton, MA: Brick House.

Tomita, Y. (2002), Chusho kigyo ni okeru migiude jugyoin: Sono kyaria to kokendo (The Right Hand Employee in SMEs: Careers and Contributions), in N. Mitani and A. Wakisaka (eds.), *Maikuro bijinesu no keizai bunseki* (Economic Analysis of Micro-business), Tokyo: Tokyo daigaku shuppankai.

Tsai, M.-H. (2006), The Myth of Monozukuri: Manufactured Manufacturing Ideology, ITEC Working paper 06–04, Doshisha University, Kyoto.

Tsoukos, H. (2005), *Complex Knowledge: Studies in Organizational Epistemology*, Oxford: Oxford University Press.

Van de Ven, A. and M. Poole (2005), Alternative Approaches for Studying Organizational Change, in *Organization Studies*, 26/9, pp. 1377–404.

—— and R. Engleman (2004), Event- and Outcome-driven Explanations of Entrepreneurship, in *Journal of Business Venturing*, 19, pp. 343–58.

Van Stel, A. (2004), COMPENDIA: Harmonizing Business Ownership Data Across Countries and Over Time, SCALES-paper N200413, EIM, The Netherlands.

—— and B. Diephuis (2004), An Empirical Analysis of Business Dynamics and Growth, SCALES-paper N200412, EIM, The Netherlands.

Venkataraman, S. (1997), The Distinctive Domain of Entrepreneurship Research, in *Advances in Entrepreneurship, Firm Emergence and Growth*, Volume 3, pp. 119–38

Verheul, I., S. Wennekers, D. Audretsch, and R. Thurik (2002), An Eclectic Theory of Entrepreneurship: Policies, Institutions and Culture, in D. Audretsch et al. (eds.), *Entrepreneurship: Determinants and Policy in a European-US Comparison*, Boston, MA: Kluwer Academic.

Vesper, K. (1990), *New Venture Strategies*, Englewood Cliffs, NJ: Prentice Hall.

Wakisaka, A. (2003), Migiude ga chusho kigyo no keiei gyoseki ni ataeru eikyo (The Influence of the Right Hand [Man] on SME Management Performance), in H. Sato and Y. Genda (eds.), *Seicho to jinzai: Nobiru kigyo no jinzai senryaku* (Growth and Human Resources: Human Resource Strategy of Growing Companies), Tokyo: Keiso shobo.

Weber, M. (1904–5, 1935), *The Protestant Ethic and the Spirit of Capitalism*, New York: Scribner.

—— (1922, 1978), *Economy and Society: An Outline of Interpretive Sociology*, 2 vols., Berkeley, CA: University of California Press.

Weick, K. (1979), *The Social Psychology of Organizing*, 2nd edition, New York: McGraw-Hill.

—— (1989), Theory Construction as Disciplined Imagination, in *Academy of Management Review*, 14, pp. 516–31.

Welter, F. and D. Smallbone (2006), Exploring the Role of Trust in Entrepreneurial Activity, in *Entrepreneurship Theory and Practice*, 30/4, pp. 465–75.

Wennekers, S., A. van Stel, R. Thurik, and P. Reynolds (2005), Nascent Entrepreneurship and the Level of Economic Development, in *Small Business Economics*, 24, pp. 293–309.

White, H. (1981), Where Do Markets Come From? in *American Journal of Sociology*, 87/3, pp. 517–47.

Whittaker, D. H. (1990), *Managing Innovation: A Study of British and Japanese Factories*, Cambridge: Cambridge University Press.

—— (1997), *Small Firms in the Japanese Economy*, Cambridge: Cambridge University Press.

Whyte, W. (1956), *The Organization Man*, New York: Simon & Schuster.

Wiklund, J. (1998), Entrepreneurial Orientation as Predictor of Performance and Entrepreneurial Behaviour in Small Firms – Longitudial Evidence, in *Frontiers of Entrepreneurship Research 1998*, Wellesley, MA: Babson College.

Wiklund, J. (1999), The Sustainability of the Entrepreneurial Orientation – Performance Relationship, in *Frontiers of Entrepreneurship Research*, Wellesley, MA: Babson College.

Wilkinson, F. (2000), Human Resource Management and Business Objectives and Strategies in Small and Medium Sized Business, CBR Working Paper No. 184, Centre for Business Research, University of Cambridge.

Yamada, K. and Y. Eshima (2003), Sozoteki chusho kigyo no keiei to senryakuteki kettei (The Management and Strategic Decisions of Creative SMEs), in *Ventures Review*, 4, pp. 13–23.

Yamamura, K. and W. Streeck (eds.) (2003), *The End of Diversity? Prospects for German and Japanese Capitalism*, Ithaca, NY: Cornell University Press.

Yasuda, T. (2004), 'Kigyoka no keireki, zokusei to kigyo no keii: pafomansu to no kankei' (The Career and Attributes of Entrepreneurs and Founding Process: Relation to Performance) in *Kigyoka kenkyu*, 1, pp. 79–95.

Zahra, S. and J. Covin (1995), Contextual Influences on the Corporate Entrepreneurship–Performance Relationship: A Longitudinal Analysis, in *Journal of Business Venturing* 10, pp. 43–58.

Index